The Latin American evangelical communi
voice has not taken a straight or an obvious |
on the outside looking in with interest and c

C000221243

In *Taking Up the Mantle: Latin Ameri*
20th Century, J. Daniel Salinas rambles expe...., ... landscape
of that process as it took shape in the twentieth century. A careful historian,
Salinas is alert both to the "conciliar" aspects of the story he tells and to the
argument that the region's "theology" has found its voice in the lived spaces
provided by the pulpit and the everyday life and service of Latin America's
"Bible people."

A good deal of the tale involves the struggle to grow out of – or break
free from – the overwhelming influence of Latin America's nearest northern
neighbor. If the evangelical gospel arrived with American missionaries,
is the shape and texture of that gospel not "good enough" Latin American
theology? Many have thought the answer must be "no," but decades passed
in the development of the positive theology that might grasp the passed
baton. A common insistence of Salinas's protagonists is that this theology
must be deeply rooted in often excruciating Latin American social realities
rather than imported in pristine form from a very different and arguably less
troubled context. The buffeting visited upon the region by ideological Left-
Right winds has made the articulate reformulation of Christian belief and
practice an ever-contested task.

J. Daniel Salinas's brief assessments at the end of each chapter of this story
are worth their weight in gold. I find *Taking Up the Mantle* an exhilarating
story, competently and courageously told by an insider who has managed a
historian's appropriate distance. It deserves to be read widely and must now
be considered the standard English-language treatment of a story that, one
trusts, has only begun.

Rev David A. Baer, PhD
Former President & CEO, Overseas Council, Indianapolis, USA

In this original work, J. Daniel Salinas corrects at least two major
misconceptions about Latin American theological reflection: that its only
expression is liberation theology and that it has been mostly non-existent
in evangelical circles. Excerpts of documents that cover more than a century
demonstrate that theological dialogue among Latin American Protestants,

from very early in the twentieth century, was already concerned with the realities of the context, and that although most evangelical theological reflection has not been the product of scholastic activity, it has not been shallow or provincial. This is a must read to get a comprehensive perspective on Latin American evangelical theologies during the twentieth century.

Elizabeth Sendek, MA
President, Biblical Seminary of Colombia, Medellin, Colombia

J. Daniel Salinas makes plain that the theological thought of the Latin churches in the early twentieth century was mainly a "repetition of whatever had arrived," not least via missionaries from the North. Moreover, some of what arrived hindered the development of a contextualized evangelical theology. The exhilarating part of Salinas's historical overview is the example of numerous towering Latin American figures who struggled valiantly and against many obstacles to articulate a theology that addressed biblically the conditions and questions of Latin America itself. Salinas explains that the task has been "chaotic, unpredictable, polarizing, and divisive." The sober message is that while these Latin American scholars and leaders have been exemplary – and in many ways successful – many challenges remain. Salinas's work underscores the reality that the task of developing a Latin American evangelical theology remains a current and ongoing challenge.

John G. Bernard, DMin
President, United World Mission

Global Perspectives Series

Taking Up the Mantle

GLOBAL LIBRARY

Taking Up the Mantle

*Latin American Evangelical
Theology in the 20th Century*

J. Daniel Salinas

GLOBAL LIBRARY

© 2017 by J. Daniel Salinas

Published 2017 by Langham Global Library
An imprint of Langham Creative Projects

Langham Partnership
PO Box 296, Carlisle, Cumbria CA3 9WZ, UK
www.langham.org

ISBNs:
978-1-78368-206-5 Print
978-1-78368-208-9 Mobi
978-1-78368-207-2 ePub
978-1-78368-209-6 PDF

British Library Cataloguing in Publication Data
A catalogue record for this book is available from the British Library

ISBN: 978-1-78368-206-5

Cover & Book Design: projectluz.com

CONTENTS

Foreword ix

Acknowledgments xi

Abbreviations xiii

Introduction 1

1 Beginnings. 3
    Panama 1916 5
    Montevideo 1925. 15
    Havana 1929. 21
    Other Theological Trends at the Beginning of the Twentieth
        Century. 25

2 The First Generation of Latin American Evangelicals Doing
  Theology: From Panama 1916 to Buenos Aires 1946 31
    La Nueva Democracia. 37
    Luminar. 42
    The Other Spanish Christ 47
    The Balcony and the Road 49
    CELA I, 1949 50

3 The Second Generation:
  From Buenos Aires 1949 to Cochabamba 1970. 55
    Certeza and *Pensamiento Cristiano*. 56
    Cuadernos Teológicos. 57
    CELA II, 1961 71
    ISAL. 77
    CELA III, 1969. 90

4 Evangelicals Searching for Their Identity and Theology:
  The Seventies and Eighties 97
    FTL 101
    Anglo-Saxon Clothing, Manifest Destiny, and Cultural
        Christianity. 108
    A New Theological Reflection 114

    Pentecostals and Historical Churches 117
    Women and Theology 120
    Pastoralia 123

5   Definition and Maturity 125
    CONELA and CLAI 128
    Multidirectional Dialogue 141
    Theological Agendas 149
    Misión 153
    Third World Theologies 156
    Dialogue with Foreign Theological and Missiological Agendas . . .160
    Female Theologians 166
    CLADE III 167
    Pentecostalism's Growth 172

Conclusion 181

Bibliography 185

Index 197

Foreword

There is a need for a book like this in English and we have to thank J. Daniel Salinas for his effort in carrying on a conscientious work of research and writing it down. As he says, outside Latin America those that do research and write about theological issues tend to think that liberation theology is the only theology that has come from that continent. This book will no doubt contribute to correct that narrow perspective.

It was necessary to identify the theology that backed the Protestant missionary activity in Latin America starting at the end of the nineteenth century and the first decades of the twentieth. An original contribution of this book is the identification and description of the dispensationalism that colored the mission theology of the faith missions that eventually surpassed the work of the denominational mission boards that had pioneered Protestant expansion in Latin America. On the other hand, the book also offers a valuable summary of the theology that was characteristic of the ecumenical missionary enthusiasts after the famous conference of Edinburgh 1910.

J. Daniel Salinas is a specialist in the development of Evangelical Theology in the last three decades of the twentieth century. His doctoral thesis on the subject was published in 2009.[1] Now in this new book he offers us a summary of those findings including references to Latin American Theologians that were part of the ecumenical movement related to the World Council of Churches.

New developments in the religious scene of Latin America include the explosive growth of Pentecostalism and significant post Vatican II changes within the Roman Catholic Church including the presence of an Argentinian Pope in the Vatican. If all this is to be understood, it is necessary to become familiar with the process of ecclesiastical and theological developments that this book so aptly describes.

Samuel Escobar
Professor in the Facultad Protestante de Teología UEBE, Madrid, Spain

---

1. *Latin American Evangelical Theology in the 1970s* (Leiden/Boston: Brill, 2009).

Acknowledgments

I thank the following persons and organizations for making this book possible:

- Global Research Institute at Fuller Theological Seminary for the generous sabbatical;
- Scholar Leaders International for their moral and financial support;
- Langham Partnership for the editorial work and willingness to publish this book;
- Latin America Mission and United World Mission for a study leave;
- Dr Samuel Escobar for reading the rough draft and providing helpful advice;
- My wife Gayna Salinas for her patience and suggesting better ways to write in English;
- and my children for putting up with me while researching and writing this book.

Soli Deo Gloria!

J. Daniel Salinas, PhD

Abbreviations

BGEA	Billy Graham Evangelistic Association
CAM	Central American Mission
CCLA	Committee on Cooperation in Latin America
CEHILA	Comisión de Estudios de Historia de la Iglesia en Latinoamerica
CELA	Conferencia Evangélica Latinoamericana
CELAM	Consejo Episcopal Latinoamericano
CEPLA	Comisión Evangélica Pentecostal Latinoamericana
CG	Church Growth
CLADE	Congreso Latinoamericano de Evangelización
CLAI	Consejo Latinoamericano de Iglesias
CONELA	Confraternidad Evangélica Latinoamericana
CT	*Cuadernos Teológicos*
EAF	Evangelism in Depth – Evangelismo a Fondo
EATWOT	Ecumenical Association of Third World theologians
ECLA	Evangelical Committee on Latin America
EFMA	Evangelical Foreign Missions Association
FTL	Fraternidad Teológica Latinoamericana
HUP	Homogeneous Unit Principle
ICOWE	International Congress on World Evangelization, Lausanne, Switzerland
ISAL	Iglesia y Sociedad en América Latina
LAM	Latin America Mission
LCWE	Lausanne Committee for World Evangelization
LEAL	Literatura Evangélica para América Latina
LND	*La Nueva Democracia*
LTEG	Lausanne Theology and Education group
PC	*Pensamiento Cristiano*
SBL	Seminario Bíblico Latinoamericano
UNELAJE	Unión Latinoamericana de Juventudes Evangélicas
UNELAM	Unidad Evangélica Latinoamericana
YMCA	Young Men Christian Association

Introduction

In personal conversations about evangelicals doing theology in Latin America I find that people usually make one of three assumptions. Most have heard of Latin American liberation theology and make the generalization that such a theology must be the only one in the region. Even some of the most distinguished evangelicals from Latin America are considered "liberationist." Others acknowledge that evangelical theology from Latin America really exists, but think that it is a recent phenomenon with only a handful of proponents. This group of people in general knows the names of televangelists or radio tycoons frequently promoted by religious literature in the northern hemisphere and concludes that Latin American evangelicals must be very similar to those in evangelicalism in the north. Finally, a smaller number of people are simply surprised to find that evangelicals have been doing and still are doing theology in Latin America. For this group, theology does not have a regional flavor, but is universal, the same everywhere.

This book describes the development of evangelical Latin American theology in the twentieth century. It follows a chronological format, intentionally including sources and quotations from each period only. Earlier events have been analyzed in later years, but the aim here is to let the voices be heard as they were originally expressed without allowing more recent views to taint our approach to the subject matter.

If this format gives the impression of spontaneity and dispersion, it is because that has been the way Latin Americans have developed their theological thought. However, this does not mean they were not serious or that they took it lightly. There has also been a variety of voices. It would, perhaps, be better to talk about Latin American evangelical "theologies," plural, since plurality has been a strong distinctive.

1

Beginnings

Wars and rumors of wars marked the Latin American ambience at the dusk of the nineteenth century and the dawn of the twentieth. Colombia greeted the new century in the midst of the bloody Thousand Days' War. Ecuador was threatened by ideological revenge from Colombia. In Cuba and Puerto Rico, the stench of gunpowder from the American–Spanish war still hung in the air. Uruguay was busy trying to quench Saravia's revolutions. The Canudos war shook Brazil with its cruelty. Venezuela was on high alert because of a possible invasion by Great Britain, who disputed the border with British Guyana. The predominant mood in the region was one of instability and revolution.

Most of the countries had experienced a century of repeated *coups d'état*. For instance, "when the republic of Peru in 1921 celebrated the centennial of its liberation from Spain, the country's leading newspaper noted that there had been 88 changes of government in 100 years."[1] Although they considered themselves democracies, "their pretended democracy is not, and never had been, more than a disguise for the rule of a caste which, with slight variations, has perpetuated itself from the days of the conquest of the Indian races by Spaniards and Portuguese and carried later by Creoles, always against the long-suffering children of the soil."[2] None of the regional economies seemed to thrive. Before the first decade of the new century was over, Panama gained its independence from Colombia with backing from the United States, the Mexican revolution against Porfirio Díaz was consolidated, the United States intervened militarily in the Dominican Republic and Cuba, and the

---

1. John A. Mackay, "Latin America and Revolution I: The New Mood in Society and Culture," *Christian Century* 46, no. 17 (1965): 1409.

2. Julio Navarro Monzó, *The Religious Problem in Latin American Culture* (Montevideo: Young Men's Christian Association, 1925), 11.

labor repressions in Chile left over four thousand dead and thousands more injured. Massacres, local revolts, civil wars, and so on, were too common in those years. This was all good material for people waiting for the apocalypses!

At a religious level there was another war going on which enraged people and provoked constant revolts. The Roman Catholic Church was thought to have full and exclusive religious control. However, some dissident groups started to challenge Rome's authority. Until that moment the religious establishment had kept the Lutheran "heresy" and its ramifications outside its borders. The Museum of the Inquisition in Lima provides evidence of the constant controls and roundups which were supposed to block the presence of other religious options in the continent. A Catholic observer described Latin American Catholicism in those years as "a sept of the Spanish type – the foster-mother of the Inquisition, the Index, and the Jesuit order – cruel, fierce, and coercive."[3] However, some international trends – humanistic philosophies and secular tendencies in Europe, besides expansionist programs, mainly British and North American – together with liberal governments in many countries, encouraged heterodoxy penetration.

In spite of early migrations of Protestants, Protestantism came to stay only after the mid-nineteenth century.[4] This arrival was a mixed process of cooperation between missionaries and local dissident groups. A variety of missionary visions and programs arrived. Not all expressions of Protestantism were the same. Starting in seventeenth-century Europe, Protestantism split into many factions depending upon their origin and founding leaders. Each group took to Latin America its doctrine, liturgy, architecture, and form of government. It was probably confusing to a people used to only one church. Henceforth, Latin American Protestantism developed its own identity as an amalgam of several of the trends that started it.

By 1916, when the Panama Congress took place, there were two distinctive tendencies in Latin American Protestantism: those Protestants who saw their religion as only spiritual, and those who understood it as touching all areas of Latin American life. The former represented mainly the tendency born of premillennialist awakenings that adopted dispensationalism as its theological framework; the latter, the majority in Panama, came from European denominations and their offices in Canada and the United States. Also,

---

3. James H. Mclean, "Theology and Citizenship in Latin America: An Appraisal," *Theology Today* 2, no. 2 (1945): 223.

4. See Gonzalo Báez-Camargo, "The Earliest Protestant Missionary Venture in Latin America," *Church History* 21, no. 2 (1952).

early in the twentieth century, Pentecostalism started (Pentecostals were not present at the Panama Congress in 1916), but it was not until a few decades later that its influence came clearly to the forefront. Latin American theology in the twentieth century followed, in general, these three interpretations.

This book includes representatives of these three main theological trends. Each one morphed, taking on new shapes as the century progressed. Each trend has had native Latin American representatives, some clearly following their foreign teachers, with others boldly taking new paths. Sometimes the three schools of thought met on the road, forming a synthesis, but most of the time they remained separate like water and oil.

Panama 1916

Panama 1916[5] was not technically a theological congress: it was a strategic meeting. Nevertheless, the theology of the participants floated at the surface of the discussions. The final documents of the congress reflect that, together with its strategies. Neither was Panama 1916 a Latin American congress. Its theme was Christian work in Latin America and participation was almost exclusively foreign. But its conclusions provide us with an approximation to a theology and doctrine that had reached the region and was being taught to new converts.

Even though the congress was about "Christian work," the reports include extensive analyses of the social, economic, and religious situation of the Latin American countries.[6] This is an important clue for understanding the theological background of the participants at Panama 1916. They made an effort to grasp as far as possible the multifaceted predicament of the Latin American peoples. The reports include topics such as education, racial integration, living conditions, and religion. Most of the people at the congress represented a theological tradition with implications for society in

5. For the history behind the Panama Congress of 1916, see Committee on Cooperation in Latin America (CCLA), *Christian Work in Latin America*. Vol. 1, *Survey and Occupation, Message and Method, Education* (New York, NY: Missionary Education Movement of the United States and Canada, 1917), 3–40.

6. Ibid.; Committee on Cooperation in Latin America (CCLA), *Christian Work in Latin America*. Vol. 2, *Literature, Women's Work, the Church in the Field, the Home Base* (New York, NY: Missionary Education Movement of the United States and Canada, 1917); Committee on Cooperation in Latin America (CCLA), *Christian Work in Latin America*. Vol. 3, *Cooperation and the Promotion of Unity, the Training and Efficiency of Missionaries, the Devotional Addresses, the Popular Addresses* (New York, NY: Missionary Education Movement of the United States and Canada, 1917).

general. Perhaps too optimistically, the reports hoped that Latin American life would improve in all areas due to an intentional and well-planned Protestant presence.

Within a complex religious context dominated in part by "medieval superstitions"[7] and by a growing rejection among educated classes of institutional religion,[8] the priority at the Panama Congress was to define what gospel message Latin America needed. Commission II said, "The task of this Commission is twofold, viz., (1) to draw up a brief statement of those aspects of the Christian message which would seem to require special emphasis at the present time in Latin America, and (2) to suggest methods of presenting and interpreting the message, and of most helpfully applying its truths in practical ways to actual conditions in the countries concerned."[9] They were intentional about considering the context in the proclamation of the Christian message. They also made it clear that "our call is to evangelize, not to Americanize."[10] They were concerned that the message be transmitted both by preaching and by the "exemplification of the Gospel."[11] They therefore emphasized that, besides evangelism, Christian work should include improvement in literacy, popular education, medical attention, and the establishment of philanthropic institutions to attend to "the spiritual, social, intellectual, and economic needs of the poorer classes."[12]

The conveners of the congress had decided beforehand to avoid a direct confrontation with the Catholic Church. Instead, they kept an open door of mutual collaboration. The year before the congress, the committee decided:

> That this Conference strongly recommends that those who are making arrangements for the Panama Conference, as well as all writers and speakers at the Conference, bear in mind that, if the best and most lasting results are to be obtained, while frankly facing moral and spiritual conditions which call for missionary work in Latin America, and while presenting the gospel which we hold as the only adequate solution of the problems which those conditions present, it shall be the purpose of the Panama

---

7. CCLA, *Christian Work*. Vol. 1, *Survey and Occupation*, 136.

8. Ibid., 79ff., 192.

9. Ibid., 245.

10. Ibid., 130.

11. Ibid., 140.

12. Ibid., 144.

Conference to recognize all the elements of truth and goodness
in any form of religious faith. Our approach to the people shall
be neither critical nor antagonistic, but inspired by the teachings
and example of Christ and by that charity which thinketh no evil
and rejoiceth not in iniquity but rejoiceth in the truth.

In the matter of Christian service, we will welcome the
cooperation of any who are willing to cooperate in any part of
the Christian program. We should not demand union with us
in all our work as the condition of accepting allies for any part
of it.[13]

Such a decision did not deny that there were problems and differences
with the Catholic Church. Robert Speer, president of the committee, had
published his conclusions and recommendations after an extensive visit to
the region.[14] He wanted to find an answer to the question, "Is our mission
to Latin America justifiable?" His question was triggered by the negative
response at the Congress in Edinburgh in 1910 to considering Latin America
as a legitimate mission field, precisely because of the presence of the Catholic
Church. Speer's answer was a resounding "Yes!" and he supported it with
several arguments. First, "The moral condition of the South American
countries warrants and demands the presence of the form of evangelical
religion which will war against sin and bring men the power of righteous
life."[15] Second, in light of the high levels of illiteracy in Latin America, the
"Protestant missionary enterprise with its stimulus to education and its appeal
to the rational nature of man is required by the intellectual needs of South
America. It is an uneducated continent."[16] He added, "The Roman Church
having had full control of the education of the continent for three centuries
must be held responsible for such conditions of popular ignorance as exist in
South America."[17] Regarding the educated classes, Speer explained,

The fact is that the men of the continent are drifting into
skepticism and the South American Church, with only here and

13. Ibid., 16.

14. Robert E. Speer, *Missions in South America* (New York, NY: Board of Foreign Missions
of the Presbyterian Church in the USA, 1909); Robert E. Speer, *South American Problems* (New
York, NY: Student Volunteer Movement for Foreign Missions, 1912).

15. Speer, *Missions in South America*, 151.

16. Ibid., 152.

17. Ibid., 153.

there an exceptional priest whose heart is burdened, is doing nothing to deal with the problem. It is issuing no literature dealing with the fundamental problem of unbelief. It is organizing no preaching missions to educated men. It is not facing the great issues rationally in the schools. The Protestant churches in Brazil are bearing the burden of the defense of supernatural religion against rationalism and fanaticism and indifference. They are needed to meet a situation which the South American Church is not trying to meet and cannot meet because it has helped to create it.[18]

Speer presented his third reason thus: "Protestant missions are justified in South America in order to give the Bible to the people." The problem was not the lack of Catholic versions either in Spanish or Portuguese, but that "the Church has discouraged or forbidden their use."[19] By contrast, missionary societies had helped distribute the Bible across the continent. Fourth, "Protestant missions are justified and demanded in South America by the character of the Roman Catholic priesthood." Speer was talking specifically about the low moral condition of the Catholic priests. "The common opinion throughout South America is, that the priesthood is morally corrupt, and the fact of its corruption is so patent that its influence, instead of being against immorality, is itself pitiably vile."[20] Consequently, Speer made a plea to the Protestant churches to confront immorality with their message and lifestyle.

The next reason, argued Speer, was "because the Roman Catholic Church has not given the people Christianity." On the basis of the devout Catholics Speer interviewed, few people in the Catholic Church knew the facts of Christ's life and fewer still knew Christ.

The very crucifixes of which South America is full misrepresent the Gospel. They show a dead man, not a living Saviour. South American Christianity knows nothing of the resurrection and of that which signifies life. We did not see in all the churches we visited a single symbol or suggestion of the resurrection or the ascension. There were hundreds of paintings of saints and of the Holy Family and of Mary, but not one of the supreme event in Christianity. And even the representations of the death of Christ

---

18. Ibid., 154.
19. Ibid.
20. Ibid., 158.

are false. Some of the figures are too terrible for description, and their whole significance is grossly untrue to the Gospel. The central place is Mary's. Often she is shown holding a small lacerated dead figure on her lap, and often she is the only person represented at all.[21]

Speer concluded that "Mariolatry is the religion of the land because the Church has taught it as true Christianity."[22] Speer was not the only one observing this: some years after him, Scottish missionary John A. Mackay described the situation in similar terms. But this is to get ahead of our story.

Speer's sixth argument why Protestant missions were justified in South America was "because the Roman Catholic Church is at the same time so strong and so weak there."[23] Even though the predominant Church claimed that almost everyone was a member, few people attended Mass. In conclusion, Speer proposed that "the South American countries must not be left to the South American religious system, because it is opposed to political liberty and popular institutions."[24] Speer based his conclusion on papal edicts and other documents of the Roman Church which explicitly said that political authorities were under the ecclesiastical ones: "The temporal authority must be subject to the spiritual power. The principle [of liberty of conscience] is one which is not and never has been and never will be approved by the Church of Christ."[25]

Amazingly, even knowing Speer's report and opinions, the organizers of the Panama Congress maintained an irenic position. Commission VIII recognized that as difficult but not impossible. Any approach by evangelicals would be met "by churchly conservatism and exclusivism, and not infrequently by aggressive opposition."[26] However, the recommendation was that, considering the wide social and religious needs of the continent, collaboration was important between the different denominations and with "all those individuals and groups, hitherto acknowledging allegiance to the Roman Church, who recognize these needs and are ready to take any step

---

21. Ibid., 161.
22. Ibid., 162.
23. Ibid., 163.
24. Ibid., 168.
25. Ibid., 169.
26. CCLA, *Christian Work*. Vol. 3 *Cooperation*, 54.

whatsoever towards cooperation with others of a different faith towards bringing about a better day."[27]

As a result of the organizing committee's decision and Speer's analysis, they tried to find out as much as possible about the situation and acted accordingly in order to avoid direct confrontation with Roman Catholic authorities. Was this due to an ecumenical understanding of Christian unity? Or was it perhaps influenced by the attitude expressed at the Congress in Edinburgh?[28] Whatever the cause, the resolution sheds light upon their theological presuppositions. They wanted Latin Americans to come to know the true gospel to improve their lives and conditions. Speer realized that in Latin America, Catholicism was not only an institutionalized religion but mostly a culture. People said they were Catholics even despite having no personal faith. That insight helped the congress to keep at a distance from the Catholic institution while defining the message which was going to offer the truth. Their public was not the institution itself, but the people who, even though they considered themselves Catholics, did not know the real, true gospel.

Commission II delineated several important points about the evangelical message Latin America needed.[29] Preachers needed to convey to their hearers that their message was the true revelation of God, a message older than Romanism – the true substance of the saving gospel of divine grace from apostolic times. The message should be fully biblical so that it would be clear to the people that the Bible was the most catholic of books and not merely an evangelical document. The Roman Catholic Church freely accepted and appealed to the authority of the Bible as the Word of God, as found in the decrees of the Council of Trent, the teachings of the great Catholic theologians, and even papal encyclicals against modernism.

The evangelical message contained two key affirmations: first, that the teachings of Christ and his apostles were preserved in the Bible, a book which could be used by anyone to know what is essential for salvation; second, that no authority could add anything to or detract anything from that which was declared by Christ to be necessary for salvation. It was of paramount importance to present the gracious fatherhood of God at the forefront of

---

27. Ibid.

28. A result of a supposed "superiority complex"? James C. Dekker, "North American Protestant Theology: Impact on Central America," *Evangelical Review of Theology* 9, no. 3 (July 1985): 386.

29. CCLA, *Christian Work*. Vol. 1, *Survey and Occupation*, 274–282.

the message and as the heart of Christ's teaching. The church was thus the community of all believers to whom the kingdom of heaven has been opened. In the church and through it faith in Christ and the knowledge of God are passed on from generation to generation. Everyone could deal directly and personally with God.

In short, in a continent with a ubiquitous crucifix, the person and the work of Christ had to be at the core of the Christian message. In Latin America, four crucial christological points needed to be emphasized, according to Commission II. First, Christ's divinity as Son of God incarnate makes him the only object of faith and worship. Second, in his life and sacrificial death Jesus Christ revealed directly and perfectly the holy love of God, and made full atonement for our sins once for all. It is blasphemy to think that someone else is needed to persuade God to have mercy on us. Third, Christ and only Christ is the risen Lord, and therefore he is the only head of the church. Here the commission recommended avoiding any direct and public attack upon the worship of the Virgin Mary because it only awakened fanatical hatred and detestation of Protestantism. However, when the message of fellowship with God through Christ the Redeemer was steadily and intelligently proclaimed, the worship of Mary and the saints went away naturally. Fourth, the teaching of Jesus is the supreme guide to our lives. We should allow no other standards of conduct, and we must learn to apply them broadly and without fear to the whole of our lives and to our industrial, political, and ecclesiastical problems; they should be demonstrated clearly in the life and character of every follower of Christ.

The evangelical preacher should invite people to a personal, loving, and intimate communion with the Father and the Savior, without any images or recommending saints as objects of trust and appeal. The only conditions for such a communion were repentance from sin and faith in the Lord Jesus Christ. By this means, the tyranny of "priestcraft" was effectively broken down. It was important to make it clear that the message of forgiveness, of justification and acceptance into God's presence, did not demand any intermediaries other than Christ.

Ecclesiological matters were vital in a continent accustomed to only one church. Protestant preachers needed to be able to explain the diverse organizational structure – Orthodox, Roman Catholic, Anglican, Lutheran, Presbyterian, and other congregations in Latin America. Chiefly, they needed to explain the differences as the result of historical, cultural, and local processes in the countries where those denominations started. But above all, the preacher needed to find clear ways to explain evangelical unity amid its diversity. It was also recommended that the architecture and furnishing of places of worship should be thought about carefully, since, for Latin Americans accustomed to ornate services full of mystery and symbolism, the simplicity and bareness of most evangelical forms of worship were repulsive. Church buildings needed to be beautiful and properly designed. Ragged and unprepared services, an informal style in the pulpit, and familiar or irreverent tones in prayer should all be avoided during Sunday services, as should a careless, offhand delivery of sermons.

> In such an environment as that of Latin America no care should be spared in the conduct of public worship to make the building and the music, the prayer and the preaching, suggest worship, awaken the sense of the presence of God, and win the spirit that is eager for the touch upon the imagination as well as for the appeal to reason and conscience, to feed on the spiritual bread that is offered to the soul.[30]

Regarding the church reaching out to the educated classes, mostly hostile to the Christian faith of any color, Commission II advised the gradual growth of strong evangelical churches where Christianity was presented "as the power of God unto salvation, where the evangelical type of sincere piety is worthily realized, where its effect upon personal character and its issue in social service manifest its full dignity and divine authority."[31] Once again, unity became a key aspect of evangelical witness and message. "The unity in which the Churches are rooted is unseen and spiritual, the boughs and branches diverge, but the tree produces the one fruitage of holy life in God." Perhaps more a wish than reality, "the Panama Congress is a brilliant proof of the fact, that the various sections of the evangelical Church feel more deeply and widely every year their inherit unity. The things that unite them are greater far than those which divide them."[32]

At the end, Commission II urged evangelical leaders to be deeply concerned about the relationship of the Christian message to the lives of people in their communities, even to the point of having significant influence over the state. They recalled significant social movements promoted by Luther, Calvin, Knox, and others. Each local Christian church and its ministers

---

30. Ibid., 281.

31. Ibid., 312.

32. Ibid., 313.

should get involved in the affairs of the community where it was located. A whole section of the final report of the congress was on what they called the "social gospel."[33]

Expecting the start of an industrial revolution in Latin America and anticipating its effects on individual and community life, Commission II argued for the message to combine the spiritual aspect with social application.

> With this new light which has broken forth from the newly understood Bible to meet the new social needs of the new civilization, missionaries and ministers of the gospel everywhere are discovering that it is their business not only to win individual souls to Christ, but to create a Christian civilization, and it has been conspicuously demonstrated at home and abroad that social work is as helpful to the one as it is essential to the other. Such work, however, has often originated in the desperate needs created by famine, flood, pestilence, or poverty rather than in a comprehensive study of the problem of human wellbeing, and in a perception of the relation of social progress to the coming of God's kingdom in the earth. The time is now ripe to take the broad view of missionary effort and to adapt methods accordingly.[34]

It seems that this proposal of a "social gospel" was the outcome of a postmillennial eschatology, in which the kingdom of God was understood as "a saved society here in the earth where God's will is done by man as it is by angels."[35] However, it was clear that such eschatology did not imply forfeiting evangelism. Instead, they went together: "Two things are necessary in order to convert the world to Christ. One is Christian truth; the other is the Christian spirit . . . A body of Christian truth without the Christian spirit is as powerless and dead as a human body without the soul. That spirit is the spirit of disinterested love." Proclamation was fruitless without the public demonstration of the Christian spirit of love.[36]

At the regional gatherings the Committee on Cooperation for Latin America (CCLA) organized straight after the Panama Congress – Lima, Santiago, Buenos Aires, Rio de Janeiro, Barranquilla, Havana, and San Juan

---

33. Ibid., 283–300.
34. Ibid., 292.
35. Ibid., 294.
36. Ibid., 297.

– the attitude to take towards the Roman Catholic Church was explained in more detail and the theological content of the message was expanded:

> Our attitude toward the Romish Church must be twofold: (a) one of sympathy and intimate solidarity towards the Christian element; (b) one of repudiation toward the element we consider anti-Christian. Affirming the truth of Christianity and repudiating the contrary errors, we declare that our purposes are frankly spiritual and religious for sincere cooperation with all the branches of Christendom that hold and profess all the Christian doctrines in their evangelical purity.
>
> Heirs of the noble religious movement of the sixteenth century, we will endeavor in the bosom of Christendom to bear faithful witness to: (a) the supremacy of the Word of God over the traditions of man; (b) the supremacy of faith over works; (c) the supremacy of the people of God over the clergy.[37]

Thus, in 1916 the Panama Congress defined as key aspects of evangelical preaching for Latin America a Christology with emphasis on soteriology, an ecclesiology that underlined unity, and the integration of the spiritual and social aspects of the message. These topics were the outcome of the various social and religious analyses of the different commissions. They showed a conscious concern for the preparation of preachers in contextual analysis and the effective adaptation of the message.

The realization of the need for better theological training and sound doctrinal teaching resulted as a reaction to the newly formed Pentecostal churches in Chile. The CCLA sounded the alarm regarding divisions in the churches caused by "mistakes and misunderstandings, the lack of harmony among missionaries, or between missionaries and national workers"; but the worst division, according to the CCLA, was that caused by the Pentecostals:

> In the Chilean Protestant churches there have arisen three separatist independent movements. In two cases the leaders have gone wrong morally and were obliged on this account to leave the church. They took with them those whose confidence they could hold. The last case was that of the so-called Pentecostal movement, where the pastor of one of the largest churches, a missionary,

---

37. Committee on Cooperation in Latin America (CCLA), *Regional Conferences in Latin America* (New York, NY: Missionary Education Movement, 1917), 426.

allowed himself to become sadly unbalanced on religion and to
be overruled by ignorant, sometimes malicious fanatics. The two
former movements were of very short duration. The enthusiasm
of independence soon gave way to discouragement and total
indifference. The Pentecostal movement carried with it a great
number of sincere people and has spread throughout two thirds
of the country. It has been entirely self-supporting and has kept
up during six years of its existence a burning enthusiasm which
has kept it alive. This movement, more than all others, shows that
there is need of a more thorough instruction of our members in
the fundamental doctrines of Christianity and a more established
interpretation of Scripture.[38]

This reaction to the Pentecostals remained unchanged for most of the
century. Ideologues from the CCLA never imagined that soon the majority of
Latin American evangelicals would identify with the Pentecostal movement.

Montevideo 1925

The Congress in Montevideo, Uruguay, in April 1925 kept the same interests
and added some new ones as a response to changing regional trends. In the
religious realm there had been two main observable developments during the
nine years since Panama: a growing spirit of materialism opposed to anything
spiritual, and a wider discontent with all traditions especially religious ones.
Taking these factors into account, Commission IV had the task of answering
the questions: What is to be our message as we seek to enter these new fields?
Are there certain elements of the Christian message that should receive
special emphasis? Have changing conditions made it necessary to shift the
emphasis in our preaching and teaching?[39]

To start with, Commission IV highlighted the need to preach in Latin
America the great teaching of the fatherhood of God. The predominant idea
was of a far-off God without any attributes to draw people to him. The report
from Brazil put it this way:

---

38. Ibid., 101.

39. Robert E. Speer, Samuel G. Inman, and Frank K. Sanders, eds., *Christian Work
in South America: Official Report of the Congress on Christian Work in South America, at
Montevideo, Uruguay, April 1925.* Vol. 1, *Unoccupied Fields, Indians, Education, Evangelism,
Social Movements, Health Industry* (New York and Chicago: Fleming H. Revell, 1925), 350–362.

There exists in the minds of the South American people a fear and an apprehension of punishment, but the realization that God is a loving father, ready and disposed to help His children, is quite foreign to their thinking. The doctrine inculcated in the mind of the Brazilian people of the necessity of human mediators and of the impossibility of having any personal communion with God has done much to destroy confidence in God.[40]

Such a concept also had implications for Christology. Together with the important message of the divinity of Christ it was necessary to emphasize his humanity. His divinity could push people away from him in terror; but his humanity helps people to feel that he understands, that he cares, that they can get close to him and trust him in a way that makes it clear that there is no need for other mediators. Also in Montevideo, Commission IX reported,

The Jesus of pure tragedy, the "Spanish Christ," must be supplemented by that powerful Personality who burned with indignation when confronted with organized deceit and oppression stalking beneath the cloak of religion. At the same time the infinite tenderness of Jesus towards the sinful, the weak, and the helpless, should receive equal emphasis. In a word, we believe that in South America the view of Christ which should be most constantly and vividly presented is that in which He appears in closest connection with sin. Let Him stand forth in the gospel message as the stern Judge of wanton evil, as the merciful Friend of struggling sinners, as the Divine Savior whose passage through Time was an event of redemptive significance and whose endless existence as the Exalted Lord guarantees the triumph of righteousness upon earth.[41]

Hamartiology, the doctrine of sin, did not come up during the Panama discussions. At the congress in Montevideo, however, individual and social sin was considered as a central ingredient of evangelical preaching: "its universality, its stupidity, its heinousness, its damming nature [and]

40. Ibid., 351.

41. Robert E. Speer, Samuel G. Inman, and Frank K. Sanders, eds., *Christian Work in South America: Official Report of the Congress on Christian Work in South America, at Montevideo, Uruguay, April 1925*. Vol. 2, *Church and the Community, Religious Education, Literature, Relations between Foreign and National Workers, Special Religious Problems, Cooperation and Unity* (New York and Chicago: Fleming H. Revell, 1925), 366.

redemption through the death and resurrection of our Lord." That was in contrast with the penal and sacramental Roman Catholic system. Then biblical preaching on sin should leave no doubt that salvation was only through faith in Christ and not simply through good works. "Here is the age-old difference of Protestant from Catholic teaching in which Protestantism was born. It still stands as one of the cardinal features in Evangelical preaching, not with any depreciation of the value of practical works, but regarding them only as fruits, and not as roots, of real Christian living."[42] Commission IX explained,

> Sin as a bloodless theological abstraction or ceremonial omission must give place to sin as a personal infraction of some eternal law of righteousness . . . Evil in all its phases must be shown to stand in eternal opposition to the will of a holy and loving God. The meaning of holiness, human and divine, must be interpreted to the people in a language they can understand . . . In a word, Scripture and literature, art and science must be made vocal, to broadcast through South American lands the eternal distinction between right and wrong and the eternal connection between sin and suffering.[43]

In addition, a more pragmatic tone was recommended, instead of the preaching of dogma. There was no consensus on this issue, but the majority of participants mentioned that the message should concentrate more on the practical aspects of the Christian life than on doctrine. "At least dogma has lost its charm. Even the ignorant people do not take the teaching of the Church seriously any more. It is not that they do not believe in religion, but that they do not believe in the dogmas in which religion is clothed. Right here, let me say that the Protestants are often as dogmatic as Catholics." This opinion seemed to be concerned with the separation of ecclesiastical rituals from daily life, which was all too common in the predominantly Catholic context. But it did not mean getting rid of dogma altogether; rather, dogma had to be balanced by ethics. "Whatever doctrinal emphasis should be given, it must be accompanied by insistence upon the practical fruits of pure and holy living."[44]

The social application of the message was also reiterated in Montevideo, even though its manner of implementation was unclear. The different reports

---

42. Speer, Inman, and Sanders, *Christian Work*. Vol. 1, *Unoccupied Fields*, 353.
43. Speer, Inman, and Sanders, *Christian Work*. Vol. 2, *Church and the Community*, 366.
44. Speer, Inman, and Sanders, *Christian Work*. Vol. 1, *Unoccupied Fields*, 353.

showed that there was a poor understanding of the wider implications of the social aspect of the Christian message. There was recognition that through medical work, student hostels, educational institutions, ecclesiastical activities, and believers fighting such social evils as alcoholism and prostitution the social gospel message was to be applied, "but even such efforts as these do not cover quite the whole range of the social applications of the gospel." How did they define the Christian social gospel? "It is the declaration that the relationship of man in every contact with human life should be organized according to the teaching of Jesus Christ and that through His Spirit, working in redeemed and transformed lives, it is possible to do it."[45] The wide range of human activity and the totality of human relationships defined the extent the gospel needed to reach: industrial, racial, commercial, governmental, and international relationships.

> Has organized Evangelical Christianity in South America anything to say on these important subjects? Has it any message to the working-man as to his relationships with his employer? Has it any message to the employer regarding his relationships with his working-men? Has it anything to say regarding the profits which a man may legitimately take from his business? Has the Church any message as to the right of the laboring classes to a larger share of the fruits of production? Has it anything to say as to the number of days a man shall work in a week, or the number of hours during which he shall work within a given day? Shall the Church have anything to say as to the age at which children may be taken from their homes and thrust into the industrial world? Has Evangelical Christianity anything to say about the peon system in vogue in so many Latin American countries? Has it anything to say as to the exploitation of the natural resources of the land by a favored few, while the great majority of the people live in misery? Has it anything to say as to the housing conditions in our great cities and in our country places? Has organized Evangelical Christianity any word regarding the health and general sanitation of our cities and country? Has it any convictions regarding the provision for mothers and motherless children and for the aged beyond an occasional orphan asylum

---

45. Ibid., 355.

or an aged people's home, in which a few people may be from time to time cared for?

Throughout practically the whole history of the organized labor movement, its adherents have seemed to think that the Church is a capitalistic organization, dominated by capitalistic interests, which seek, through the Church, to keep in submission the less favored portions of society. Has Evangelical Christianity in Latin America done anything to disprove this statement? Have its leaders shown themselves in any special way to be the friends of the exploited groups in the national life?[46]

Through these and similar questions an agenda of social commitment for the Latin American evangelical churches was proposed. Commission IV recognized that the reason why the influence of evangelicals in society was minimal was possibly because of the small number of believers. Yet even a weak voice is better than silence. The social implications and applications of the gospel were a practical consequence of Jesus' teachings and not a mere appendage. They reflected the theology and especially the Christology of the organizers of the congress.[47]

Interestingly, when talking about the evangelical message, Commission IV mentioned Latin American missions to the world. Many Latin American missionary societies were already in existence. For instance, Argentinian missionaries had been sent to Spain and Brazilian missionaries to Portugal. Brazilian churches financially supported a Japanese missionary in work among Japanese farmers in southern Brazil. There were exchanges of Christian workers between several countries. The Spanish pastor Agustin Arenales traveled extensively in Latin America collecting gifts to support evangelism in his country. From the beginning there was a clear missionary conscience among Latin Americans.

The need for better preparation of preachers, which was briefly considered at Panama, was described as "the greatest problem which confronts the Montevideo Congress."[48] The pulpit continued to be the most used and the most effective means for evangelism. However, in spite of sufficient financial resources, people, and methodologies, the whole ministry was compromised for lack of well-trained preachers. Initially, when the message was new to the

---

46. Ibid., 356.
47. See the report of Commission V on the social movements, ibid., 389–494.
48. Ibid., 363.

region, ministers with little preparation did a fairly good job; but the situation had changed.

> With the majority of the Latin people it no longer is a question, What does the Bible teach on this or that important issue of life, but how can an educated man, who is alive to what modern science teaches, still believe that it really makes any difference what some Oriental said 2,000 years ago? What is the will of God? is no longer a question. God to the average Latin of the educated classes, and to thousands who are not educated, simply does not exist. Or if He does exist, it is only in poetry and in the fancy of those who secure their living by propagating this belated falsehood.[49]

Besides training in theology and homiletics, preachers needed in-depth spiritual preparation and a deeper study of the needs and problems of the people. This was urgent since one of the main struggles churches experienced was to build on the results of evangelism. Young people especially, while accepting the message, did not become members of the churches and most of them did not stay long enough to experience any significant growth. The proposed solution was to develop high-level theological and ministerial institutions, some of which were in the process of consolidation.

The question remains whether the leadership at Panama and Montevideo were able to convince Latin Americans to adopt their strategic and theological agenda. If so, why did most of the evangelical churches in Latin America develop in such a different way from the one described by the congress reports? There is no doubt that the model that became predominant was another one. Perhaps, in spite of the detailed analysis of the many conditions in Latin America, they failed to reach the educated classes. Actual results showed that, after Montevideo, the working classes responded more positively to the gospel than any other group. Perhaps the social agenda was too big a program for an infant church still in diapers. Were there any key external factors of which they were unaware? Reviewing the conclusions of the Havana Congress in 1929 and other contemporary trends may shed some light on these questions.

---

49. Ibid., 364.

Havana 1929

Mexican Methodist journalist Gonzalo Báez-Camargo was named president of the Hispanic American Evangelical Congress at Havana in June 1929. In his analysis, Báez-Camargo named several factors that worked against Protestant plans to expand in Latin America, starting with the suspicion that they were political agents sent by the United States.

> The suspicion and the lack of trust, as our people observe the political and international maneuvers of the northern country, reach us, enfold us, and confront us, Hispanic American Protestants, even while we oppose the policies the United States implements in the rest of the continent as strongly as our fellow countrymen. Those who have led the United States government to write shameful pages of international politics in the history of its dealings with Latin America, would never imagine how unjustly, but understandably, they have hindered the evangelism of our peoples.[50]

The question remains, though, whether it was possible to get rid of that stigma which was well known by some missionaries. Samuel Guy Inman, general secretary of CCLA, for instance, had written explicitly about the influence North American policies had on missionary work:

> It would be folly not to recognize the obstacle to foreign missionary work in Latin America created by the real or supposed policies of the United States toward her neighbors to the south. The facts themselves are rather embarrassing, with or without explanation. The seizure of Panama by President Roosevelt, the taking over of Santo Domingo's custom-houses to ensure the payments of debts to foreign creditors, the actual occupation of Santo Domingo by United States troops, the practical conquest of Haiti by United States marines, the seizure of Vera Cruz by the United States Navy in 1914, the punitive expedition into Mexico

---

50. Gonzalo Báez-Camargo, *Hacia La Renovación Religiosa En Hispano-América: Resumen E Interpretación Del Congreso Evangélico Hispano-Americano De La Habana* (Mexico City: Casa Unida de Publicaciones, 1930), 24.

under General Pershing in 1916 – these are facts open before all the world.[51]

The Congress in Montevideo had delineated a threefold response on the subject: to avoid any association of the evangelical movement with "pan-Americanism" as a North American policy, to advise missionaries not to get involved in any local politics, and to accelerate the passing on of evangelical work to locals.[52] But there were still many reasons for people to connect the two. Inman had concluded that a "Northerner" visiting Latin America would note differences in everything except evangelical churches.

> If remembering that he is a Protestant, he visits his church, speaks with a Protestant minister, looks in private or public at Protestant work, he will find that it is in a large part a copy of the Protestantism which he has already known in his own nation. The churches may be larger or smaller, more or less beautiful, but they will be copies of what he has already seen in North America. The preaching may be with more or less eloquence, with more or less knowledge of the text, but it will be a copy of the theology which he knows, a duplicate most likely of what he has already heard. Even the gestures of the orators, the citations of the preachers, will show him that they prefer translated work; that for them their masters and teachers are Protestants who lived years ago or who are today popular in the cold lands of the North. Scarcely will he find either differences of originality to show that Protestantism is not an exotic plant, but indigenous to Spanish-speaking people, a part of their civilization and culture. He will notice this further if he gives attention to the literature, studies the hymns, the form of service, and organization of the church. Among these people who have been so original in their music, in their hymnology, and in their literature, he will find little more than imitation of hymns in English, many times badly translated, with English melodies, not always adapted to the delicate ear of the Spanish-speaking people; with ceremony and religious manifestations that may be now almost archaic among

---

51. Samuel G. Inman, *Ventures in Inter-American Friendship* (New York, NY: Missionary Movement of the United States and Canada, 1925), 134.

52. Speer, Inman, and Sanders, *Christian Work.* Vol. 2, *Church and the Community*, 360.

the North American people and yet constitute the liturgy and the ceremonies of Spanish-speaking churches of today.[53]

Attention to this issue had come up before. The same year of the congress in Montevideo, Argentinian Julio Navarro Monzó, an influential leader with the YMCA in the Southern Cone, recommended that Latin American Protestants should avoid being just a copy of the Anglo-Saxon and German religious institutions of the sixteenth-century Reformation. That was to make "as great a mistake" as when the nascent Latin American republics copied European political institutions "without having passed through the historic experiences which created the social condition of which those forms are the crystallization." Navarro expected a new Reformation since, for him, the "Reformation is a spirit, a movement, while Protestantism is an organization. The Reformation, the spirit of the Reformation, is something eternal. Protestantism is something temporal."[54]

> It will be a new reformation, the reformation of the twentieth century. It will be a synthesis of the efforts of Latins, as well as Anglo-Saxons, of the Germanic peoples as well as of the Slavs, of the peoples of the West, as very probably also the East, to find a solution for the moral and spiritual problems of the modern world, the problems raised by science in its conflict with the traditional theologies, the problems which have arisen in industrialism and the gradual awakening of the laboring classes, the problems which arise because of the approximation of the different peoples, the narrowing of their economic relations, and the necessity for establishing friendly relations between them.[55]

Báez-Camargo also mentioned the "Roman scholasticism" as another cause of the rejection of Protestants, mainly by the educated classes. "Bookstores are willing to sell Buddhist, Mahometan, Theosophical, Spiritist, pornographic, radical in many ways, unbelieving and atheist works, except Protestant." He asked: "Maybe our Protestantism does not adapt well to the temperament of these peoples, it does not satisfy their religious aspirations, neither does it fulfill their spiritual needs – in a word, it does not take root,

---

53. Samuel G. Inman, *New Churches in Old Lands: Thoughts Concerning the Evangelical Movement in Hispanic America, Especially in View of Discussions Related to the Havana Congress* ([n.p.], 1929), 1.

54. Navarro Monzó, *The Religious Problem in Latin American Culture*, 56.

55. Ibid., 58.

it does not stick, it does not identify with them." He concluded that "perhaps we have been unable to connect with our people. We are estranged from our race."[56] This shift in perspective is interesting. Instead of finding the causes in external elements, Báez-Camargo turned his gaze onto the Protestant movement to reevaluate and suggest reorganizing it.

> It is urgent to examine carefully our Protestantism; to review our way of presenting the message, our organization, the forms of our meetings; our methods; our attitude toward the social longings of our peoples; our elements, our physiognomies.
>
> Our Protestantism does not have any roots or any relationship with the spiritual traditions of our race . . . It is a pity that in our dealings with Catholicism we have gone so far as to reject even whatever is Christian, and glorious, of the religious experience of our race.[57]

Consequently, Báez-Camargo proposed to "Latinize" Protestantism, so that instead of a religious invasion there was a religious reformation. For him, the fact that the Congress in Havana was led and directed by Latin Americans was a step in the right direction, although he knew that "this great enterprise of better assimilating Protestantism is not something instant, violent, or hurried."[58]

Regrettably, at Havana the opportunity to Latinize the message was lost when the declaration of the International Missionary Congress held in Jerusalem the previous year was officially adopted for the Havana Congress. It was not that this declaration had any theological or doctrinal errors; the problem was that it set a precedent very difficult to break with. It seemed as if the initial efforts in Panama and Montevideo to define a message which would take the context into account were abandoned in Havana. Discussion was therefore more about strategy than content. But Inman's, Navarro's, and Báez-Camargo's observations give us an idea of the struggles evangelicals faced in defining their identity and mission. They give us a window into the theological thought of the Latin American churches at that time. Mainly, there was a repetition of the theologies that had arrived. There were some evangelicals who started to think their faith within their context while balancing external pressures: for example, Uruguayan Eduardo Monteverde,

56. Báez-Camargo, *Hacia La Renovación Religiosa En Hispano-América*, 25.

57. Ibid., 27.

58. Ibid., 138.

who presided over the Panama Congress in 1916; Brazilian Erasmo Braga, president of the Congress in Montevideo in 1925 and one of the honorary presidents at Havana; Mexican Gonzalo Báez-Camargo; Mexican writer and journalist Alberto Rembao, editor of *La Nueva Democracia* for many years (see next chapter); and Argentinian Julio Navarro Monzó.

Other Theological Trends at the Beginning of the Twentieth Century

The theological position at Panama and the following congresses was not accepted by all the mission agencies working in Latin America. For example, the *Bulletin* of the Central American Mission (CAM) said in January 1916:

> We are delighted to know that our missionaries are of one mind in opposition to the proposed Panama Congress that expects to meet next month in Panama. Being convinced that it is a delusion and a snare, and not gotten up for the glory of the Lord, we can have nothing to do with it. It started into shared fellowship with Rome, but she being too worldly-wise to have part in a Congress she did not alone inaugurate and control, repudiated the whole thing. Now that this thing was gotten up for the vowed purpose of having fellowship with Rome, and that has failed, why not call it off altogether?[59]

CAM was one of the many mission agencies that arrived in the nineteenth century to evangelize Latin America. It was founded in 1890 by Cyrus Ingerson Scofield, mostly known for authoring the notes of the Scofield Bible. The purpose of CAM was to "preach the Gospel to every creature in Central America."[60] Scofield's hermeneutical and theological framework was the dispensational system developed in Ireland by John Nelson Darby (1800–1892) at the beginning of the century as a response to the lack of authenticity Darby found in the Anglican churches. Darby taught his doctrine in the United States, a country he visited frequently. Many people of different denominations accepted his scheme. It is important to note that when Darby went to the United States similar systems had already been developed, independently of his influence, by pastors such as James Inglis and William

---

59. CAM, *The Central American Bulletin* 22, no. 1 (1916): 4.

60. CAM, "Origin and Purpose of the Mission," *The Central American Bulletin* 3, no. 2 (1897): 2.

Miller.[61] These theologies taught people to understand the issues raised by the Civil War as prophetic fulfillments. The theological and ideological discussions leading to the birth of Protestant fundamentalism in the United States prepared the soil for the acceptance of Darby's system.

Scofield was not the only ecclesiastical leader who adopted premillennial dispensationalism (PD). A good number of influential men accepted it completely or with minor modifications: for example, Adoniram J. Gordon, a Baptist and founder of the Missionary Training School in Boston (Gordon College and Seminary), and main editor of the periodical *Watchword*; Presbyterians Arthur T. Pierson and James H. Brookes, the latter a graduate of Princeton Seminary and editor of the pamphlet *The Truth*; Methodist William Blackstone, founder and first dean of the Bible Institute in Los Angeles, later known as Biola University, and founder of the Hebrew Mission in Chicago; William J. Erdman, pastor of the Moody Church in Chicago and one of the founding fathers of the Moody Seminary; evangelist Dwight L. Moody, one of the founders of Dallas Theological Seminary; and the founder of the Christian and Missionary Alliance, Albert B. Simpson.

The key elements of Darby's dispensationalism were as follows:

- The division of history into seven periods called "dispensations:" Innocency (from creation to the judgment of the expulsion), Conscience (until the deluge), Human Government (until Abraham), Promise (until the Sinaitic covenant), Law (until Christ's death), Grace (from Pentecost to the second coming of Christ), and Kingdom (until the last judgment).

- A dichotomy between the church and Israel, as two completely separate realities. One becomes part of Israel by natural birth; one becomes part of the church by spiritual birth. There are exclusive promises and prophecies for each. In a future millennium, the church will reign as the "Bride of the Lamb," while Israel will be restored to their ancestral land and will inherit an earthly kingdom announced by the prophets.

- A distinction between the true church and the universal church. "The true church could not possibly be identified with any of the large denominations, which are riddled with heresy, but could only

---

61. See Alan Thomas Terlep, "Inventing the Rapture: The Formation of American Dispensationalism, 1850–1875" (dissertation, University of Chicago, 2010).

be formed by individual Christians who could expect to be saved from the impending destruction."[62]

- A literal hermeneutics applied to the Bible, especially to the prophecies related to the second coming of Christ, the return of the Jews to their original territory, a secret rapture, a great tribulation, a millennium, and the final destiny. Such literalism was not used for all literary genres in the Bible: the Song of Songs, for example, was interpreted as an allegory of Christ and the church.

- An understanding of the kingdom as a postponed reality, completely futuristic, and only for the Jews: the hope of a full restoration of Israel to their promised land. During his first coming, Christ wanted to establish a literal, physical kingdom, a theocracy, but it did not happen because the Jews rejected him. Therefore, at his second coming, Jesus will establish a kingdom with 144,000 Jews, survivors of the tribulation.

- A narrow view of the church. "The true Church can never be an organization but must remain a spiritual fellowship of individual Christians."[63] The church as a new spiritual body was unknown to the prophets of the Old Testament and it was called a "mystery" in the New Testament.

- The need to be ready for a secret rapture of the true church. That will happen before seven years of great tribulation. God opened at Pentecost a soteriological parenthesis which he will close at the rapture of the church.

- A second opportunity for the Jews during the millennium to receive the kingdom. Israel will accept Jesus as their Messiah and the salvation of the Jews will be completed.

- A literal millennium in Jerusalem, when unfulfilled promises made to Israel will be fulfilled.

- A sharp distinction between law and grace. God's expectations for the church are not the same as those for Israel, resulting in a different treatment toward each group. The law was the basis for the "gospel of the kingdom" for Israel, and grace for the "gospel of grace" for the church.

---

62. Ernest R. Sandeen, "Toward a Historical Interpretation of the Origins of Fundamentalism," *Church History* 36, no. 1 (1967): 69.

63. Ibid.

- The categorization of the Bible. The Pauline letters and some texts from the other letters are the only scriptures for the church. No text of the Bible applies to more than one dispensation. Only the texts directed to those who were born spiritually are for the church. The others are for Israel.[64]

Premillennial dispensationalism (PD) was a key factor in the development of evangelical theology in Latin America. It was the theological framework for most of the missionaries sent by the "faith missions" at the end of the nineteenth century and the beginning of the twentieth century. Those missions passed PD dogmatically on to the new converts in the field. By the mid-twentieth century, with only a few minor variations and adaptations, PD had become absolute orthodoxy. It was "sound doctrine" for the majority of evangelicals. Even Pentecostal denominations adopted much of it.

Premillennial dispensationalism helped define evangelical identity in Latin America. Among its positive elements were a high view of Scripture, an emphasis on personal conversion together with individual ethics, and a sense of urgency for world evangelization based on the belief in an imminent personal return of Christ. The US–Mexico war and World War I added fuel to the eschatological fire, making evangelism seem even more urgent because the Lord was coming again anytime soon, according to the PD scheme. Also, the participation of all believers in the mission of the church – the priesthood of all believers – was more at the forefront in PD than in the CCLA. Most of the missions, like CAM, had from their beginnings local workers who were recent converts. The only thing they needed was the Bible, nothing else.

In contrast with the Panama Congress and the other congresses that followed, PD as a worldview did not have any interest in social involvement. CAM's publications and other documents have many references to spiritual conditions but social, political, and economic analysis is absent. The same could be said about most of the other "faith missions" working in the region. Schools, clinics, and orphanages were opened and run by missionaries. But, as William Cameron Townsend said at the time in Guatemala, "Of course we have a few schools and do some medical work and some of us want to develop these two branches even more but they are and always will be made

---

64. This summary of dispensationalism is taken from C. I. Scofield, ed., *The Holy Bible Containing the Old and New Testaments, Authorized Version, with a New System of Connected Topical References to All the Greater Themes of Scripture, with Annotations, Revised Marginal Renderings, Summaries, Definitions, Chronology, and Index* (New York: Oxford University Press, 1917). Many of these interpretations were revised during the twentieth century.

only servants of the work of evangelization."[65] The supremacy of evangelism, understood as the oral preaching of the dispensational message together with an invitation to accept Jesus personally, was an integral part of missionary practice. At the beginning of the twentieth century the inherited conflict between evangelism and social work had an important influence on the practical application of the message.

Within faith missions and their churches attitudes toward the predominant Church were those of direct confrontation, in contrast with that proposed by the CCLA. Missionaries as well as converts were convinced that Catholicism had not offered the true gospel and therefore they were responsible to fill that vacuum. As Scofield said: "Christians acquainted with Romanism only in the United States have no conception of how utterly debased and idolatrous it is in Spanish America."[66]

In Latin America PD inhibited the development of a contextual evangelical theology because it was a closed system. There was almost no possibility of change or adaptation; it looked like the Catholic theology they had opposed so eagerly. This kept the churches and denominations that started those years with little or no interest in producing a different biblical and theological response from the one they had received. It was important to learn the eschatological charts, the differences between Israel and the church, to believe in a secret rapture of believers and in a literal millennium. What else was necessary? Questioning the package was not encouraged.

We see during the first three decades of the twentieth century that the model the CCLA proposed at the different congresses was quickly eclipsed by the impetus and growing numbers of those who followed the dispensational model. We also need to take into account that, since early in the century – 1909 to be exact – there was an increasing Pentecostal presence, both native and foreign.[67] Soon CCLA's proposal became the minority and never represented Latin American Protestantism. The many internal revolutions, World War II, and the establishment of the State of Israel in 1948 seemed to validate PD and gave it the final thrust it needed. The sense of urgency became more intense;

65. Quoted by Bill Svelmoe, "Evangelism Only? Theory Versus Practice in the Early Faith Missions," *Missiology: An International Review* 31, no. 2 (2003): 197.

66. Quoted by George Irwin Ferris, Jr., "Protestantism in Nicaragua: Its Historical Roots and Influences Affecting Its Growth" (dissertation, Temple University, 1981), 121.

67. For the beginnings of the Pentecostal movement in Latin America see Luis Orellana, *El Fuego y La Nieve: Historia De Movimiento Pentecostal En Chile: 1909–1932* (Concepción, Chile: Centro Evangélico de Estudios Pentecostales [CELEP], 2006).

the eschatological hope of a secret rapture and the imminent return of Jesus Christ became stronger and more deeply entrenched across the continent.

2

The First Generation of Latin American Evangelicals Doing Theology: From Panama 1916 to Buenos Aires 1946

D aniel Enrique Hall, a Methodist minister from Buenos Aires, Argentina, recognized in 1927 that "the Roman Catholic Church in Latin America has departed from true Christianity in both belief and practice, and has invented and imposed upon its communicants traditional and superstitious rites and doctrines which are completely foreign to the mind and spirit of Christ."[1] A large part of the population, convinced that they were being deceived by the official Church, was openly rejecting all forms of religion, including the Protestant message. Hall acknowledged the evangelical contribution to Latin America in education, distribution of evangelical literature, especially the Bible, reduction of alcoholism, social work among the lowest-income workers, betterment of public health, and similar activities. All of that was carried out together with a key spiritual work, "making Christ known, winning disciples to him from every walk of life, organizing these believers into groups for corporate worship and united service, and extending Christian beliefs and ethical standards to community life."[2] Hall thus showed

---

1. Daniel Enrique Hall, "The Protestant Movement," in *As Protestant Latin America Sees It*, ed. Milton Stauffer (New York, NY: Student Volunteer Movement for Foreign Missions, 1927), 89.

2. Ibid., 98.

the integration between the social and spiritual aspects of the mission of the church at the beginning of the century.

By the end of the 1920s, evangelical churches had many needs on several fronts. Another Methodist from Argentina, Gabino Rodríguez, mentioned nominal Christians, former Catholics, who had converted but "have never borne the fruits of their new belief."[3] They were indifferent and ineffective witnesses, satisfied with observing rules of conduct and believing a set of doctrines but with no visible evidence of their new life. Rodríguez also mentioned the difficulty of getting new generations, specifically the children of believers, involved in the church. He attributed this to the fact that

> Unfortunately too much of our preaching and teaching has been dogmatic in character, controversial, and not very high quality intellectually. We have failed in two very important respects, it seems to me. In the first place, we have thus far failed to make our preaching and teaching a challenge to young people. And because the gospel has not been presented in a form and manner designed to challenge these young people, many of them have either become indifferent to it or have accepted it as something wished upon them, rather than as a gift of life which they have desired for themselves. In the second place, we have failed to hold the young people because we either did not or could not give them a proper social environment in which to express their social natures. Not finding an attractive or satisfying social life in the church, they have been lured away from the church in their quest of social activities and entertainment.[4]

Besides this, Rodríguez mentioned the pressing need of evangelical churches in Latin America to find ways of self-government, self-support, and self-diffusion. Two essential areas were part of this: leadership and finances. Regarding finances, Rodríguez asked: "Is it fair to be dependent any longer on our Christian friends, in Protestant North America and in Europe, who have been aiding us with their money and some of their best sons and daughters? Ought we not, even though still young, to begin to walk alone? Or will we

---

3. Gabino Rodríguez, "The Evangelical Churches," in *As Protestant Latin America Sees It*, ed. Milton Stauffer (New York, NY: Student Volunteer Movement for Foreign Missions, 1927), 110.

4. Ibid., 112.

continue for years to live an indigent life, holding fast to our foreign crutches longer than we need to or ought to for our good?"[5]

To meet the need for a Latin American leadership, Rodríguez called for extensive high-grade educational theological facilities with higher entrance requirements and better selected students. "This in turn calls for better theological schools, equipped with better library facilities and with better teaching staffs." For him, it was necessary to have well-prepared leaders in order to gain independence from foreign missionary supervision. There was also "a dearth of good Christian literature" and a need for "up-to-date textbooks for theological students and ministers, of sermons, commentaries, and devotional books." In short, there was a need for "literature that inspires, literature to guide and feed the mind, to strengthen the heart, and to move the will of our young generation."[6] This was even more pressing since "Protestant fanatics" were offending the religious sensibilities of Latin Americans and giving an erroneous impression of the Protestant faith.

In order to combat the idea most Latin American intellectuals held that the Christian faith was contrary to scientific investigation and progress, Rodríguez identified the need for "strong men in our ranks to disabuse people's minds of these misconceptions, both with the living voice and with the pen." These men had to be Latin Americans "well-equipped mentally, abreast of the latest scientific methods and discoveries, and will also need to have a knowledge of our Latin temperament and point of view, of our history and of our literature."[7] About the swift industrialization of Latin America, the challenges brought about by urbanization, and the conflict between labor and capital, Rodríguez commented,

> In the face of such pending disaster, will the Protestant church, regardless of the attitude of the Roman Catholic Church, still hesitate to preach a social gospel? Too long has she hesitated; too long the missionaries and native evangelists have concerned themselves almost exclusively with preparing men and women for life beyond the grave. They have preached an individual gospel and have left social problems largely in the hands and at the mercies of politicians and millionaires. Today the socialists are telling the Protestant Christians to "step aside, give us room,

---

5. Ibid., 114.

6. Ibid., 116.

7. Ibid., 117.

and we will show you how to create a new social order." Will we give way to them? We jeopardize our cause daily by insisting on being merely "other-worldly." Christ came to bring Latin America abundant life now. The time has come when to preach this gospel in these countries is to stress its social message and to challenge Christians with its social implications and demands.[8]

For Rodríguez, preaching needed to demonstrate "that the Christian religion is not dogma but life; it is not one special brand of theology better than all others, but a living spirit." To confront popular religiosity of rituals and formalities the message had to show "that Christianity is a power giving life to the spirit and fortitude to the soul, that it inspires, remotivates, and transforms." Believers had the responsibility to show "that evangelical Christianity is more than intellectual acceptance of a set of so-called orthodox beliefs, that it is life more abundant."[9] Gabino Rodríguez and his colleague Daniel Enrique Hall help us to see that by the third decade of the twentieth century the evangelical church in Latin America had taken root and was growing steadily. Both men had a genuine interest in the nationalization of the churches and their leadership. The evangelical message had a space and it was relevant for the spiritual and social realities in the region.

A few years later, John A. Mackay published a similar analysis. Mackay considered evangelical Christianity to be "the greatest single movement in the history of Latin America since the dawn of political independence."[10] The main contributions of the movement were fourfold: the availability of the Bible where reading it had been forbidden; the existence of new Christian communities; new schools and other educational options; and community service. "The Bible was the pioneer of the Evangelical movement in Latin America," and, according to Mackay, "the Book has been doing its transforming work and delivering its redemptive message."[11] Besides this, "after eighty years of missionary effort, an indigenous evangelical community in Latin America is a reality to be rejoiced in." It was a minority that in most countries "exerts an influence out of all proportion to its numbers, and constitutes a religious, ethical, and cultural force of no small importance."[12]

---

8. Ibid., 119.

9. Ibid., 120.

10. John A. Mackay, *That Other America* (New York, NY: Friendship Press, 1935), 145.

11. Ibid., 151.

12. Ibid., 154.

Mackay also mentioned, as positive examples of evangelical growth, the names of various evangelical Latin American intellectuals. In Mexico there was Presbyterian Moisés Sáenz, a diplomat in Ecuador, and his brother Aarón Sáenz, the head of the Federal District in Mexico and "a possible future president of the republic." There was also Methodist Andrés Osuna, former minister of education under Carranza's presidency, former governor of Tamaulipas, and for many years director general of education in the state of Nuevo León. From a younger generation, Gonzalo Báez-Camargo, "one of Mexico's leading editorial writers," possessed "a combination of qualities which one rarely met with in wanderings through many lands." From Brazil, Mackay listed Erasmo Braga, who had already passed away and who the authorities of Rio de Janeiro recognized by naming a street in his honor. Braga was remembered "as an educator and a writer of school textbooks, as a champion of every good cause in the country, as a father of cooperative movements in Brazilian Protestantism and secretary of the Committee on Cooperation in Brazil, as an international figure in the councils of the Christian church." Also from Rio de Janeiro was Presbyterian pastor Àlvaro Reis, who after his death the municipality "enshrined . . . in the memory of the citizens of Rio" by calling a plaza by his name. From Argentina was Dr George Howard, who for over two decades did evangelism in many countries "without any of the ordinary trappings associated with regular church services," and who was "a magnificent example of a pioneer evangelist, with the kind of message and the way to deliver it that the present hour in South America needs." Julio Navarro Monzó, also from Argentina and a lecturer for the YMCA, "in theaters, public lecture halls, and university auditoriums confronted the great unchurched masses with the reality of religion and especially of the Christian Savior and Lord."[13] It seems that the strategy of the CCLA to reach the educated classes was bearing some fruit.

As we will see below, Mackay described how some evangelical circles in Latin America, reacting to the popular concept of the "poor Christ," had deprived "the cross and the Crucified of the centrality which belongs to them in New Testament Christianity." That was responsible for a shallow presentation of the cross. He quotes an article in *La Nueva Democracia* in which Spaniard Juan Orts González raised some important christological questions: "Which ought to be our Christ, Velázquez's or the North Americans'? Is the Christ

---

13. Ibid., 156–174. Mackay writes a whole section about Monzó in John A. Mackay, *The Other Spanish Christ: A Study in the Spiritual History of Spain and South America* (New York, NY: Macmillan, 1933), 213–230.

of the North Americans deficient or complete? Is the Christ of the Spaniards the ideal for humanity or does he need to be completed? When one listens to North American speakers, or reads devotional books written in North America, one observes that the predominant note in these writers and preachers is that of the living Christ, triumphant and omnipotent, the Christ who is all action, service, power and stimulus."[14]

Mackay agreed with Orts González that Anglo-Saxon Protestantism had emphasized the risen Christ "who is all light and power." This was underlined by the absence in the new churches of any Christian symbolism representing "the tremendous realities of suffering and atonement in the life history of Jesus Christ." Spanish Catholicism, in contrast, had emphasized exclusively the crucified Christ. However, for Mackay, all Roman Catholicism "has been gloriously and consistently aware that something of cosmic importance happened when Jesus died on Golgotha."[15] In consequence, "Spanish and Latin American Catholicism have lost in ethical power; North American Protestantism is losing in religious depth." Therefore, concluded Mackay, the Christ needed by Spain and Latin America – and also by North America – was "the risen Crucified one."[16]

Mackay also delineated an ecclesiology for Latin America. The future of Christianity was linked to the existence and spiritual energy of organized Christian communities: "the future lies with those who make an absolute and irrevocable commitment to the revelation of God in Jesus Christ, and who, bound together in an intimate fellowship of love, according to the mind of Christ, take it as their supreme aim to make that fellowship coextensive with human society."[17] For Mackay, even a small Christian community should be an important influence in society. Nevertheless, he said, "let it not be thought that the new Christians in Latin America should immediately assume all the responsibilities toward society which are the inescapable obligation of mature, consolidated churches whose membership is in a position to exert a dominant influence in civic and national affairs." Here he proposed something that sounded like an exaggeration: "Nascent churches have a great deal to

---

14. The Christ of Velázquez (*Christ Crucified*) was a painting from 1632 by Diego Rodríguez de Silva y Velázquez. Mackay, *That Other America*, 190. For an account of the development of Christology in Latin America see J. Samuel Escobar, *En Busca De Cristo En América Latina* (Buenos Aires: Kairos, 2012).

15. Mackay, *That Other America*, 191.

16. Ibid., 192.

17. Ibid.

learn from the organization and work of communist 'cells.'"[18] To the question "What is our ideal for the new Christian churches in Latin America?" Mackay gave this answer:

> One of their chief concerns must be the expansion and consolidation of their fellowship, but not in order that this fellowship may become an end in itself; not that it should exist merely for services; not that its round of activities should be an everlasting treadmill. The church must be "edified" in the Pauline sense "for the work of ministering," for the task of serving men and women in the spirit of Christ. Church leaders must see to it that an opportunity is provided for the expression of every talent that can be used in the service of truth and goodness. They must equally show concern that human needs in the community in which the church is located are being faced by the membership. Nothing is more pathetic than to find from time to time that a member of an Evangelical church in a Latin American country wishes to devote himself to a philanthropic task in which the church is not interested because it is exclusively concerned with itself.[19]

Mackay was echoing the agenda the CCLA's congresses had defined for the evangelical churches: growth and social service. There was a clear danger of their not seeing beyond their four walls. For him, evangelical communities were elements of spiritual and social, as well as individual and community, change.

La Nueva Democracia

The congresses convened by the CCLA provided the incentive for several literary and journalistic initiatives. Latin American theological thinking found in those publications its best distribution channel. Samuel Guy Inman, professor of Inter-American Relations at Columbia University, New York, general secretary of CCLA, and an active participant at the various congresses,

---

18. Ibid., 193.
19. Ibid., 195.

started the magazine *La Nueva Democracia* (*LND*) in January 1920.[20] *LND* appeared monthly for twenty-three years and then quarterly until the last issue in 1963. The main editor was Spaniard Dr Juan Orts González. Alberto Rembao was its director from 1939 until its closing, which coincided with Rembao's death.

> Our main purpose? To make our magazine a public platform from which the ideals, in part latent, of the American continent come out and crystallize in public ways; everything being directed, not to subordinate Latin American civilization to the Anglo-Saxon civilization or vice versa, but, on the contrary, to try to show that both civilizations can complement and perfect each other, through co-penetration and mutual influence. After both civilizations are convinced of this fact, to procure that both might offer spiritual, social, artistic, and economic help to a Europe battered and in imminent danger of complete ruin. No doubt we are living in critical days; humanity is currently going through the most tremendous crises of its history. We depend on America to solve these terrible problems. If not, they threaten to bring down the present civilization, with the same ease Barbarians brought down the Roman Empire.[21]

Initially it would seem that *LND* was more interested in political and economic questions. However, the editors made it clear that "our first section will be eminently religious." It was not the religion "of rigid dogma, a series of mechanical rituals, or complicated ceremonies; of temples, basilicas, and cathedrals; of an organism settled in its forms of ministers, pastors, bishops, and popes." Instead,

> The religion we are going to talk about is the pure and simple religion of Golgotha's martyr, Jesus Christ; this religion which was sought out by the great seers of past revolutions, which was their inspiration; this religion which in its original purity attracted such illustrious poets and writers, so noble and opposite in their political views, as Victor Hugo, Chateaubriand, Castelar and

20. In *LND*, "without any doubt many Latin American intellectuals found for the first time a Protestant theological expression at academic level." Samuel Escobar, *La Fe Evangélica y Las Teologías De La Liberación* (El Paso: Casa Bautista de Publicaciones, 1987), 51.

21. Redacción, "Nuestro Saludo y Nuestro Programa," *La Nueva Democracia* 1, no. 1 (1920): 2.

Tolstoi, Rivero and Nocedal, etc.; this religion which when loyally and sincerely interpreted can solve all the present problems; in a word, we are going to talk about the sociological aspects of Christianity. We are convinced that readers who will constantly and impartially read all the facts and reasons we will argue for will be convinced that if there is a solution to today's problems, it is based only on a well-thought-out Christianity; that without the high concept Christianity has of the law and obligations, of authority and obedience, of social justice and distribution, of human personality and the home, of individual liberty and the workplace, not to mention other problems, society cannot evolve. It will lack foundations or will have more than enough tyranny; complete chaos will come upon it, an incomparable chaos, worse than the eruption of the Barbarians over the Roman Empire.[22]

The first issue of *LND* included, besides the editorial, four main sections: Sociology and Morality, Science and Inventions, Art and Education, and Global News. These four themes continued until the last issue. In December 1921, book reviews were included. Most of the articles were written by Hispanic Americans. Inman was able to recruit famous people as writers, such as Uruguayan former president Baltasar Brum; José Vasconcelos, a former minister of education in Mexico; and Chilean poet and 1945 Nobel Literature Prize-winner Gabriela Mistral. Journalists, writers, and educators, including women, had in *LND* a wide platform to reach primarily the educated classes of the continent.

The content and contributors of *LND* maintained the framework on Christian work that the CCLA had delineated at the congresses. There was no problem, from a Christian standpoint, with talking about world events such as the European war or Latin American social realities. Interest in society at large did not inhibit *LND*'s apologetic and evangelistic interest. For instance, the article "Why Do Many People Reject Religion?" stated the following:

There is no doubt that ninety-nine percent, not to say one hundred percent, would reconcile themselves to religion – and here by religion we mean Christianity – if they knew its whole magnificence, splendor, simplicity, and truth. This is the supreme problem the churches have today: to introduce

---

22. Ibid.

true Christianity to humankind. There has never been such an opportunity for the Christian message to be offered satisfactorily to all peoples and all social classes. Never before has humankind felt bigger perplexities, greater longings, and a more vivid desire to investigate whether Christianity can save it from the horrible present conflicts. But the Christianity which can save humankind is not a mere liturgical Christianity or entirely ecclesiastical: a tolerant and harmonious Christianity like Christ's is needed; a fertile and vital Christianity like the apostles'; a transforming Christianity which will apply, without any conditions or human prejudices, the Christian principles to all the current problems, private, public, belonging to capital or labor, relating to government or those under government, about domestic problems or international relationships; a Christianity fearlessly telling the truth and all the truth to capital and labor, kings and populace, clergy and laypeople. Woe to the churches if in these times they are unfaithful to their mission, because of selfishness or through dangerous partiality, and do not offer the message, the whole of the Christian message, to today's society! May God forbid it! The Christian churches will be swept away by the present revolutionary whirl and they will perish in a worldwide cataclysm leaving nothing but confusion, anarchy, and chaos.[23]

In the next issue, *LND* was even more explicit about its ecclesiological agenda. The editorial read:

Humankind requires during these days full of instability and anguish that the Christian churches stay not with placebos, nor that they offer fictions and shadows, or remain content with unfriendly and partial messages; instead humankind requires them to present in its fullness the whole program of Christ that consoles those who are suffering and the needy; and in all its terrifying majesty for those who abuse power, riches, and their political influence. Only this kind of Christianity can survive the threatening and invading Bolshevism, only this kind of Christianity can be a fraternizing flag between capital and labor, only this kind of Christianity can be like a rainbow in the current

23. Redacción, "¿Por Qué Rechazan Muchos La Religión?," *La Nueva Democracia* 1, no. 2 (1920): 4.

squall and storm and guide people to the only fountain of truth, justice, and salvific and transforming love: to Jesus Christ.[24]

Inman and his team did not hesitate to mix their version of church with politics. Henceforth, their call to evangelicals to get involved was bold, especially because evangelicals in Latin America were a small minority. For *LND*, though, the fact that they were few was not an excuse. Previously Erasmo Braga had called the evangelical churches "the biggest social organization of Latin America, after the Roman Church."[25] Maybe evangelicals did not have any idea of their numerical strength, and that kept them from getting involved in the public arena. *LND* mentioned, for instance, the fact that slavery had been tolerated and many times even promoted by Christians, the complicit silence of the churches regarding the administration of justice in favor of the powerful and the unfair distribution of wealth, the lack of intervention of the churches to prevent the war, and the diminishing evangelistic zeal, "whilst churches found satisfaction in building new places of worship with better organs and greater comfort for their few members."[26]

The question remains whether the position taken by *LND* about the churches being involved in the politics of their countries was realistic. A historian had a completely different take on the situation.

> The Protestant community of Central and South America at that time (ca. 1918–1930) was suffering from an acute inferiority complex. Most churches were small chapels or rented halls on back streets. The congregations felt themselves to be an oppressed, persecuted minority. Their evangelistic activity was limited largely to a modest and somewhat timid personal witness and to preaching in their unpretentious chapels. National leadership, except in the large cities, was mediocre and not well prepared.[27]

Contrast this opinion with what Alberto Rembao wrote in 1948:

---

24. Redacción, "Cristo y Las Iglesias Cristianas," *La Nueva Democracia* 1, no. 3 (1920): 3.

25. Erasmo Braga, *Pan-Americanismo: Aspecto Religioso. Una Relación E Interpretación Del Congreso De Acción Cristiana En La América Latina Celebrado En Panamá Los 10 a 19 De Febrero De 1916*, trans. Eduardo Monteverde (New York, NY: Sociedad para la Educación Misionera en los Estados Unidos y el Canadá, 1917), 49.

26. Redacción, "Cristo y Las Iglesias Cristianas."

27. W. Dayton Roberts, "The Legacy of R. Kenneth Strachan," *Occasional Bulletin of Missionary Research* 3, no. 1 (1979): 2.

Today, the twenty Latin American nations may well be classified as Protestant, in the sense that in each one of them the Evangelical community is already too numerous to be regarded as a minority and strong enough to cause the general public to stop and look and listen. In any event, that community, anywhere, is not the feeble congregation of outcasts hanging around the philanthropic skirts of foreign missionaries, but rather a most powerful ferment with sufficient energy of radiation to alter for good the social atmosphere and the spiritual climate of the whole continent.[28]

Do these two extremely different opinions provide evidence of the gulf between the Protestantism of the CCLA and that of the churches started by the faith missions – or maybe an indication of a chasm between the two theologies? Was the optimism of the CCLA a reflection of what was really happening, or was it just wishful thinking? The fact that many years needed to pass before the realization of the ideal *LND* proposed for the churches does not take away its merit of being at the forefront of the Protestant efforts to spread the yeast of the gospel in Latin America.

Luminar

La Nueva Democracia was in its seventeenth year of continuous publication when in Mexico Gonzalo Báez-Camargo started another magazine. *Luminar*, a "revolutionary and independent" magazine, came out in December 1936 as the world was going through the period between the two great wars. Báez-Camargo had also invited important people to contribute: Colombian politician Guillermo de la Torre; William N. Montaño, a Bolivian author; Angel M. Mergal from Puerto Rico; the director of the Institute for Philosophy and Literature of Mexico, Antonio Caso; and Argentinian Augusto J. Durelli. Women also had a place to write in *Luminar*, as in *LND*.[29] The purpose of

---

28. Alberto Rembao, "The Presence of Protestantism in Latin America," *International Review of Missions* 21, no. 1 (1948): 57.

29. Mexican historian Carlos Mondragón asserted, "*Luminar* represents the most important Protestant publication in Mexico during the 1930s and 1940s. Not just because of its critical and antidogmatic editorial criteria, but mostly because of such an editorial philosophy, it counted on the best quills of the Mexican, Latin American, and European intellectual world. Neither before nor since have evangelicals published in Mexico a magazine with the level and quality of collaborators *Luminar* was able to have during its fifteen years of productive existence." Various, *Gonzalo Báez-Camargo: Una Vida Al Descubierto* (Mexico D.F.: Centro de Comunicación Cultural [CUPSA A.C.], 1985), 126.

Luminar was to "project light upon the problems and perplexities that agitate the conscience of our times and to show, within the criteria of our convictions, a dynamic orientation for the crossroads put forward by collective and individual life." Not to leave any doubt that it was Christian magazine:

> Such light, such orientation, such dynamism, can derive only from a supreme source of energy. That supreme source of energy, Luminar professes, is found in Christ. Luminar will be, thus, a Christian magazine, and for this we do not offer any excuses or apologies. We believe the time has come, once again, to interrogate Jesus, to bring him out of the tomb in which many of his enemies and even some of his friends have wished to keep him under seven seals; to again examine his message in detail without any prejudice, so that orientations and dynamic principles can be found in him once more, to convert this world which is crumbling away into a newer, younger, and better one. Wasn't it he who promised not only new heavens but also a NEW EARTH? To say that Luminar is a Christian magazine does not in any way mean a dogmatic or confessional magazine. Luminar believes the truth is in Christ. Nevertheless, it does not believe that the truth can remain definitely enclosed, packed, and poured into dogmatic declarations or finished recipes. Christ is the Way, the Truth, and the Life. But that Way is not fenced in by ecclesiastical hedges; that Truth is not monopolized by doctors and scribes; that Life is not exhausted by traditional forms, nor deposited inside hardened casks, dried riverbeds, and waterproofed cisterns. The Way advances, the Truth is marching on, and the Life is opening up in perpetual bloom.[30]

Here is found the same attitude towards dogma held by the CCLA and *LND*. Did such a position discourage local theological production within the area of influence of the CCLA? Báez-Camargo wrote after the Havana Congress of the need to "Latinize" Protestantism, to make it into a native plant. In the first issue of *Luminar* he explained what he meant. Each epoch must take into account its concrete problems and realities, he said, and search inside the message of Christ for its own applications and practical solutions.

---

30. Pedro Gringoire, "Presentación," *Luminar* 1, no. 1 (1936): 4.

Otherwise, Jesus' teachings would not have any positive or real value at any time. He explained,

> It is necessary, therefore, to delineate the projections his message has for the concrete problems of our day; to delineate the points of immediate application of his doctrine; to outline the results, in today's terms, of the forces he liberated and put into action within history. This task, for our generation, is still undone. To achieve this, it is necessary to get rid of any dogmatic tyranny, to put on internal strength with no other limitations but those imposed by a genuine love for truth, and go forward with the heroic task of building upon Christ's eternal principles a new economical, social, and spiritual construction which will bring solutions to the deepest problems of today and a solid push in our march for an ideal world.[31]

Evidently, early in the century there were solid proposals to work towards, if not a theology, at least a contextual message that would consider the particular situations and conditions of the countries in Latin America. Antenor Orrego, a Peruvian sociologist, called that process the "Americanization" of Latin America.[32] About a decade later, in 1945, Mexican writer Francisco E. Estrello described the same challenge. Estrello was convinced that, even though Christianity was the only adequate spiritual message, it had lost relevance, "vitality and freshness, not because of Jesus but because of the Christians."[33] Thus, it was necessary to "enter a time of renewal of our former processes as well as of our spirit," since believers were "giving a dead show to the world." Instead, the Christian message needed to "share the pain, miseries, yearnings, anxieties, hopes, and struggles of men; it must identify with them, to become like one of them."[34]

> We Christians today are committed to demonstrate to the world that the Christian religion is not made of tradition, that it is linked to life and that it is as real as life; that the Lord did not live fantasies and did not feed people with them; that the kingdom of heaven is not an imaginary kingdom but a true kingdom

---

31. Ibid., 5.

32. Antenor Orrego, "El Destino Trascendente De América," *Luminar* 1, no. 4 (1937).

33. Francisco E. Estrello, "El Cristianismo De Hoy y De Mañana En El Mundo," *Luminar* 9, no. 4 (1945): 50.

34. Ibid., 51.

made out of experiences that are far from fantasy; that Jesus is not yesterday's reality, but also today's; that he is not one reality among many, but the Supreme Reality; that all life is under his authority; that everything real belongs to him.[35]

Believers needed to recover what Estrello called a "simple lifestyle" in contrast to "the spirit of selfish commercialism" of his time. A simple lifestyle included living for the dignity of human life and for the service of others. It meant to stop being concerned with "an altar Christianity" and to start living "Jesus' Christianity." It meant to live according to the principles of "justice, altruism, and love" with generosity, sacrifice, service, and holiness. It meant to live out a prophetic Christianity recognizing that "human personality is sacred" and therefore "every system that tends to diminish it is a system that goes against God's plans and, as Christians, we are neither willing nor obligated to support it."[36]

We must preach Christianity which unites, erases borders, and eliminates prejudices; we must live this Christianity which does not leave alive even the smallest speck of hatred, but instead sparks a fire of love; a fire of love to warm up not only our friends but our neighbor, whoever he might be. The man left at the side of the road, robbed and beaten by thieves, was a Jew; the man with compassionate hands and a heart full of love, who washed the wounds and poured oil on them, was a Samaritan.

The world needs our Christianity to have compassionate hands and a heart burning with the Samaritan love, because there is much pain spread out on the road demanding to be alleviated, and much need from which we cannot just walk away.[37]

Such a Christianity would return happiness to people, because "the kingdom of heaven was not a task just for the disciples in the first century, it is a task for us, the Christians of today, and for the Christians of tomorrow." Estrello concluded,

Our Christianity is facing a crisis, and if it wishes to know how it should behave and how it should act, the only thing to do is to turn and face Jesus, to be inspired by the heroic dignity and

---

35. Ibid., 53.
36. Ibid., 56.
37. Ibid., 58.

glorious majesty of his actions at a time when the destiny of humankind was at stake. Today, as it was then, we are living in a time when the destiny of humankind is at stake; the world awaits the living and profoundly spiritual message of Jesus' followers.[38]

Báez-Camargo and Estrello were not the only writers of *Luminar* carrying a strong christological banner, as a review of its table of contents would show. As we have seen above, Christology was also highlighted at the congresses of the CCLA. That was a reflection of a trend in the general cultural atmosphere during those years. "The most cheering element in the Latin American situation today is the way in which Christ is attracting to himself the gaze of an increasing number of people in the other America," wrote John A. Mackay in 1935 after several years of traveling across the continent presenting the Christian faith to academics.[39] Such an interest in Jesus, Mackay explained, was stoked by some nonreligious literature: two books by the French communist writer Henri Barbusse –*Jésus* and *Les Judas de Jésus* (1927) – which had been widely distributed in Latin America among the "radicals"; and a book by another Frenchman, Ernest Renan – *The Life of Jesus* (1863) – "the only life of Christ known to many Latin American intellectuals." There was also a book – *The Invisible Christ* (1928) – by Argentinian author Ricardo Rojas, considered "the most brilliant man of letters in the twenty southern republics."[40]

One of the most prolific evangelical writers of those years was Argentinian Baptist pastor Juan Crisóstomo Varetto (1879–1953), an author of historical, pastoral, and theological books which showed a clear Latin Americanization and key relevance for that time. For instance, he wrote the first biographies of Diego Thomson, Rogerio Williams, Federico Crowe, and Juan F. Thomson; books about the Latin American religious situation and Protestant history; pastoral works and sermon outlines – all of which served as textbooks in many Bible institutes. Varetto had originality and clarity together with a deep understanding of the evangelical identity of his and other denominations in general.[41]

---

38. Ibid., 62.

39. Mackay, *That Other America*, 131.

40. Ibid., 134. Mackay includes a short analysis of Ro *The Other Spanish Christ*, 205–213.

41. Here is a partial list of works by Juan C. Varetto: *Diego Thomson, Apóstol De La Instrucción Pública E Iniciador De La Obra Evangélica En La América Latina* (Buenos Aires: Imprenta Evangélica, 1918); *Discursos Evangélicos* (Buenos Aires: Junta Bautista de Publicaciones, 1919); *Rogerio Williams: Héroe De La Libertad Religiosa* (Buenos Aires: Junta de Publicaciones de la Convención Evangélica Bautista, 1921); *Hostilidad Del Clero a La*

The Other Spanish Christ

No other book had more influence on the development of Latin American evangelical theology in those years than John A. Mackay's *The Other Spanish Christ*, 1932. It was mostly unknown in Latin America until the Spanish translation came out twenty years later, whereupon it immediately became one of the most quoted by Latin Americans who wanted to think their faith in a relevant and contextual manner. After a lengthy analysis of what Mackay called "The Iberian Soul" he developed the theme of the figure of Christ in South America:

> But however much overshadowed by His Mother, Christ too came to America. And yet, was it really He who came, or another religious figure with His name and some of His marks? Methinks the Christ, as He sojourned westward, went to prison in Spain, while another who took His name embarked with the Spanish crusaders for the New World, a Christ who was not born in Bethlehem but in North Africa. This Christ became naturalized in the Iberian colonies of America, while Mary's Son and Lord has been little else than a stranger and sojourner in these lands from Columbus's day to this.[42]

Commenting on what the great Spaniard Miguel de Unamuno wrote about the Spanish Christ, Mackay came to the conclusion that in "Spanish religion Christ has been the center of a cult of death." Consequently, "details of His earthly life are of slight importance and make relatively small appeal." Hence, continued Mackay, Christ was "regarded as a purely supernatural

---

Independencia Americana (Buenos Aires: Imprenta Metodista, 1922); *Las Biblias En Castellano* (Buenos Aires: Junta de Publicaciones de la Convención Evangélica Bautista, 1925); *Separación De La Iglesia y El Estado* (Buenos Aires: Junta de Publicaciones de la Convención Evangélica Bautista de las Repúblicas del Plata, 1927); *Héroes y Mártires De La Obra Misionera Desde Los Apóstoles Hasta Nuestros Días* (Buenos Aires: Convención Evangélica Bautista, 1934); *Federic Crowe En Guatemala* (Buenos Aires: Junta Bautista de Publicaciones, 1940); *El Apóstol Del Plata, Juan F. Thomson* (Buenos Aires: La Aurora, 1943); *Refutación Del Adventismo* (Buenos Aires: Junta de Publicaciones de la Convención Evangélica Bautista, 1948); *La Reforma Religiosa Del Siglo XVI* (Buenos Aires: Junta de Publicaciones de la Convención Evangélica Bautista, 1949); *Una Conversación Familiar Con Los Que Quieren Bautizarse* (Santiago: Wilson, 1950); *Los Hechos De Los Apóstoles Explicado* (Buenos Aires: Editorial Evangélica Bautista, 1952); *Cuatro Conversaciones Familiares Sobre Samson* (Buenos Aires: Editorial Evangélica Bautista, 1952); *Bosquejos Para Sermones* (Buenos Aires: Editorial Evangélica Bautista, 1955); *La Marcha Del Cristianismo: Desde Los Apóstoles Hasta Los Valdenses* (Buenos Aires: Junta de Publicaciones de la Convención Evangélica Bautista, 1973).

42. Mackay, *The Other Spanish Christ*, 95.

being, whose humanity, being only apparent, has little ethical bearing upon ours."[43] The Christ of the predominant religion in South America was a "docetic Christ" resulting in a type of faith "which was utterly devoid of both intellectual and ethical content." He concluded,

> A Christ known in life as an infant and in death as a corpse, over whose helpless childhood and tragic fate the Virgin Mother presides; a Christ who became man in the interests of eschatology, whose permanent reality resides in a magic wafer bestowing immortality; a Virgin Mother who by not tasting death became the Queen of Life – that is the Christ and that the Virgin who came to America! He came as Lord of Death and of the life that is to be; she came as Sovereign Lady of the life that now is.[44]

But Christ "remains to be known as Jesus, the Saviour from sin and the Lord of all life,"[45] an astonishing descriptive declaration from a continent which considered itself Christian. At the end of the book Mackay defined what he thought evangelical work in Latin America should look like. He advised foreign missionaries to "identify themselves absolutely with their community," avoiding the founding of "little Britain" and "little America" in their adopted countries. "The word from abroad must become indigenous flesh, or it will fail to obtain a hearing for the eternal Word it presumes to echo."[46] He made an urgent appeal for unity and cooperation among mission organizations working in the area because the "demonstration of the fundamental unity and solidarity of the evangelical forces would make a profound impression in the Latin American world."[47] Here Mackay struck a chord constantly found in subsequent evangelical literature – the lack of unity among evangelicals.

For the local churches, Mackay encouraged reverent conduct in the worship services: "Preaching and worship have fallen on evil days when religious thought has to be spiced by the banal prelude of a joke." Besides this, he recommended the adoption of "a new type of pioneer evangelism" to take religious ideas "into the open air, and there proving that they are worthwhile being considered for their own sake, and not merely as part of

---

43. Ibid., 98.
44. Ibid., 102.
45. Ibid., 117.
46. Ibid., 265.
47. Ibid., 266.

a ceremonial act."[48] He predicted that when "the officials representative of Protestant Christianity in Latin America step out into the open, and become interested in presenting the faith that is in them in such a way as to challenge the man in the street, a new day will have dawned in the spiritual history of the continent."[49] The Christian message was "not a system, but a personality." The main concern of Latin American believers "should be not whether the Continent will become Protestant, as we with our institutional-mindedness understand Protestant, but that it shall become Christian."[50]

The Balcony and the Road

As influential as Mackay's book was on the new generations of Latin American evangelicals, so was his metaphor of the balcony and the road in the search for truth. "The first precondition necessary for achieving insight into God and man is that the seeker place himself in the appropriate perspective for this."[51] The "balcony" and the "road" defined that perspective. A balcony was a common feature of Spanish architecture and it can still be seen in many of the old cities in Latin America. The perspective from the balcony was that "of the perfect spectator, for whom life and the universe are permanent objects of study and contemplation." The road was "the place of action, of pilgrimage, of crusade." Mackay intended to convince his readers that the road was the proper perspective because "religious truth is obtained only on the Road."

> The Road is the symbol of a first-hand experience of reality where thought, born of a living concern, issues in decision and action. When a man squarely faces the challenge of existence, a vital concern is aroused within him. He puts to himself the question, what must I do? He is eager to know, not so much what things are in their ultimate essence, as what they are and should be in their concrete existence.[52]

Whoever assumed the perspective from the road was concerned about righteousness and committed to righteousness, someone who "hungers and thirsts after righteousness." For Mackay those "who seek righteousness as

---

48. Ibid., 267.
49. Ibid., 268.
50. Ibid., 264.
51. John A. Mackay, *A Preface to Christian Theology* (New York, NY: Macmillan, 1941), 27.
52. Ibid., 44.

the 'pearl of great price,' however they may interpret it, must be prepared to sacrifice everything on its account." For Mackay, doing theology had direct ethical implications. Theology and ethics went together. For example, when someone was searching for personal truth in Jesus Christ, that was "the moment to descend from the Balcony to the Road. For Christ can never be known by men who would be His patrons, but only by those who are prepared to become His servants."[53]

In his books, Mackay provided for subsequent generations of Latin Americans a model for reflection, an acute and academic analysis, a rigorous literary methodology, a theological agenda, an ecclesiastical paradigm, and a challenge to be autochthonous and relevant. It was hard to ignore his calling. When the Spanish edition of *The Other Spanish Christ* and some of his other books came out, they fell upon fertile soil. Many young people were inspired and encouraged in their faith through Mackay's writings. Samuel Escobar, for instance, told how before he went to college in 1951, Mackay's book *El Sentido de la Vida* helped him in his conversion to Christ.[54] Escobar also wrote,

> The writings of Latin American ecumenical theologians like Emilio Castro and José Míguez Bonino, or evangelicals like René Padilla and Pedro Arana, show Mackay's pervasive influence. In Latin America he pioneered a new form of evangelism to reach the unchurched and paganized elites, especially university students. He drafted documents that are points of reference of church history in our time and created metaphors and aphorisms that are part of the theological heritage of the church universal. His life and career were a unique blend of the best of the evangelical and ecumenical worlds.[55]

CELA I, 1949

Gonzalo Báez-Camargo and John A. Mackay participated at the First Latin American Evangelical Conference (Primera Conferencia Evangélica

---

53. Ibid., 71.

54. Samuel Escobar, "Heredero De La Reforma Radical," in *Hacia Una Teología Latinoamericana: Ensayos En Honor a Pedro Savage*, ed. C. René Padilla (San José, Costa Rica: Editorial Caribe, 1984), 53.

55. Samuel Escobar, "The Legacy of John Alexander Mackay," *International Bulletin of Missionary Research* 16 (1992): 116.

Latinoamericana, CELA I), Buenos Aires, 18–30 July 1949, a year after the World Council of Churches was formed. There were fifty-six official delegates and forty-seven visitors representing eighteen denominations. CELA I was organized "by the entities for inter-denominational cooperation representing most of the evangelical forces in the countries of Latin America." In contrast with the previous congresses convened by the CCLA, this conference "was not about a study of the mission fields by the organizations on the field, but rather the reflection of the national evangelical churches on their situation and mission."[56]

Although CELA I was not a theological gathering, its final reports reflected a statement of faith. Commission II condensed in six major points their conclusions about the evangelical message for Latin America:

- Our message for America and the world is Jesus Christ and His gospel. Jesus Christ, Son of God and Son of Man, is the Revelation of the nature and designs of God as Father, perfect and infinite in love, justice, and holiness.

- This message is in the Bible. The Bible is the supreme source of our knowledge of God and His redemptive revelation in Jesus Christ. Reading the Bible is, then, indispensable for the spiritual life of every Christian. The Christian church should make it available and proclaim its teachings to the whole of society.

- Humankind was created by God in His image and likeness for a life of filial communion with Him and a fraternal relationship with their neighbor. People rebelled against God's will and tried to be a law unto themselves. From this rebellion, the essence of sin, proceeds human disorder with the consequences of misery and evil. Incapable of saving themselves, people need conversion, forgiveness, and regeneration.

- We find in the gospel God's answer to our need. God, in His infinite love, has taken the initiative to save humankind. He came to us, in His wholeness, in Jesus of Nazareth, who conquered sin and death. His redemptive suffering and death on Calvary give us the assurance of the Father's forgiveness. His resurrection guaranties the triumph over sin and death for all those who trust in Him.

---

56. CELA I, *El Cristianismo Evangélico En América Latina. Informes y Resoluciones De La Primera Conferencia Evangélica Latinoamericana, 18 Al 30 De Julio De 1949, Buenos Aires, Argentina* (Buenos Aires: La Aurora, 1949), 18.

- Together with His gift of Christ, God has bestowed and bestows His Holy Spirit, Counselor and Spirit of Truth, in order to constitute and preserve the church, the communion of those God has called "out of darkness into His wonderful light." Also, through the Spirit's direction and power the church proclaims to the world the salvific work of Christ for the conversion of unbelievers and the sanctification of believers. The church teaches people the love of its Master and Lord, and approaches them by preaching the gospel of grace; practicing the ministry of mercy, teaching, and healing; striving for peace and reconciliation among people; standing up against iniquity and injustice; and praying to God for the pain and distress of those who suffer.

- Christ impels his followers to seek first the Kingdom of God and His righteousness, meaning to accept joyfully God's sovereignty over everything and everybody. The presence of the Kingdom on earth implies not only individual regeneration but also the transformation of all levels of human society by the work of the Holy Spirit on renewed lives, and it is manifested through the obedient acts of His followers. Christ will establish his Kingdom of love and justice and, at the end, under God's absolute dominion, there will be "new heavens and a new earth."[57]

CELA I recognized the need for theological institutions to prepare pastors, institutions with programs adaptable to specific needs. The backbone of the instruction should be "the study and interpretation of the Bible," together with history and theology, including the basics of the original Bible languages. It was important to also include pastoral practice. The faculty, so far mostly foreign, should soon include more native professors who "have studied at the best universities to better their teaching." Theology professors should maintain close relationships with local churches, "but they should not be so loaded with ecclesiastical work that they will be left with little time to prepare their lectures, keep up with their theological studies, and make original contributions to evangelical literature."[58]

Regarding evangelical literature, before CELA I the CCLA had been publishing works penned by Latin Americans – such as *Reformismo Cristiano y Alma Española* by Angel M. Mergal; *Discurso a la Nación Evangélica* by

---

57. Ibid., 35–37.
58. Ibid., 68–73.

Alberto Rembao; and *Radiofonía Evangélica* by Manuel Garrido Aldama. This publishing was the result of a strategic conference on Christian literature held in Mexico City in 1941 for Spanish-speaking countries. There were two similar conferences for Brazil: São Paulo 1936 and Rio de Janeiro 1947. The plan was to continue to publish books on the Bible, the church, doctrine, apologetics, Christian life, Christian education, and children's books. CELA I defined goals for the preparation of national writers, including journalists, and called the churches to help in the distribution of whatever was being published.[59]

The theology of CELA I and its final recommendations stayed within the boundaries marked out by the previous congresses. What was new at Buenos Aires was that the delegates represented churches and denominations, making it more likely that its directives would be followed. There was a clear awareness of the needs and a commitment to keep expanding. However, one might ask whether CELA I really represented Latin American evangelicals. The participating denominations were few and mostly of Reformed convictions – Waldensian, Methodist, Nazarene, Baptist, Lutheran, Presbyterian and Episcopalian – with a minimal Pentecostal and faith missions presence – Disciples of Christ and Christian and Missionary Alliance. There was no one from Central America, where churches mostly followed the dispensational and anti-ecumenical line. There was only one delegate from Colombia and Mexico. In this way, CELA I maintained the chasm that had existed from the beginning between the CCLA and the faith missions.

---

59. Ibid., 76.

3

The Second Generation: From Buenos Aires 1949 to Cochabamba 1970

When idealistic marauders ousted dictator Fulgencio Batista on New Year's Day 1959 and established Cuba as the first communist government in the Americas, the Cold War reached its peak. Since the evangelical presence in Latin America was mostly the result of conservative North American missionary proselytism all kinds of alarms went off, sending evangelicals into panic mode. For most it was clear which side Christ was on: he was definitely not with the "leftists." Communism and socialism became in the evangelical world the "unpardonable sins," the Antichrist, obnoxious diseases of apocalyptic proportions. Evangelicals developed strategic schemes to keep them out of the region and to exorcize them wherever even the faintest suspicion of their ugly presence was encountered. Dominican Juan Bosh described the situation:

> More or less, by 1961 Latin America has become the field of the most hateful political battle in the world. Reactionary forces – continental and hemispheric – have deployed all their weapons for a fight with no surrender. By saying that the Cuban revolution is communist, the whole media, owned by the land-owning oligarchies, financial and commercial, beat the masses day and night with psychological terror. Their plan is to start in America the persecution of communists, and later, as always, of the non-communist revolutionaries.[1]

---

1. Quoted in *Panorama Iberoamericano, 1962* (Huampaní: II Congreso de Comunicaciones Evangélicas, 1962).

However, on the university campuses, Christians could not keep their heads hidden in the sand. They were thrown into an intense discussion with their Marxist classmates on the options Latin America had for bringing about social equality and bettering the living conditions of millions of people. Most evangelical university students had not faced these questions before and their spiritual answers seemed out of place and superficial. Ecclesiastical leaders were not prepared to deal with the situation, and this gave the students the idea that their faith was irrelevant. Many left their churches, since they could not reconcile their beliefs with the demands for answers.[2] There was an urgent need for well-thought-out, biblically sound responses that did justice to the complex situation and the Latin American context.

Certeza and *Pensamiento Cristiano*

Argentinian Alejandro Clifford (1907–1980) was a pioneer opening up opportunities for theological reflection. In 1928 he founded *El Despertar*, a magazine for young people within his denomination, the Plymouth Brethren, which ran for four decades. In 1953 he also started publishing *Pensamiento Cristiano* (*PC*), a non-denominational magazine, as a platform for theological dialogue and reflection. Clifford was also the first editor of *Certeza*, a magazine aimed at university students and young professionals mostly in the context of the International Fellowship of Evangelical Students (IFES). *Certeza* started in 1959 and closed in 1980. For almost three decades the two magazines presented the theology being forged by evangelicals in Latin America. In these magazines were found the first writings of some who later became well-known theologians, such as Miguel Zandrino, David Powell, and René Padilla from Argentina; José Grau from Spain; and Peruvians Samuel Escobar and Pedro Arana. There were articles on sociology, psychology, education, and society in general.

Samuel Escobar, who was part of the editorial team of both *PC* and *Certeza*, described them as "a laboratory of theological, journalistic, and educational learning."

> In Certeza we wanted to make it possible for the Gospel of Jesus
> Christ to reach the university student in a relevant manner, in
> proper Spanish, and without losing evangelistic zeal. The goal of

2. Samuel Escobar, "La Nueva Generación Evangélica." *Pensamiento Cristiano* (1969): 188–193.

Pensamiento Cristiano was to present to the thinking evangelical a panorama of what was being produced on Bible, theology and history, in Europe and North America, while at the same time to stimulate Latin American evangelical authors. It was in that magazine that for the first time appeared the names of F. F. Bruce, James Packer, A. Rendle Short, D. J. Wiseman, and John Stott, representatives of a school of serious and responsible evangelical thought.[3]

In addition to producing the magazine, the editorial team of *Certeza* labored in publishing books, both translated and written by Latin Americans. The first published title was *Basic Christianity* by the British author John R. W. Stott. In this way, Editorial Certeza promoted theology, biblical studies, historical and sociological analyses, and general literature. It also published works by lesser-known local authors on relevant topics.

Cuadernos Teológicos

A year after CELA I, and within the context of ecumenical Protestantism, *Cuadernos Teológicos* (*CT*) was launched, a theological periodical under the auspices of four seminaries and schools of theology: Buenos Aires, Matanzas (Cuba), Mexico, and Rio Piedras (Puerto Rico). *CT* had the goal of treating theological themes from the point of view of Latin American Protestantism.

The initial preoccupations of the "young" churches from Asia, Africa, and Latin America did not center on theology but on evangelism, church organization, classes for children and youth, and preparation of national ministers. In all these continents, though, the time has come, in the life of the evangelical churches, when theology must occupy a more important place, for their spiritual sake and for their intellectual contributions within the current issues in their own countries.[4]

CT included articles written by Latin American scholars on the church, Christian faith, history, and interpretation. It also included translated articles, book reviews, and historical documents of different theological and ecclesiastical gatherings, local as well as global. It wanted to maintain a link

---

3. Escobar, "Heredero De La Reforma Radical," 59.
4. "Editorial," *Cuadernos Teológicos* 1, no. 1 (1950).

between the graduates of the four theological schools involved. "The editorial of *Cuadernos Teológicos* will give preference to original contributions in Spanish and Portuguese. It will try to present, every year, articles on some aspect of any of the following themes: Old Testament, church history, history of Christian doctrine, Christian dogma, Christian ethics, practical theology, and the missionary and ecumenical movement."[5]

One of the factors that may have encouraged the publication of *CT* were the evaluations by two European observers at CELA I, Marc Boegner from France and Spaniard Manuel Gutiérrez Marín, who agreed that the conference was weak in its theological content. Argentinian Methodist Adam F. Sosa reacted to their comments by asking: "Is it true that Latin American evangelicals do not have any theology or that we even despise it? Are we wrong in how we cherish and express the basic tenets of our faith? Might not our different ways of presenting the message be manifestations of our theology in gestation? What is it about this theological situation that alarms our brothers?"[6]

"Every preacher is a theologian, a bad one or a good one, but in the end, a theologian," wrote Puerto Rican Angel M. Mergal. For Mergal, theology was not an occupation exclusively for experts. Instead, it was the very science of preaching: "Theology cannot be other than the experience of a revelation expressed by human words; the coupling of the Word of God and the word of men."[7] Mergal showed that even though there were no theological treatises or encyclopedias produced by Latin Americans, theology came from the pulpits. Theology meant delivering the truth "in small doses to the congregation." Theology should start with the Word of God, since "*Theos*, God, and His *Logos* (His rationality) are the objects of preaching" and the objects of theology.[8]

In line with Mergal, Sosa recognized that despite the lack of academic theology, theology was being done by preaching the gospel. However, Sosa came to his conclusion about theology and preaching through a different analysis from that of Mergal. "Undoubtedly, Latin American evangelical thought revolves around the Bible, for the work of evangelism which is the primary task of our churches, the simple explanation of the plan for salvation

---

5. Ibid.

6. Adam F. Sosa, "Algunas Consideraciones Sobre La Actual Posición Teológica De Los Evangélicos Latinoamericanos," *Cuadernos Teológicos* 9, no. 2 (1960): 152.

7. Angel Manuel Mergal Llera, *Arte Cristiano De La Predicación* (Mexico: Comité de la Literatura de la Asociación de Iglesias Evangélicas de Puerto Rico, 1951), 50.

8. Ibid., 64.

– with which Peter conquered his first three thousand converts and which for Paul was the most convincing theology – Christ and Christ crucified, still has the same power today as then."[9] Sosa explained that evangelical thought in Latin America was influenced more by the English and North American revival than by the European Reformation. This was mainly due to the fact that the revivalist movement came after the Reformation and consequently had a more powerful influence in the origin of the churches that arrived in Latin America. "The sign of this preaching was evangelism, and Latin American evangelical churches, independently of their denomination, have been born under this sign and have in common to live by that sign. Their doctrinal emphases – even if we do not want to call them theological – are the same of that movement and its North American twin."[10]

Besides revivalism, Sosa identified pietism as a key influence on the theological thought in Latin America. Evangelicals in the region emphasized experience over doctrine without necessarily rejecting the latter. Evangelism was dominant in the churches and, although "the theologian could be satisfied by proclaiming that God saves people, the evangelist cannot be satisfied until he is sure that people have actually been saved." Personal experience was within the evangelical movement "a doctrine common to all evangelistic groups."

> The word "experience" is quite discredited in theological circles where it is associated almost exclusively with mystic and subjective positions and with Schleiermacher. Here we have a different position than most of Protestantism. For Latin American evangelicals the term experience – with its clear mystic and pietistic meanings – does not refer only to a subjective position – we should say that entire generations of preachers did not know the name Schleiermacher. It designates a condition of a most authentic objectivity inseparable from the concept of conversion. Actually, it is probably more appropriate to talk about "experimental religion," that is, a live faith with visible results.[11]

Sosa also characterized Latin American theological thought, in contrast with its European counterpart, as integration between the concepts of

---

9. Ibid., 153.
10. Ibid., 156.
11. Ibid., 157.

mission with evangelism, lay apostleship (when "the faithful witness of an authentic laborer will always be more worthy than that of a cleric disguised as a laborer"), the doctrine of Christian stewardship ("unknown by European theology"), and the idea that churches ought to influence society positively, finding solutions for endemic maladies such as alcoholism.

It was important, though, to learn from European churches, where "theology has at its service the sharpest minds and liturgy has reached its maximum development, but where the people, in general, do not participate in the life of the churches, or better said, churches do not have any influence over people's lives, and where the only thing stopping their church buildings from closing is that they are paid by the state." Sosa warned,

> Theology and liturgy are good only as helps for religious life; they can never be substitutes for it. The same is true about morality and ecclesiastical activities. We do not believe it is illegitimate to paraphrase the words of the Lord saying that theology, liturgy, the various ecclesiastical activities, and morality "were made for man, not man for them." At the same time as, with sound theology, we affirm that God is sovereign, our due gratitude to him obliges us to humbly recognize the fact that we are God's supreme object of interest (John 3:16). If at times we highlight too much the latter idea it should be to exalt the greatness of the former one. If we forget either part, or emphasize only one, we may have "theology" but not faithfulness to the gospel.[12]

Sosa's analysis gives the impression that Latin American evangelicals were starting to explore their identity independently of foreign tutelage. His questions and comments reflect a commitment to the church, a more autochthonous understanding of the mission of the church, and an incipient clarity about evangelical reality in the continent. Sosa showed that received theology and ecclesiastical models had experienced an adaptation to local situations and were starting to develop their own characteristics with both inherited and Latin American traits. Other thinkers were also on the same track.

Thomas Liggett, for example, president of the Evangelical Seminary in Puerto Rico, argued that for Protestantism to respond to the Latin American challenges it must "affirm its compatibility with the Latin culture. We have

---

12. Ibid., 161.

unreservedly accepted, for too long, the Roman Catholic thesis that Latin culture and Roman Catholic Christianity go together and that Evangelical Christianity is something strange to Latin culture."[13] Liggett considered it a false thesis since the European Reformation in the sixteenth century was not limited to the northern countries but affected also Italy, France, and Spain. To support his argument, Liggett mentioned John Calvin from France, and Spaniards Juan de Valdés, Francisco de Enzinas, Juan Pérez de Pineda, and Cipriano de Valera among others. "If we add to these names, and others from literature, the hundreds of thousands who enter into the evangelical churches in Latin America, it becomes more obvious that we can emphatically affirm that evangelical Christianity touches a sensitive chord in the Latin heart, and provides an atmosphere free of oppression and intimidation; it feels at home amidst Latin culture as in any other culture within Christendom." However, Liggett pointed to the lack of unity as a serious obstacle before the monolithic religious culture of the Catholic Church. "We must unite to achieve two goals: maximal use of our resources for the task in front of us, and a clear manifestation of unity that is evident not only for those inside the church but for the outsiders too."[14]

Samuel Escobar also explored evangelical identity, asking if Latin American evangelicals were fundamentalists.[15] It made sense to ask this, because most of the faith missions that had arrived in Latin America identified themselves by that adjective, and since most evangelicals in Latin America were descendants of those missions they inherited the same identity. Escobar perceived that, although "we have now among us new generations of Latin Americans whose evangelical faith is a native plant, we have not yet reached full maturity, neither have we broken institutional, cultural, and spiritual ties with our brethren from North America and Great Britain."

Reviewing history, Escobar explained that fundamentalism started as a reaction against liberalism and theological modernism at the end of the nineteenth century. Liberalism "tended to reject any supernatural element in the biblical message, embracing some optimism about man." This had an influence on all doctrinal aspects including theology, soteriology, Christology, and the doctrine of the Bible, affecting the moral and ethical aspects of the

---

13. Thomas J. Liggett, *Latin America: A Challenge to Protestantism* (Rio Piedras, Puerto Rico: Evangelical Seminary of Puerto Rico, 1959), 8.

14. Ibid., 9–10.

15. Samuel Escobar, "¿Somos Fundamentalistas?," *Pensamiento Cristiano* 13 (1966): 88–96.

message. Initially, fundamentalism was "a movement that protested against such a radical disfiguration of the Christian message."

Although at its beginnings the movement helped to undermine liberal theology, "in its campaign against the so-called 'social gospel' fundamentalism started to reduce 'all the counsel of God,' feeling little need to present Christianity as a comprehensive overview of the world and life."

> Due to its failure to relate the Christian revelation to the wider concerns of civilization and culture, and by reducing religion, with narrow criteria, to just personal piety, fundamentalism was in danger of degenerating into a simple, morbid, and sick excitement. At the bottom of this pietistic tendency lies an indiscriminating antithesis between heart and mind, to which most fundamentalist pastors and educators adhere. Such obstruction of the intellect and the expression of religious experience by a phraseology using only emotional and volitional terms is a tendency which really agrees more with modernist theology than with biblical theology.[16]

According to Escobar, fundamentalism failed to offer a "biblical, solid, and orthodox" alternative to liberalism. In addition, in North America the movement took an extreme conservative position with the political right defending, by all means, the "American way of life." To be a fundamentalist in this sense was to bear a name with which Latin American evangelicals did not identify. Nevertheless, within Latin American social reality, neo-liberalism called "fundamentalist (together with the adjective 'retrograde') any evangelical who disagrees with it."

How did Escobar finally answer his question?

> Are we fundamentalists? No, if it is understood as the theological degeneration described by Henry,[17] simplistic anti-intellectualism, lack of seriousness in studying the Bible, and the basic reactionary stance. No, if it is understood as racial segregation, the political extreme right, and the naiveté to believe that the American Way of Life is the kingdom of God on earth. No, if it is understood as denying the application of the gospel

---

16. Ibid., 92.

17. Carl F. H. Henry, *Evangelical Responsibility in Contemporary Theology* (Grand Rapids, MI: Eerdmans, 1957).

to all areas of life and culture. But we believe that there are clear fundamentals, we believe in the authority of the Scriptures, we believe in the legacy of twenty centuries of biblical Christianity, because we realize it is the only one which with realism, with truth, reveals, diagnoses, and responds to human need, because it is the Word of God. We also believe that new generations of evangelicals, especially students, have the task to comprehend the application of the gospel to all areas of life, to elaborate a theology faithful to the Bible and aware of the needs of Latin American people today. We believe too that we must live the gospel in today's convulsive world in faithfulness to Christ and his Word. That will mean being light and salt, being present in all areas of service and struggle when necessary, but as Cristoforos, someone who carries Christ. In other words, as free men who do not fall into slavery to the many idols and myths of our times.[18]

In another analysis of fundamentalism, Ecuadorian Washington Padilla stated that such a theological system was supporting the capitalist society and its values. Even though fundamentalism called people to a separation from the world, it was just an external separation and not a total one. Therefore, according to Padilla, it was a system that became "an ally of the established order and lost the dynamism of the concept of the Kingdom of God."[19] It was not, though, indifferent to human needs. Fundamentalism considered evangelization to be urgent, "so that men and women will be saved from the coming judgment and will participate in the blessings in a celestial kingdom." Fundamentalism invested lots of resources in huge evangelistic campaigns and in creating missionary societies to spread its version of the gospel to the four corners of the earth. "Such a unilateral emphasis on evangelization against a wider Christian action in society was linked to an individualistic concept of the church and of the Christian life."[20]

Padilla contrasted fundamentalism's program with the one proposed at Panama 1916. The organizers of Panama 1916 had recommended a program which, according to Padilla, was an integral mission, "which included the

---

18. Escobar, "¿Somos Fundamentalistas?," 96.

19. Washington Padilla, *La Iglesia y Los Dioses Modernos: Historia Del Protestantismo En El Ecuador*. Biblioteca De Ciencias Sociales, Volumen 23 (Quito, Ecuador: Corporación Editora Nacional, 1989), 183.

20. Ibid.

spiritual and the material, people's encounter with Jesus Christ and social and material betterment through education, institutional changes, and the exporting of North American civilization to the southern countries." Padilla argued that fundamentalism was a more negative influence for Latin American evangelicals:

> For the organizers of Panama 1916 – with all their limitations and distortions – the message of the gospel had to do with life here and now; for the fundamentalist critics of Panama 1916, the message of the gospel was a message of death, not of life: it was a message for beyond the tomb, not for human beings who faint and suffer and need an integral salvation that includes all dimensions of life in this world. In reality, when one reads the reports of some of the fundamentalist missions, one gets the impression that those brethren were more preoccupied – obsessed we would say – with death, and almost completely disengaged from life. And if they had any worry about life it was to limit it with their absurd legalisms.[21]

For Padilla, the main problem with fundamentalism was not its commitment to Truth but its disregard of unity and love; therefore "its contribution to a continent with open wounds from bloody racial fighting between classes, races, ideologies, and interests of all kinds is minimal."[22] Padilla concluded,

> Protestantism has not completely fulfilled its mission mostly because it is hostage to the liberal–capitalist mentality that is in the atmosphere and interprets the Bible with that mentality. This leads it, though involuntarily, to put the gospel and the church institution to the service of this world and its false gods, instead of putting them exclusively to the service of the true God: the God of love, justice, fraternity, and peace, the God of the poor and oppressed, society's victims.[23]

In Padilla, Escobar, and Sosa we find an analysis that distances itself from the received tradition, criticizing it respectfully but decisively. Escobar showed an understanding of the background behind the imported doctrines,

---

21. Ibid., 311.
22. Ibid., 312.
23. Ibid., 428.

their demands, and their sociopolitical framework. However, his criticism was constructive, proposing a way of reflection for Latin Americans who were thinking about their faith with a local accent. It was possible to evaluate these foreign theologies without capitulating to modernism. The time had come to define Latin American evangelical identity separately from its foreign parents.

Of course, as mentioned above, there was not only one evangelical voice in Latin America. When Argentinian-born Kenneth Strachan was invited to present his view on evangelism, his speech received several reactions that help us understand what was going on theologically at the time. Strachan shared the evangelistic experience he had, as president of the Latin America Mission (LAM), during the years following World War II. It was time, said Strachan, for evangelism to be passed over from missionaries to the national churches. "Most of us are constantly convicted of our failure as witnesses."[24] There was a feeling of dissatisfaction with evangelism. Many churches were turned inwards, insulated from society, and heavily dependent upon professional ministry, resulting in a passive irresponsibility among the members. Furthermore, new political realities, the resurgence of the Roman Catholic Church, the increase and spread of sects, and the relentless permeation of Marxist and socialist ideas called for a careful re-evaluation of evangelistic programs and practices. Strachan's conclusion was that "the expansion of any movement is in direct proportion to its success in mobilizing its total membership in continuous propagation of its beliefs."[25]

Strachan then delineated four principles applying his conclusion to evangelism. First, "every Christian without exception, according to his gifts and situation, is called upon to be a witness for Christ." This was to achieve the mobilization of the total membership of the church. Second, "personal witness must center in the fellowship and communal witness of the local congregation." Third, "individual and communal activity must relate constructively to the total witness of the entire Body of Christ." Unity, in this case, was essential. And fourth, the outreach must be "nothing less than total and complete." The command was to every creature, among all nations, in the entire world.[26] These principles were practiced in several countries where the program Evangelism in Depth, organized by LAM, was in place.

---

24. Kenneth Strachan, "Call to Witness," *International Review of Mission* 53, no. 2 (1964): 191.

25. Ibid., 194.

26. Ibid., 195.

Responding to Strachan, Victor Hayward questioned some aspects of both methodology and content.

> Is Christ the Saviour of the world, or Saviour only of the Church? Is He the Saviour only of "them who believe," the Lord only of the Church? Or is He "the Saviour of all men," though "especially of them that believe," and Lord of the world, as well as of the Church? Do we proclaim His coming as a secular, or as a religious event? Is His salvation a means of escape for men's souls from this wicked world, or dare we announce "the redemption of the world by our Lord Jesus Christ"? Do we speak of redemption of men's bodies and minds, as well as of their souls – in other words, of their total personalities in all their relationships with their environment both here and hereafter? Or have we lost sight of the concern of the Creator for the whole of the secular world He has made?
>
> The question is, how big is our Gospel? Do we proclaim, as of secular importance, that Jesus Christ who came will come again, to be made manifest as the One through whom God has been reconciling all things to Himself, as God's appointed center for all creation, as the meaning of the total history of all mankind? Do we proclaim Him as the Word through whom all things were created, and as Him who is even now ruling in this world, though His rule is hidden and will be universally acknowledged only at the End? Does His reign apply to secular affairs? Does His salvation concern more than individual souls? The fact that Christ is our personal Saviour does not mean that He is our private Saviour. We are clear about this in respect of ourselves as individual Christians. But are we equally clear that Christ is not the private Saviour of His Church?[27]

Hayward referred to a narrow definition of evangelism which, "in limiting its proclamation to a call to individual conversion, seems to leave out of account whole sections of biblical doctrine." For him, evangelism ought to focus on the world instead of on the church. If it did not, the church would repeat the same terrible mistake made by the Jews "when they mistook election for witness, service, and suffering as being election for self-centered

---

27. Victor E. W. Hayward, "Call to Witness – But What Kind of Witness?," *International Review of Mission* 53, no. 2 (1964): 203.

privilege." The objective for witness should be all creation, "men in their social and corporate structures of existence."[28] The gospel pertained to all areas of human endeavor.

Strachan answered Hayward's comments by recognizing that within conservative evangelical circles in Latin America were "emphases which contribute to an ultra-individualistic, falsely pietistic, church-centered way of thought and life that constitutes an imperfect and somewhat distorted representation of our sacred calling and mission in Christ."[29] Strachan rejected Hayward's "false dichotomy between the world and the church."

> Must we not recognize that, regardless of failures in its attitudes or conduct, the Church of the present age is in the world, and that the Gospel has been entrusted to it for the world? So that the Gospel is not a correlate of either the Church or the world, but rather relates through the Church to the world. There is therefore no real choice.[30]

The key questions Strachan considered were: What essentially is the gospel? and, What of the gospel is it essential to preach to the world? Strachan agreed with Hayward that the gospel had "implications that go far beyond the individual and the church, that embrace all of creation and the whole range of human life." However, the danger of overlooking entire sections of Scripture was present in both those who emphasized individual regeneration and repentance and those who overlooked or minimized them. Both parties were in need of correction in the light of Scripture.

There were also practical questions regarding the understanding of gospel witness. Strachan distinguished between the initial proclamation, which included the "basic facts of the Gospel," and the "subsequent teaching on the part of the Church." He explained that "it does not seem to me a fair demand to make of any organized evangelistic effort, that it bring forth in its initial presentations more than those basic facts of the Gospel which are required to command that response which God desires and exacts."[31] Finally,

---

28. Ibid., 206.

29. Kenneth Strachan, "A Further Comment," *International Review of Mission* 53, no. 2 (1964): 209.

30. Ibid., 210.

31. Ibid., 212.

Strachan called the church to self-criticism and renovation, "but in complete faithfulness to the terms of the Gospel and her essential mission."[32]

Emilio Castro, a Methodist pastor from Uruguay, also contributed to this conversation. Castro agreed that "the greatest obstacle to evangelization is the church which is preoccupied with its own existence."[33] He pointed out the need evangelical churches and denominations had, not only to proclaim reconciliation but also to live it out by showing Christian unity. Strachan's distinction between the initial witness of the essential part of the gospel and the teaching that would come later was rejected by Castro. He explained,

> It is a question of proclaiming Christ, His promises and His commands, in such a way that the new convert accepts his responsibility in the world and is not self-centered. It is a message of repentance, and this includes not only sorrow for our sins, but a radical change in our outlook on life; a crucified Christ, who has taken upon Himself the lot of all sinners and invites us to bear with Him the cross of service in the world; a resurrected Christ, who calls us to live the reality of the new man. In short, the convert should not have a religious dimension only, but should really live according to the Gospel and have a total dimension.[34]

There were, as Castro explained, two latent dangers in what Strachan proposed. First, if it was "a mere technique placed at the disposal of self-centered and socially irresponsible churches, it would only increase that irresponsibility." Churches had to reconsider their message, taking seriously all of Latin American reality. Second, an evangelism which would take believers away "from their places of responsible witness in society" was "a tragedy for the Gospel in Latin America," resulting in a "socially irresponsible" church.[35]

This dialogue between Strachan, Hayward, Castro, and others was paradigmatic of what evangelical Christianity in Latin America was going

---

32. Ibid., 215.

33. Emilio Castro, "Evangelism in Latin America," *International Review of Mission* 53, no. 4 (1964): 452.

34. Ibid., 454.

35. Ibid., 455. To see other contributions to this dialogue and Hayward's counter-response, see Markus Barth, "What Is the Gospel?," *International Review of Mission* 53, no. 3 (1964); Martin Conway, "A Permanent Argument," *International Review of Mission* 53, no. 4 (1964); Victor E. W. Hayward, "Call to Witness," *International Review of Mission* 54, no. 2 (1965).

through. It was a moment of questioning, definition, and evaluation. Key questions were being asked about the identity and mission of the church, its relevance, the content and reach of its message, its relationship with society in general, and its involvement in the lives of the people. All evangelicals, both those closely involved in the ecumenical movement and those holding more conservative positions, were searching to better understand their place in a complex age in Latin America. Everyone was experiencing growing pains. This dialogue also showed clearly that the two sides were quickly moving further apart. Each had its hobby horses. But it was important to keep the conversation open.

A few years later, Dayton Roberts, a close friend of Strachan's, evaluated the Hayward debate as positive because through it Strachan became aware of two shortcomings in his evangelistic scheme. First, Strachan's proposal "was heavily *methodological* rather than *theological.*" Second, "Ken came to see that the concepts of Evangelism-in-Depth needed to be set appropriately in a broader context of correct, biblical missiology. He realized that a better theological foundation had to be laid for the adequate communication of his burden."[36] And that is exactly what Strachan did a few months before his premature death on 24 February 1965.

Strachan defined "redemption" as the central theme of the Bible, a redemption centered in Jesus Christ. "Salvation then, in biblical terms is rooted in the transformation of each individual in order that he may be thus incorporated into the family of God. It is not merely a call to service and a partnership in action; it is first a call to repentance and faith, to sonship and to a new life, marked by holiness and obedience, worship and fellowship."[37] The mission of the church is, then, "to proclaim the good news of salvation to every creature in all the world and to attest the reality and power of the gospel through the holy lives and genuine love of its members, their devoted service to mankind everywhere, and their patient endurance of suffering."[38]

The incarnation of Christ was for Strachan the hermeneutical key to understanding discipleship and the mission of the church, "the pattern of mission for every disciple." Furthermore, the incarnation became for all who

---

36. W. Dayton Roberts, *Strachan of Costa Rica: Missionary Insights and Strategies* (Grand Rapids, MI: Eerdmans, 1971), 116.

37. Kenneth Strachan, *The Inescapable Calling: The Missionary Task of the Church of Christ in the Light of Contemporary Challenge and Opportunity* (Grand Rapids, MI: Eerdmans, 1968), 45.

38. Ibid., 48.

called themselves a disciple of Christ "the pattern for the methods he employs to carry out his mission."[39] Here Strachan found biblical support for mass evangelism: "as we follow Christ in the Gospels, we are forced to recognize that much of his ministry was carried out in the midst and on behalf of the multitudes." Jesus' ministry to the multitudes was seen "in the demonstration of supernatural power over the adversary, in the compassionate healing of the sick, in comfort for the sorrowing, and in ministry to the poor."[40]

The ministry of the Holy Spirit was also indispensable when defining the community of believers and its mission: "any effort to define the Christian mission or to provide for its execution in other terms is to miss the mark and to doom the church of Christ to failure."[41]

> The apostolic strategy was to involve every Christian in constant responsible service and witness in every situation of secular and religious life. In these witness-situations, through the teaching ministry of leaders specially gifted and called for the task, a continuous process of disciple-training was carried on. The fruitful end of such activity was a reproductive fellowship and witness on the part of the cells and congregations that make up the one church of Christ.
>
> Discernible in this simple strategy were the following elements: (1) the indispensable operation of the Holy Spirit; (2) the fundamental mediation of prayer; (3) the constant itinerant witness from man to man and from house to house; (4) the opportune proclamation of the gospel to the masses; (5) the intense teaching ministry in the formation of disciples; (6) the outreach of service through healing; and (7) the warmth of fellowship.[42]

At least, in this case, a conversation with people with different points of view helped Strachan in his own theological reflection. Evangelical theology would have greatly profited had theologians more often been in dialogue.

---

39. Ibid., 54.
40. Ibid., 57.
41. Ibid., 59.
42. Ibid., 65.

CELA II, 1961

Benjamín Moraes, president of the Second Latin American Evangelical Conference (CELA II) in Huampani, Lima, Peru, said,

> This hour is extremely grave; we cannot be content repeating phrases that have been common "slogans" in evangelical pulpits for decades. It is true we continue with our proclamation of the eternal biblical truths the Holy Word of God teaches. So, a new inquiry into the political, social, economic, and religious situations in Latin America is imperative, so that we speak the eternal truths in a language that is suitable for new listeners, being trained to receive the Divine Logos who becomes incarnate for each generation. The Latin American general panorama has changed much in the last decade. Our churches are more conscious of this in order that their witness might become more appropriate and convincing.[43]

Among the important changes Moraes pinpointed were rapid industrialization with an increase in manual laborers, Marxist proselytism mainly among students, and a spiritual awakening within Roman Catholicism. Within evangelical Protestantism, Moraes mentioned the growth of independent groups with no relationship to any of the traditional denominations, and the ultra-conservative tendencies with messianic pretensions which condemned any who might think differently. Moraes was probably referring to Carl McIntire's organization, the International Council of Christian Churches, that led the police in Lima to interrogate several CELA II leaders, even John Mackay, accusing them of having communist links.

CELA II highlighted the theme of unity and evangelism "in order to not only add members to our congregations but overall to increase the number of witnesses of Christ in the World." Evangelism was not only verbal but also the active participation of believers in all areas of society.

> We observe with deep empathy and in a spirit of solidarity the eager search of our people for a better future. We long for justice, a more equitable distribution of the wealth God has placed in our land, the yearning of great masses of our continent for social

---

43. CELA II, *Cristo La Esperanza Para América Latina: Ponencias-Informes-Comentarios De La Segunda Conferencia Evangélica Latinoamericana, 20 De Julio a 6 De Agosto De 1961, Lima, Perú* (Buenos Aires: Confederación Evangélica del Río de la Plata, 1962), 12.

and economic independence, cultural equality, and a fuller participation in the life and direction of our nations. We are in solidarity with the desire for liberty in Latin America. We do this because we know justice and liberty are undeniable consequences of the gospel, gifts given by God to humankind and for which we must struggle.[44]

Argentinian Methodist José Míguez Bonino presented the theological speech at CELA II. Míguez defined the evangelical message as, besides the obvious verbal proclamation, "the attitude in life of believers in the world, their struggles and sufferings, well, every word and action by which we bear witness to Christ."[45] His starting point was that which CELA I had defined: "Our message for Latin America and for the world is Jesus Christ." However, Míguez questioned whether evangelicals had been "faithful to the fullness of Jesus Christ as found in the Scriptures." He identified three different emphases among evangelicals regarding Christology. First, the "conservatives" (Míguez made it clear he did not like labels) emphasized Jesus Christ as the "expiation victim." Second, the "liberal" churches presented Jesus Christ as the teacher "whose teachings about God as Father, the law of love of the Kingdom of Heaven, from the Sermon on the Mount, had occupied the first place." And third, other groups presented Jesus Christ as the "Judge who comes at the end of the age to complete his work."[46] Míguez's response to these emphases was:

Unilateral insistence on Christ as Teacher results in mere powerless moralism. Exclusive emphasis on the second coming produces a passive ultra-worldliness, a sort of fanaticism, and the separation of Christ's sacrifice from his life and teachings gives us the picture of a passive Christ whose true humanity is of little importance. It is necessary to keep these three aspects in unison: Jesus Christ as sacrifice for our own sake, Jesus Christ as teacher, Jesus Christ the Judge and King coming in glory.[47]

Moreover, Míguez added two aspects lacking in Latin American evangelical Christology: recognition of the practical consequences of the incarnation and the sovereignty of Jesus Christ over the whole universe

---

44. Ibid., 25.
45. José Míguez Bonino, "Nuestro Mensaje," in ibid., 70.
46. Ibid., 72.
47. Ibid., 73.

today. Regarding the former, Míguez asked if perhaps "our evangelical work lacked a sense of identification with the Latin American people that goes along with the incarnational message, a sense of solidarity with the lost, the sinners and the disoriented? Have we not tried to save people from outside without getting too close to them, being afraid of contamination? Have we not loathed our people, feeling better than them, too holy to get entangled with their messy problems and passions?" Míguez recommended a profound meditation on the incarnation of the Son of God.[48]

Jesus Christ's sovereignty over the universe also led Míguez to question evangelical practice in Latin America:

> Doesn't it seem as if we evangelicals act on the basis that Christ has the right of sovereignty only in the church and that the world does not belong to Him? Have we not recognized as Satan's some rights to sovereignty over the world which are not his but that he usurped, and therefore we do not have to bow to him? Has this not resulted at times in a dual morality, as if in the world Satan were sovereign and we obey him, and Jesus Christ were Lord only over the church where we need to follow His will – while other times it has resulted in some indifference toward the world, because we think that only whatever happens inside the church concerns Jesus Christ and that He is not the sovereign Lord who holds the destiny of humankind and nations?[49]

Míguez condensed in one brilliant phrase his christological concern: "A reduced Christ will always result in a reduced Christianity and a rachitic witness." Regarding the centrality of the Bible for Latin American evangelicals, Míguez recommended that sterile controversies should be kept at bay, most of them having been imported. He pleaded for unity in the church, and for the avoidance of excessive individualism in order that a real fraternal communion might be lived out among churches. For instance, Míguez mentioned the impossibility of celebrating the Lord's Supper at CELA II since not everyone felt free to participate because of denominational differences. Furthermore, he highlighted the aspect of the Christian life within the evangelical message: "The evangelical church in Latin America has insisted that a believer is a changed person, and shows evidences in his life of that change. I believe

---

48. Ibid., 74.
49. Ibid., 75.

we must keep and increase this in our Protestantism." However, there was a danger that "such Christian life might fall into a cold and negative legalism" closer to the Pharisaism of Jesus' time.[50]

What did it mean to preach that message in the Latin American context? Míguez mentioned four key aspects. First, Latin America was a continent "in revolution and hungry for a total transformation"; that was why "Jesus is the hope for a revolutionary Latin America. The hope for a revolution where any person might be respected and given dignity." Second, Latin Americans lived in absolute "disorientation and human searching." Here, Míguez again pointed to Jesus as the model for human existence: "Jesus is not only the model of true humanity, but the source of true humanity."[51] Third, proclaiming the message in Latin America meant taking into account the almost five centuries of Roman Catholic influence. Míguez emphasized that the most important thing was not "the confrontation of the evangelical church with Rome. More important is the confrontation of Jesus Christ with Rome. We are only servants in that confrontation. Christ, and not us, is the Judge of the Roman Catholic Church. But Christ is also the Saviour of Roman Catholicism." Fourth, the message was to be proclaimed inside the evangelical churches. For him, evangelicals were like "strangers to Latin America's life." He finished with a clear call for theological depth:

> The word theology has been vilified, sometimes assimilated to extreme dogmatism and other times to some sort of philosophy being done in the clouds. Theology is no more than the effort of the Church to obey Him with the Lord's mind. It is simply the effort of the Church to confront the preached message with the Word of God. I believe there is a big need in our Latin American Church for theological profundity.[52]

Míguez' speech at CELA II was comforting and prophetic. His evaluations give us a positive and realistic view of the theological and ecclesiastical situation at the beginning of the 1960s. There was a disposition to be critical and constructive within the evangelical movement. His observations about deficiencies in Christology – namely Docetism (see below) – agreed with Mackay's three decades earlier. It seems that there was not much change on this issue. Moreover, Míguez set out a proposal for change and growth.

---

50. Ibid., 82–83.

51. Ibid., 85–86.

52. Ibid., 91.

Within the evangelical message were seeds that would produce an authentic crop for the kingdom of God. Evangelicals, though, sowed selectively, within denominational boundaries. It was time for unity and for integration of the message so that real transformation for the church and for all areas of life in the continent might be experienced.

Besides Mackay and Míguez, another person who analyzed the Docetism in Latin American evangelical theology was Cuban historian Justo Luis González. His springboard for the discussion was the affirmation that "the center of our faith is the incarnation." González presented two historical extremes which denied the incarnation from the onset of the Christian era: Docetism and Ebionism. According to Docetism, matter was inferior and the spiritual was emphasized. Ebionism, on the contrary, reduced faith to the material realm because the distance between God and man was impassable; the eternal did not mix with the temporal. For González, both positions were present but veiled in evangelical faith:

> Too often we as Christians, after rejecting any insinuation of Docetism in regard to the person of Christ, fall into a practical Docetism that is an implicit negation of the incarnation of God in Christ. Such Docetism is characterized by a spiritual interpretation of Christianity as if it had regard only for some supra-heavenly and spiritual realities. According to this, everything material is far from having any relation with Christianity. The duty of the believer is to pray, go to church, and read the Bible. Politics, business, and public life in general are nothing more than a manifestation of sin and a trick of the forces of evil to keep us away from spiritual life.
>
> All of this is nothing but a veiled Docetism that has to do, not so much with the person of Christ, but with how God relates to the world. Such veiled Docetism is not less dangerous than its antecedent from the first centuries of this era because every tergiversation of God's relationship with the world leads to a tergiversation of the central moment of such a relationship: the incarnation.[53]

González's proposal for confronting the veiled Docetism was a "Christian materialism": that is, "that our God is not the God who reveals himself in a

---

53. Justo L. Gonzáles, *Revolución y Encarnación*. Vol. 1, Colección Universitas (Río Piedras, Puerto Rico: Librería La Reforma, 1965), 22–23.

supposed spiritual sphere that exists apart from matter. No. God is the Creator of this world and its matter. Our God is the God whose supreme revelation is given to us in a man of flesh and blood." The practical implication of the error of those who emphasized the spiritual was that it led Christians to a lack of interest in the world, and they "deserved the accusation that they worry too much about heaven and forget the earth where they live." Consequently, "Christianity is a placebo to help men to forget their miseries instead of fighting to solve them, and Karl Marx's accusation that religion is the opiate of the masses is justified."[54] It was a tragedy that the church had abandoned the world where it was supposed to be light and salt.

Since Latin American reality was definitely one of revolution, González delineated three options for evangelicals. First, the church could align itself with the "conservative forces" to stop the oncoming changes. Of course he did not recommend this option: "There is no bigger blasphemy than to establish an equation between God's will and the status quo." Second, the church could ignore the revolution, a church hidden in an "ivory tower," oblivious of the social changes. That was, according to González, "a flagrant negation of the message of the incarnation." Third – the only real alternative – the church could "get into the situation in which the world is, participate in it as our Lord participated in our infirmities, and do everything possible to lead it." However, González warned that "if we sin by not wishing to be revolutionary Christians, we also sin when we fall into the temptation to be Christian revolutionaries. The first one is the Docetic error, which pretends to meet with the divine outside of concrete reality. The second is the Ebionist error, which believes that the divine is found simply in an extension and culmination of the human."[55]

González's words and analysis provide an example of what it meant to do theology in Latin America during the 1960s. It was impossible not to see and live the social, political, and economic changes without being affected by them; but it was difficult for an evangelical community which had mainly kept itself at the margins of history to accept González's proposal. González was not the only Protestant to see the circumstances as a unique opportunity the church could not simply allow to pass by. That was also the thesis of the movement Iglesia y Sociedad (Church and Society; ISAL).

---

54. Ibid., 25.
55. Ibid., 53–54.

ISAL

A week before CELA II, at the same venue (Huampani, Lima, Peru), the First Evangelical Latin American Consultation on Church and Society took place. It was convened by the confederations of churches from Argentina, Brazil, and Uruguay. It had a threefold thematic: Christian responsibility in the light of the rapid social and cultural changes, the prophetic participation of Christians in Latin American politics, and Christian preoccupation with progress and economic development. It was the first meeting of "evangelicals from the whole continent to consider specifically the significance of Christian responsibility before a situation of swift social transformation."[56] The most important outcome of this consultation was the formation of the Junta Latinoamericana de Iglesia y Sociedad, better known by ISAL, officially founded in February 1962.

For ISAL, Huampani meant two things: becoming aware of the situation and defining a key analytical method for ISAL's methodological approach. The method consisted in "separate analyses of the basic aspects of Latin American reality (economic, political, social, and cultural) and . . . [relating] afterwards those evident characteristics and needs to the church's situation." The evangelical church and Latin American society had so far remained separate, according to ISAL, and the relationship between the two had been "premeditatedly and inexplicably" ignored.[57]

> The social reality was a fact the church could not contain; the church had tried to analyze a process of "rapid social changes" undoubtedly as a bewildering and evolving process, but also as an external process of a different nature than the proper substance of the church. Current analysis leads us to discover the deep and global nature of such a change. That radical transformation of the social order, already called the "Latin American revolution," went through the very axis of ecclesiastical life and organization. It was a fact – that was precisely the discovery in Huampani – enfolding and conditioning the church. Nothing is more false than, with a passive and objective attitude, to determine beforehand what changes need to happen in the life of the church

---

56. ISAL, *América Hoy: Acción De Dios y Responsabilidad Del Hombre* (Montevideo: Iglesia y Sociedad en América Latina, 1966), 11.

57. Ibid., 13.

to adapt or modernize its strategy. The deep impulse and sense of transformation originated in the core of society, and the church experienced the same tensions and splits as the society in which its body was shaped.[58]

The ecclesiology reflected here, even though considered new, resembled in many ways what the CCLA proposed early in the century, when churches were encouraged to become active participants in society and to avoid looking like alienated and exclusive clubs. Yet the fact that Huampani 1961 considered it a "discovery" pointed to a church wrapped up in itself, locked inside its church buildings and irrelevant to society in general.

ISAL defined itself as a new attitude of "Christians interested in society as such, the place of people in that society, the social and economic conditions which determine human frustration and suffering in a limited and concrete environment, Latin America; furthermore, [as] a formula we found to express a new concept of Christian witness through service and fulfillment of social and political responsibilities believers share with every citizen."[59]

Was ISAL forgoing the evangelistic mission of the church? By that time there were mainly two positions on the topic among evangelicals. One subordinated social responsibility to evangelism. The other, seemingly that of ISAL, considered social responsibility and evangelism as equally important parts of Christian mission. "While practicing social responsibility, Christians have witnessed; their proclamation of Jesus Christ followed different methods and responded to new circumstances, but that did not mean it was not essentially evangelism. Social preoccupation was a way to witness as worthy and important as traditional ways used as evangelistic action."[60]

Confronting what ISAL called the biggest structural change ever in Latin America, the church was called to be in continuous dialogue with various societal aspects such as the transition from a rural to an industrial society, the breakup of family life, high demographic growth, the changing social role of women, the new power of the working class, and the challenges of the media.

Luis Odell, ISAL's secretary, explained that when talking about social responsibility churches understood it to be mostly "to resist and fight against the traditional catalogue of vices from our pietistic and puritan roots: alcohol, social vices in general, sexual abuse, and only in a more peripheral way the

---

58. Ibid., 14.

59. Ibid., 12.

60. Ibid., 13.

misery, physical suffering, etc."[61] For Odell, Latin American churches were socially illiterate, leading believers to reactionary positions, supporting the bourgeoisie, without the means to understand social, political, and economic processes. He challenged the church:

> It is time to leave behind the traditional philosophy for social action within the churches – "assistentialism" as the best expression of Christian charity and piety – and go forth to discover and apply new ways of action and service, capable of making a positive and definite contribution for a holistic renovation of the Latin American countries. The situation forces us to action, allowing us, by its intensity and outreach, if not to recover the time that has gone by, to advance in our comprehension of our responsibility so that we are not left behind in the race during this historical time in which we are living.[62]

At Huampani the political participation of Latin American evangelical churches was also discussed, defining the purpose of such participation as to provide all human beings with adequate conditions for an abundant and fulfilled life. Since the political participation of the churches was inevitable, the consultation encouraged believers to get involved individually so that the church would not be considered a specific political party. It was not going to be easy, there were tensions and threats, but it was to be done in obedience to the Lord of the church. The main objective was the search for social justice.

> People have realized recently that the misery, material suffering, and other maladies they bear do not have to be part of a society with the technical and economic resources to resolve such problems in a short time. The Christian notion of social justice is not just to give to each one what belongs to them. In the Bible, social justice is God's action to tear down whatever oppresses and enslaves human beings, making a new society possible where human dignity is wholly recognized. The goal of Christian social justice is to provide men with the appropriate means for a legitimate life in Christ.[63]

---

61. Luis L. Odell, "Junta Latinoamericana De Iglesia y Sociedad (Jlais): Origen, Definición, Objetivos," *Cristianismo y Sociedad* 1, no. 2 (1963): 3.

62. Ibid., 4.

63. ISAL, *Encuentro y Desafío: La Acción Cristiana Evangélica Latinoamericana Ante La Cambiante Situación Social, Política y Económica* (Montevideo: ISAL, 1961), 48.

Christian responsibility regarding economic development was defined as "working to establish systems that provide each human being with the opportunity of a decent life and of spiritual and cultural development." For ISAL the system should promote liberty, justice, and progress. However, the church should avoid identifying itself with a particular economic system. Neither capitalism nor collectivism completely satisfied people's needs. That was why Christianity was needed to help to find a new way to overcome the deficiencies and danger of these two rival systems. Churches were to consider these questions seriously in order to reach this goal.

Gonzalo Castillo-Cárdenas, also associated with ISAL, said that although the evangelical movement arrived in Latin America with a contagious mystique, evangelism, and with a powerful instrument, the Bible, and had initially experienced considerable growth, by the 1960s it had reached a point of stagnation and crisis. At its beginning, the evangelical movement had offered a real alternative to Roman Catholicism:

> The evangelical movement confronted a superficial religiosity with the need for a deep life of spiritual communion with Christ; syncretistic practices with the supreme centrality of Jesus Christ in the Church and in personal and collective piety; the divorce between religion and morality with the absolute need of a new birth with visible fruits in the private life; ignorance of Scriptures with the demand to read and study the Bible in order to be a member of the Church; passive religiosity of the people with the most complete lay participation and responsibility in evangelism and Church governance. These were, and still are, the great motives which justify and give power to the Latin American evangelical movement.[64]

For Castillo-Cárdenas, in spite of a great start, after its infancy and early youth the evangelical movement had found itself not knowing how to evangelize Latin Americans. This was mostly caused by rigid doctrinal orthodoxy, legalistic personal piety, the rites and meetings that made up traditional church life, and programs which were perceived by the people as alien to their problems and offensive to God and men. As the solution he proposed that those who called themselves Christians should first accept their responsibility for the people's new human predicament and give up

---

64. Gonzalo Castillo-Cárdenas, "El Cristianismo Evangélico En América Latina," *Cuadernos Teológicos* 2, no. 5 (1964): 61–65.

their lives to change it. In other words, evangelical Christians needed to make an active commitment to Latin American revolution. Consequently, the new evangelism was "to participate as Christians in both demolition and construction, with all the risks, and to live fully the revolution."[65]

Received theologies, liberal and fundamentalist together, were the reason for churches not participating in the revolution, according to Hiber Conteris, one of ISAL's ideologues; instead they helped to preserve the status quo.

> Except for few and unimportant exceptions, these two tendencies determine Latin American Protestantism's basic attitudes toward social change. In an attempt to provide an elemental characterization, we can say: (1) Churches that answer to the "Social Gospel" seem to recognize the need for change. However, such a change has to be made preserving the "Christian" values of traditional society. By "Christian" values we mean invariably a conceptualization of life from the epoch and society the churches identify themselves as at the origins of the Protestant movement in Latin America. The root of these values is found in individualism as the basic philosophy to understand liberty, political democracy, human rights, economical action and systems, etc. (2) The second attitude corresponds to the fundamentalist groups which postulate a radical separation between "the Gospel" and "the world." The mission of the church is to preach the Gospel and to attend to the "spiritual" salvation of men, without any preoccupation with the determining economic and social factors of their condition. This has led them to a Manicheism, affirming the spirit as the true reality while the social dimension corresponds to "the world," a secondary and false reality.[66]

Conteris identified a third option: indigenous and Pentecostal churches all over the continent with members primarily from the lowest sectors of society, peasants or native populations in rural areas, and the growing urban proletariat. For Conteris, these churches, in spite of a fundamentalist and otherworldly theology, were active agents in the revolution. Since the revolution demanded a great display of violence, the church was in need of

---

65. Ibid., 65.

66. Hiber Conteris, "El Rol De La Iglesia En El Cambio Social De América Latina," *Cristianismo y Sociedad* 3, no. 7 (1965): 55.

a radical structural change in order for believers to participate in a violent revolution, because, according to Conteris, that was the only way left to achieve structural transformation in Latin America.[67]

ISAL held its second consultation in El Tabo, Chile, 12–21 January 1966. Since Huampani, ISAL maintained an intensive program on several fronts. Regarding publications, besides the quarterly journal *Cristianismo y Sociedad* started in 1963, they published several books about social reality and the church's responsibility, presenting ISAL's theological reflection and pragmatic agenda. They also convened a Consultation on Service and Social Action in Rio de Janeiro in September 1963, where they reiterated that social action, as a ministry of the church, should be a dimension of the proclamation of the gospel. At Rio, a special secretariat started to coach churches on project formulation, conference organization, and publications. It seemed that ISAL did not linger long on theory but went straight into practical application. They also gave a key role to training leaders in the topics ISAL was promoting, through consultations as well as regional and national gatherings in at least eight countries.

At El Tabo, ISAL fine-tuned its theological method. They recognized the need for an ideological mediation for theology. The sociological and economic concept of "structure" was used to interpret the nature of social change in Latin America and to call it "revolution." They also introduced the category of "theology of history" to interpret that change from the church's perspective.

> The characteristics of social change in Latin America, the global nature of its process, gave rise to the need for a holistic reflection on history; it was absolutely necessary to find a current interpretation starting with an all-encompassing process that makes sense. This process, from a Biblical standpoint, is history itself: history considered not exclusively as human endeavor, but mainly as God's accomplishment, as the development of his will for human redemption, anticipated, known, and interpreted in light of the revelation of Jesus Christ. Humans become, thus, subjects and objects of historical transformation. The "humanization" of people is history's provisional telos, the immediate and penultimate goal that precedes the final gathering of everything in Jesus Christ.[68]

---

67. Ibid., 56–58.

68. ISAL, *América Hoy*, 17.

Since the church is at the hub of history, ISAL declared that "social revolution is also the church's revolution." The question was, "Can a Christian participate in a direct attack on the established legal structures (revolution) when there is no other possibility in sight for transforming them by current political and social movements?" Answering this question, ISAL explained that there were already in Latin America many forms of active violence which "are killing Latin Americans by hunger and sickness and are depriving them of opportunities to live." Thus, for Christians to act in a violent revolution was not to introduce violence in a society without violence.

> Violence could restore in our society an order closer to God's will for humankind. In this context, Christians' immediate task would be to identify and uncover forms of invisible and white-collar violence, to find its causes and possible remedies, to put into practice those remedies with the least exercise of direct violence, to study and use preventive mechanisms for every kind of violence. And finally, when a decision has to be made either way, and they are not sure about their decision, they should remember that perhaps they will never have absolute and definite assurance that their decision is the only possible one; and at this time they should maintain fraternal communion with those brethren who decided differently.[69]

This shows the direction ISAL was taking. The church ought to become more active in the revolution. There was no place for neutrality. This was a hard pill to swallow, especially since until that moment it had supposedly been a non-political church, dedicated exclusively to spiritual matters.

El Tabo called the church to become more Latin American. It had to better reflect the characteristic nature, culture, and ways of the region. The situation, as ISAL described it, was that the church's "liturgy, hymns (the religious service in general), Sunday school lessons, youth work, its constitution, theology, everything is distant, in form and content, from autochthonous Latin American culture. How can we incorporate in our meetings, in their liturgy and hymns, our language, our rhythm?" We remember that Inman in 1929, and others since, had mentioned something similar. The question was, How many of the cultural traits of European and North American Protestantism

---

69. ISAL, "II Consulta Latinoamericana De Iglesia y Sociedad 'El Tabo': Chile, Enero 12–21, 1966," *Cristianismo y Sociedad* 4, no. 9–10 (1966): 95.

were incompatible with the way of life and the nature of Latin Americans?[70] Furthermore: "What are the good and bad fruits of an evangelism which came from outside? Having arrived from countries where the Gospel was already known, how could they take root among us without foreign clothing and forms?" We have seen this already. The need to break with imported models started to be defined more accurately. Here the cultural element was what defined the "Latin Americanization" of the church. Moreover, El Tabo asked: Might Pentecostalism represent a change, the Latin American form of Protestantism? Can Pentecostalism serve as the basis for the expression of a new Christian life in our continent today?[71] Interestingly, ISAL recognized the Pentecostal influence, which up to that point had been mostly ignored.

ISAL's summary of the state of evangelical theology in Latin America said,

> It is possible to see that Latin American Protestantism has incorporated into its preaching and message a "doctrine" directly inherited from its missionary origins: the conviction that the inner transformation caused by conversion to Jesus Christ has consequences for the personal life resulting in a better social and economic situation. Although there is no theological formulation of this doctrine, the general consensus seems to validate it. Paradoxically, in this case, this conviction appears to contradict the need for social solidarity demanded by the development process the countries of the continent are going through. The "doctrine" of personal improvement (eminently an individualistic concept of success) has led the church to create a series of institutions equivalent to a Protestant sub-culture, like a cyst inside the national culture. It is like a microcosm where believers tend to isolate themselves and find refuge, like the educational system created by several evangelical traditions parallel with the prevalent public system. "Doctrine" and institution, then, are supporting each other, provoking a certain Protestant "mentality," often conceptually confronting the Latin American environment.[72]

In the final document, *Message to the Evangelical Churches of Latin America*, ISAL proposed that "the only way for a significant participation

---

70. ISAL, *América Hoy*, 122.

71. Ibid., 125.

72. Ibid., 130.

of the church in this revolution, and to take the message of Jesus Christ to the new structures of Latin American society, is found in the search for its renewal." They meant a renewal both of form (the religious services and liturgy) and content (its message). Without any renewal, they concluded, the church would not find a way to fulfill its permanent and unique mission. It was not an easy task; it was difficult and painful, yet not impossible.[73]

The Third Latin American Consultation of ISAL was held in Piriápolis, Uruguay, in December 1967. It was a time to redefine the identity and mission of ISAL, to evaluate what they had done so far, and to define goals for the future. ISAL made it clear that it was not a political group, that it did not identify itself with a specific political program, but that it had concrete proposals on politics: the "need for liberation from the hegemony the United States of America exercises over the continent and the dominance that the leading classes enjoy for their own sake, as well as the conceptualization of new economic, social, and political structures, to help in creating the new man Christianity has always wanted."[74] It is clear that the discussion had moved from the kingdom of God to the concept of humanization and a new man.

ISAL considered itself neither a church nor a specialized ministry of the church only for Christians. Instead, it "also aspires to meet those under oppression who are searching for potential transformation." Whether intentionally or without noticing it, ISAL started to drift away from the evangelical churches it wanted to serve. For instance, within its program ISAL offered its members "the necessary elements so that they can get involved in the effort to conceive and attain a more just society." Undoubtedly this sounded good; however, in its documents, churches were not included – only individuals. Could it be that churches started to be suspicious of the evangelical character of ISAL? A study of ISAL's publications reveals that the topic of evangelism disappeared while social, economic, and political ones came to the forefront. It was hard to convince outsiders that it was not a political group. This does not mean that ISAL was not calling attention to important realities the churches in general had overlooked almost completely. The situation in the continent was harsh and there was no way out in sight. ISAL's questions were real. However, by alienating itself from the community which had supported it from the beginning, it lost its best opportunity for tangible change.

---

73. ISAL, "II Consulta Latinoamericana De Iglesia y Sociedad 'El Tabo,'" 102.
74. ISAL, "III Consulta Latinoamericana De Isal," *Carta de Isal* 1, no. 1 (Abril 1968): 2.

It was in Ñaña, Peru, in July 1971, that the Fourth Continental Assembly of ISAL took place. The theme was "bases for a strategy and program for ISAL." Much water had gone under the bridge since Huampani ten years before. The minutes of the assembly clearly reflected the process of radicalization ISAL was going through. The main topic had to do with the involvement of Christians in the liberation experience in Latin America. Liberation was defined as "rupture with the system of economic dependency and exploitation our people are suffering which is generated by the actions of imperialism in alliance with national dominant classes."[75] Why a process of liberation of Latin America? ISAL answered that it was "to create a more just society in which odious class distinctions disappear and a more rational organization of production is established in accordance with the proper needs of workers. It will be a society where power will be in the hands of the popular classes currently being exploited. To achieve this goal it will be necessary to socialize production means and to democratize power. It will be a new society in which social issues will prevail over individual ones."[76] The change in direction since El Tabo, where ISAL specifically said it did not support any specific political project, is clear.

Within this social and political understanding, evangelical churches were "exposing the cultural forms and values of class interests linked tightly to the past which need to be overcome," and "are linked also to the centers of imperialistic dominance." Therefore, it was recommended to "nationalize the churches, understanding this not only as a step to allow the adoption of autochthonous and regional cultural forms, but also as the identification of the church with the interests and historical destiny of the people they ought to serve."[77] This action would affect theological reflection too.

> Given the peculiarities of the current Latin American theological situation for an authentic theological renewal, we should not understand it as repetition of theologies formulated in opulent societies (theology of the death of God, theology of hope, etc.). Instead it is an intention to comprehend the faith symbols and categories within the framework of the liberation process

---

75. ISAL, "Bases Para Una Estrategia y Programa De Isal. IV Asamblea Continental, Julio 1971. Ñaña, Perú," in *América Latina: Movilización Popular y Fe Cristiana*, ed. Rafael Tomás Carvajal et al. (Montevideo: ISAL, 1971), 140.

76. Ibid., 143–44.

77. Ibid., 148–49.

propping it up without obstructing it. Mere changes in the life forms of the church (liturgy, pastoral care, songs, etc.) in themselves are not very helpful for implementing our liberation. That's why the strength comes from the popular classes that want a new tomorrow, a new society. The church, then, must serve those classes and, if possible, be attentive and formulate a "theology of the people" instead of a "theology for the people."[78]

Uruguayan Methodist Julio de Santa Ana, a main ideologue for ISAL, compared the initial presence of evangelical churches in Latin America and their proposal for social change with the Protestant Reformation of the sixteenth century. However, from the very arrival of Protestants in Latin America, according to De Santa Ana, two trends were in confrontation: those who defended the "social gospel" and those who insisted that Christian action was only or firstly spiritual. He explained that these opposing trends "dominated theological production in Latin America for the largest part of the twentieth century; of those two the most dynamic has been the fundamentalist which has been predominant in the majority of the churches in the continent."[79] The confrontation between those two trends wore out evangelical work.

On one side, the social gospel lost sight of the particular social conditions in Latin America and often fell into an attitude of emphasizing behavioral change instead of societal change. On the other side, fundamentalism insisted so much on the other-worldliness of Christianity that it lost sight of the social dimension of the gospel. While the social gospel urged Christians to influence society and lost whatever is specific to Christian action, fundamentalism denied importance to social, economic, and political structures as if upon them the lordship of Jesus Christ should not be proclaimed. The saddest thing here is that such a polemic has not come up after considering the Latin American situation and its problems, but as the projection of debates and discussions that took place at the end of the last century and the beginning of this century in the countries where evangelical missions toward these lands started. Consequently,

---

78. Ibid., 150.

79. Julio De Santa Ana, *Protestantismo, Cultura y Sociedad: Problemas y Perspectivas De La Fe Evangélica En América Latina* (Buenos Aires: La Aurora, 1970), 112.

besides wearing out the strength of the evangelical movement by centering it on a discussion alien to the Latin American situation, it provoked a bigger alienation from our people, bringing out a difficult evil to repair for Latin American Protestantism.[80]

From the fifties, De Santa Ana said, the theologies of Barth, Brunner, Tillich, Niebuhr, Aulen, and others had become better known in several Latin American seminaries, particularly the emphasis on the incarnation of the body of Christ in the world and its implication to take seriously temporal structures through social service. This perspective did not eliminate internal debates, but it helped Latin American Protestantism to include in its theological thought particular questions such as the following: why numerical growth did not necessarily bring about the signs of the new world, which should go together with the proclamation of the message of salvation as the fulfillment of the mission of the church, according to the Bible; and how much preaching from the pulpits was about a lifestyle alien to Latin Americans. Regarding such preaching, De Santa Ana said, "instead of fulfilling the mission of the Church, what the evangelical movement had been doing consisted mostly in propagating certain beliefs and ideals for life that had little to do with our people's existence."[81]

For De Santa Ana, depending on foreign help was an impediment to taking the incarnation of evangelical work seriously. The incarnation of the message and the indigenization of the churches were imperative.[82] Furthermore, churches had to widen their understanding of mission to include all dimensions of human reality, especially the relationship of the church with society. However, a deficit in biblical knowledge, exegesis, and hermeneutics had resulted in a deterioration in theological reflection.

Today, on one side, because of fundamentalism, we are faced with a constant reference to biblical texts generally extracted from their context, and this produces a false interpretation. On the other side, those concerned about proper exegesis read commentaries, which may help a little, but often coming from other situations and other countries they sidetrack the

---

80. Ibid., 113.
81. Ibid., 117.
82. Ibid., 119.

interpretation of the message, making it meaningless for our
Latin American predicament.[83]

De Santa Ana highlighted the lack of good reflection in pastoral theology
and historical theology related to Latin American situations and culture.
Besides this, a renovation of theological education was imperative not only
to prepare people to lead churches but, in general, to prepare ministers to be
true servants of human beings and society. Consequently,

> Only when Latin American evangelical theologians become men
> of their people and men of God, while living even to the point
> of rupture – the tension produced by the encounter between
> the living God and people and their hopes – and when out of
> that tension thoughts turn into concrete and creative actions of
> solidarity with the people of Latin America, will we see a full
> awakening of real Latin American theological reflection. That
> day, the molds of foreign theologies will be put aside, not because
> of any opposition to them but because they do not respond as
> effectively as our own to the problems we have. Then theology
> will stop being bookish: it will became both an act of obedience
> to God and a sign of solidarity with our people and their destiny.[84]

ISAL was the first group to do contextual theology in Latin America.
Before, it had been done mostly by individuals. ISAL grasped the historical
moment and was able to enroll Protestant intellectuals to study the church
and its social involvement within Latin America during those years. In that
sense, ISAL became the first Protestant theological team in Latin America.
Its contribution to theological debate was an interdisciplinary method
introducing sociological instrumentation to theology, two disciplines which
did not mix much until then. Moreover, ISAL began bridging theology with
the historical, social, and economic situation of the continent, something
rarely explored beforehand. In general, before ISAL, theology had been related
only to the spiritual and religious issues of Latin Americans. ISAL widened
the area of influence of theology, taking advantage of available resources in
other sciences. Its questions about how to do theology and what it meant
to be the church at that particular historical moment changed subsequent
theological reflection.

---

83. Ibid., 143.
84. Ibid., 150.

ISAL provided an example of what can happen when a group swiftly distances itself from evangelical churches. In the end it isolated itself and its agenda attracted more unbelievers than evangelicals. Internal tensions and political repression eventually forced it to dissolve while some of its members continued publishing books and dialoguing.[85] ISAL's work prepared the setting for several theologies in the seventies: the so-called liberation theologies, mainly from Catholicism, and evangelical radical theologies such as those of the FTL (Fraternidad Teológica Latinoamericana).[86]

CELA III, 1969

Luis P. Bucafusco, president of CELA III, Buenos Aires, 13–19 July 1969, defined the mission of the church as a debt owed to the Latin American people, a debt of concrete responsibility and commitment with a holistic approach. For him, "the mission of the church as debt dissipates any possibility of isolation." He added,

> Feeling like debtors forces us to ask seriously and sincerely about the awareness of evangelical presence and our actions in these moments of change and intense searching. Because it is not enough to know we should serve; we want to deeply understand how far this service to people should take us. We are

85. For example, Hugo Assmann, "The Christian Contribution to the Liberation of Latin America" ["El Aporte Cristiano Al Proceso De Liberación De América Latina"], trans. Paul Abrechtin, in *Anticipation* 9 (Oct. 1971); Hugo Assmann, *Theology for a Nomad Church* (Maryknoll, NY: Orbis Books, 1975); Julio De Santa Ana, *Good News to the Poor: The Challenge of the Poor in the History of the Church* (Maryknoll, NY: Orbis Books, 1979); Julio De Santa Ana, *Separation Without Hope? Essays on the Relation between the Church and the Poor during the Industrial Revolution and the Western Colonial Expansion* (Maryknoll, NY: Orbis Books, 1980); Julio de Santa Ana, *Towards a Church of the Poor: The Work of an Ecumenical Group on the Church and the Poor* (Maryknoll, NY: Orbis Books, 1981); Julio De Santa Ana, *Is There Hope for the Third World?* (Amsterdam: VU Boekhandel/Uitgeverij, 1988); Julio De Santa Ana, *Through the Third World Towards One World* (Amsterdam: Vrije Universiteit, 1990); Julio De Santa Ana, *Sustainability and Globalization* (Geneva: WCC Publications, 1998). Pablo Richard, *The Church Born by the Force of God in Central America* (New York: New York Circus Publications, 1985); Pablo Richard, *Death of Christendoms, Birth of the Church: Historical Analysis and Theological Interpretation of the Church in Latin America* (Maryknoll, NY: Orbis Books, 1987).

86. For an analysis of ISAL's influence on liberation theologies, see Alan Neely, "Protestant Antecedents of the Latin American Theology of Liberation" (PhD diss., American University, 1977). For another study of Protestant precursors for liberation theologies, see Angel Daniel Santiago, "Contextual Theology and Revolutionary Transformation: The Missiology of M. Richard Shaull, 1942–2002" (ThM thesis, Princeton Theological Seminary, 2000).

committed to the process of transformation and development of our people since we are concerned for their wholeness. We are not for substituting one misery for another, a laboratory for hatred and violence. Instead, we are for meaningful and radical change erasing those irritating and annoying inequalities, allowing every human being to live in the fullness of his potential and reach the abundant life promised by our Lord. A debt as mission forces us to be there, in the battlefield, to fight for a new and more human order, more full of God's presence. Jesus Christ's sovereignty should be seen in the whole of human life, and within the political, economic, social, cultural, and religious context. We are debtors, we should pay off the debt![87]

Paternalism and theological dependence within evangelical churches led Bucafusco to recognize that structures and theology were contaminated with imported vices and problems. The situation was messier since, besides ideology, finances were also part of it. Many Latin Americans were wanting freedom from obsessive paternalism and were searching to define their identity, to work out their personality. This didn't mean a total break with the global church or a rejection of the gospel. In contrast, "we want to *be*, we want to have our life structured according to Latin American circumstances and the situation of Latin Americans and to be able to formulate a theology relevant to the condition and situation of people in Latin America. Such a theology should be the fruit of Latin American thought and reflection of those who *live* and *labor* in the continent, who are embedded into the reality of Latin Americans."[88]

Bucafusco's words highlighted what was happening during those years. Latin Americans started to break their dependency and search for their way around, not only structurally but also theologically. It was a time of growth when they wanted to continue the trajectory they had followed so far, only without foreign tutelage. They intended to be relevant and conscious of the Latin American context at that time. From the sixties onward, this was the tendency and there was no going back. Latin Americans started on their own path, to the surprise of outsiders.

---

87. Luis P. Bucafusco, "Impresiones Personales Sobre La III CELA," in *Deudores Al Mundo, III Conferencia Evangélica (CELA)* (Montevideo: UNELAM, 1969), 14.

88. Ibid., 15.

Uruguayan Methodist pastor Emilio Castro used a metaphor to explain this:

> The Gospel came to us like a plant in a pot that was transplanted into the native soil of our situation. Only we planted it together with the pot and forgot the importance of breaking the pot with the effects of the power of the Gospel so that, deeply rooted in our autochthonous soil, it would yield its most authentic fruit, legitimately Latin American. The idea is not, then, to repeat Christian forms perhaps useful in other times and places, but to express the faith here and now in our continent, being sure that, by relating the Gospel to the problems and opportunities of each local and national situation, we fulfill our missionary responsibility and also we achieve the goal that moved the preachers from the past who came to our countries: to plant the Church of Jesus Christ in the solid and fertile Latin American soil.[89]

José Míguez Bonino said that the influence of Protestantism had visible ambiguities. For example, while for many people conversion meant a subversive experience of freedom, he asked whether that subversion originated in the gospel's demands or if it was just religious, dominated by liberal capitalist ideology, keeping Latin America dependent, underdeveloped, and exploited. He said,

> Can we say that conversion brought liberation when it just replaced one alienation by another one, providing a refuge, a substitute society (church), and therefore moving people apart from the battle front where society's destiny is defined? Finally, was the Gospel really the source of our polemics against Roman Catholicism, or was it the pietistic individualistic and subjective theology that led us to a legalistic pharisaism on one side and to bourgeois conservatism on the other side?[90]

We find a similar analysis in Samuel Escobar's presentation at Cochabamba, Bolivia, in December 1970, when the FTL (we will look at

---

89. Emilio Castro, *Un Pueblo Peregrino: Reflexiones Sobre La Misión De La Iglesia En El Mundo Actual* (Buenos Aires: La Aurora, 1966), 56.

90. José Míguez Bonino, "Protestantism's Contribution to Latin America," *Lutheran Quarterly* 22, no. 1 (February 1970): 94.

this in detail in the next chapter) was founded.[91] Escobar called an attitude related to the theological dependency of Latin American evangelicals "Anglo-Saxon clothing." He identified four historical factors related to this attitude: the social origin of the missionaries (most of them belonged to the middle class), the anti-Hispanic polemic regarding whatever was Hispanic, the fundamentalism–modernism debate in North America, and pietism with a monastic inclination. Any evangelical theologian needed to recognize these factors to reflect on "how much his preferences and perspectives are conditioned and determined by missionary political and social heritage; and how those preferences and perspectives for his theological labor correspond to the teaching of the Word of God and are not just a reflection of the middle class cultural mold." Escobar warned that to do theology a Latin American had to be careful not to anger his missionary sponsors and become suspected of heresy – not the best atmosphere for creative work. Pietism, as a spiritual element of the missionary movement, could degenerate into a selfish individualism and create a monastic attitude.

> Among us, the pietism of the missionaries was emphasized because of the strength of Christendom represented by Rome, with its variety of badly disguised syncretism and paganism. A minority complex was added to pietism and, after losing the vigor of the first generation, it has become a factor in stagnation and a scandalous vacuum of evangelical presence in the whole Iberian-American life and culture. This has been reinforced by the predominance of a dispensational theology providing another justification to reject culture, a separation from the world, a pharisaism produced by a remnant complex, and the adoption of an easy and closed doctrinal scheme. All of this makes difficult the inquisitive attitude that belongs to any theological labor.[92]

To confront such theological dependence, Escobar called on Latin Americans to determine what was permanent in their "precious heritage" and to get rid of everything that was accessory. Here Escobar defined seven lines of action: to reappraise everything Hispanic; to rediscover and value the

---

91. Samuel Escobar, "El Contenido Bíblico y El Ropaje Anglosajón En La Teología Latinoamericana," in *El Debate Contemporáneo Sobre La Biblia*, ed. Peter Savage (Barcelona: Ediciones Evangélicas Europeas, 1972). For a historical account of this meeting, see Daniel Salinas, *Latin American Evangelical Theology in the 1970s: The Golden Decade* (Leiden: Brill, 2009).

92. Escobar, "El Contenido Bíblico," 31.

Protestant Reformation, especially its Latin elements; to create an atmosphere of freedom and maturity; to stand against the parties and labels coming from different ecclesiastical and missionary fronts; to provide a pastoral dimension to theological labor; to understand the revolution; and, finally, to recover hope. For Escobar the theological task had an important ecclesiastical element.

> A theologian under the influence of the Word of God can help the church to distinguish between mere ecclesiastical traffic and the mission of the church. A biblical theologian can show the possible danger of the people of God missing the way. For example, when the community of believers confuses numerical growth with growth according to biblical teaching, it needs an alarm call. The same happens when we confuse ecclesiastical activism with fulfilling the mission. A theologian cannot produce doctrines to justify such practices. His role is to discover biblical truths to correct errors. It is an unpopular task, certainly, the task of the prophet. The opposite danger might be a theologian in his ivory tower not realizing the work of the Holy Spirit among his people, as the revealed Word teaches.[93]

Also at Cochabamba, Peruvian Presbyterian pastor Pedro Arana Quiroz defined Latin American theology as "an expression of our Christian faith containing Iberian-American cultural and historical factors, conscientious and contemporaneous in its approach to our continent's reality, that is, in close relationship with daily life and pertinent in its transmission of the message."[94] Arana proposed that to do theological work theologians needed to know and take a position on certain issues affecting evangelicals: liberal rationalism and Comte's humanism; fundamentalist subjectivism, where experience is the supreme authority on faith issues; existentialist absolutism; and ISAL's proposal of revelation in revolution. Those factors were obviously working against the biblical message.

For René Padilla, the evangelical movement in Latin America was mostly theologically conservative, characterized by submission to the authority of the Bible. However, it was a purely formal submission, without any practical consequences for doctrinal definition, ethics, and preaching. This resulted

---

93. Ibid., 35.

94. Pedro Arana Quiroz, "La Revelación De Dios y La Teología En Latinoamérica," in *El Debate Contemporáneo Sobre La Biblia*, ed. Peter Savage (Barcelona: Ediciones Evangélicas Europeas, 1972), 42.

in an almost complete absence of theological reflection among evangelical conservatives in Latin America. He said,

> One of the most common characteristics of preaching in evangelical churches in Latin America is its lack of biblical roots. Notwithstanding a common submission to the authority of the Bible, in practice there is an astonishing lack of seriousness towards biblical revelation. The text is often used as a pretext, as a sounding board for preachers to throw away their rumblings and exhortations with no regard to relating them to the written text. If we also throw in the distance between the message and the questions the modern world asks the Christian faith, it is not surprising that most evangelicals in our continent have little idea how the authority of the Bible affects practical life. The evangelical pulpit in Latin America is in crisis. A unilateral emphasis on evangelism divorced from teaching has resulted in a distortion of preaching and consequently of the life and mission of the people of God in the world. Wherever the objective Word of God is replaced by human opinions, and subjected to circumstantial conditioning or the ideologies of the times, Christian experience gets reduced to a subjectivism destroying the very essence of what it means to be Christian because the connection between religious experience and the objective reality of the revelation given once and for all is destroyed.[95]

Padilla characterized Latin American evangelicalism as "sad doctrinal superficiality, gospel intellectualism indebted not so much to theology but to simplistic foreign-made doctrinal formulations, and lacking judgment to discern between purely religious experience and genuine Christian experience, between pietism and piety, between professionalism and discipleship, between rationalism and orthodoxy, between intolerance and conviction."[96]

The "Evangelical Declaration of Cochabamba" invited believers to confess that God has revealed himself in a clear and definite way through Jesus Christ, as the Bible says. This was to be the foundation for a theological

---

95. C. René Padilla, "La Autoridad De La Biblia En La Teología Latinoamericana," in *El Debate Contemporáneo Sobre La Biblia*, ed. Peter Savage (Barcelona: Ediciones Evangélicas Europeas, 1972), 138.

96. Ibid., 153.

reflection which took into account the context in the continent. Believers were invited to return to the Bible to question evangelical traditions in light of the written revelation, to really be disciples within the complex social, political, and economic reality in Latin America. There was a need for a new biblical movement among Latin American churches.[97]

The FTL brought consolidation after a time of searching for identity and a definition of what it meant to do proper Latin American evangelical theology. It was a group effort, non-denominational, with ample continental representation (from Mexico to the Southern Cone), and willing to put aside doctrinal and ideological differences to achieve a common good. The FTL catalyzed the concerns of Latin Americans who were already doing theology, and provided the platform for unity and teamwork needed at that particular time in history. Unity and mutual collaboration were imperatives for the 1970s, a decade that shook Latin American theology, changing it completely, and taking it on new paths not even the visionaries of the CCLA had imagined.

---

97. Peter Savage, ed. *El Debate Contemporáneo Sobre La Biblia* (Barcelona: Ediciones Evangélicas Europeas, 1972), 225–28.

4

Evangelicals Searching for Their Identity and Theology: The Seventies and Eighties

In 1971 a book by Peruvian Dominican priest Gustavo Gutiérrez, *Liberation Theology: Perspectives*,[1] launched Latin American theological reflection to the world. Gutiérrez's thesis and conclusions were immediately translated in over twenty languages, such that theologies of liberation became known globally simply as "Latin American theology." Evangelicals who were already thinking theologically and producing theology were totally eclipsed and even, in many places inside and outside Latin America, were also labeled "liberationists." But there was no unified response to liberation theologies from the evangelical camp. There were some who rejected them completely, while others embraced them unreservedly. The evangelical community in Latin America became even more fragmented because of the new theologies. Political, social, and economic questions demanded a biblical response but it was hard to break with received patterns.

For example, Manuel J. Gaxiola, a Unitarian Pentecostal from Mexico, recognized that liberation theology made Christians aware of the sad and hard conditions of life for most Latin Americans. He considered it an antidote to those who "blatantly try to mix the baptism of the Holy Ghost with material progress, and measure their spiritual success by the size of their bank account and the amount of their riches."[2] Regarding the reception of liberation

---

1. Published in English as Gustavo Gutiérrez, *A Theology of Liberation: History, Politics and Salvation*, trans. Sister Caridad Inda and John Eagleson (Maryknoll, NY: Orbis Books, 1973).

2. Manuel Jesús Gaxiola, "The Pentecostal Ministry," *International Review of Mission* 66, no. 261 (1 January 1977): 61.

theologies by Pentecostals, Gaxiola made four keen observations. First, the "theology of liberation cannot be accepted by the majority of Pentecostals because they differ in their concepts of what liberation and involvement are." He explained,

> Whereas the theology of liberation seems intent on reaching its goals through political means (as politics are understood in the traditional sense), and by the changing of all kinds of structures, most Pentecostals believe that liberation is essentially a spiritual operation of Christ, irrespective of political or economic conditions either before or after this operation. Even if they admit that socio-economic and political conditions should be changed, Pentecostals would agree that this is a secondary concern, and they would differ in the degree to which they would participate in a liberation movement of any kind.[3]

Gaxiola's second observation was that most Pentecostals would equate liberation theology with Marxism, mostly understood "as the political system of countries like the USSR, China, or Cuba." Consequently, most people were hardly convinced that they wanted it implemented in their own societies. Their dilemma, according to Gaxiola, was that "they perceive the faults of the capitalist system (better than we give them credit for), and appreciate the conveniences and disadvantages of Marxism, yet without being convinced that they want it for themselves."[4] Third, Pentecostals had a different take from liberation theology on who were the poor:

> The theology of liberation seems to have a very romantic, almost paternalistic, idea of the poor. This theology seems to offer a very simplistic reason for their condition: they are poor because they have been traditionally exploited or abused. Nobody can deny this, but it seems to me we should go farther and deeper, and see the poor not only as fellow human beings worthy of our love and solidarity, but also as sinners in need of forgiveness, many of them as willing and capable as their exploiters of becoming heartless exploiters of their own brethren. Pentecostals know that poverty is caused by the greed of the rich, but this is not the exclusive cause. Sometimes the poor oppress the poor (Prov

---

3. Ibid.
4. Ibid.

28:3), and in their greed are as unjust as the rich (Matt 18:23–35). Pentecostals know this also, and for that reason they expect both the rich and the poor to avail themselves of God's saving grace and then to live peacefully and justly with one another.[5]

The fourth assessment of liberation theology by Pentecostals, according to Gaxiola, was that the former did not have a "viable plan of action, and seems to consist of endless talk between one theologian and another." Despite the fact that most liberation theologians were Catholic, in Gaxiola's evaluation the Catholic Church as an institution had shown no significant change. Things were not much different on the Protestant side where Gaxiola saw many inconsistencies, such as the fact that "the most vocal attacks against the capitalist system come from those who benefit from it: indigenous ministers and seminary professors who derive their income precisely from the countries they criticize most virulently." In order to achieve honesty and be more effective, these Protestants "should renounce all support and every benefit they receive from other sources, so as to be able to speak with the authority of those who live without their means."[6]

Gaxiola's assessment was right on the mark. On the one hand, Pentecostals came mostly from the lowest strata of society; they were the poor liberation theology wanted to liberate. But they did not adopt liberation theology. Gaxiola demonstrated that anti-Catholic sentiment was not the main reason for the Pentecostal rejection of liberation theology: rather, it was because their theology and ecclesiastical experience had good enough answers to help them in their predicament. There were many elements in Pentecostal theology and doctrine, as well as in communal life, that reached the poor without patronizing them. On the other hand, Pentecostals did not think they needed any liberation besides the spiritual one they had experienced by the power of the Holy Spirit. All the liberation theology talk about changing their oppression was foreign to them. They had hope, they had freedom, in Christ, and they had the baptism of the Holy Spirit. What else did they need? They had it all – something liberation theology did not consider.

Another evangelical analysis of liberation theology came from Baptist theologian René Padilla. He described Gutiérrez's book as the magnum opus of liberation theology. However, it left much to be desired from the biblical standpoint. Padilla said,

---

5. Ibid., 62.
6. Ibid.

For Gutiérrez, Christianity is taking shape in the praxis of small groups of Christians involved in the struggle for a new free society. Theology is essentially the reflection on that praxis in a concrete historical situation. By tying itself down to a particular revolutionary praxis which is considered exempt from judgment, this theology makes its first mistake even before starting the formulation of its basic tenets. Never has it tried to demonstrate why that specific praxis is chosen, and not another one, as the object for reflection and what gives it its Christian character. Too easily it is taken for granted that the liberation sponsored by the political left coincides with the liberation proposed by the Christian faith. The praxis adopted by the theologian is never subject to a critical analysis of its basic presuppositions. One gets the impression that everything regarded as the kind of action expected from a Christian in a revolutionary situation has been defined a priori, that the role of theology is then merely to provide a façade to that particular political option. Biblical exegesis has no importance whatsoever for liberation theology.[7]

However, such ideologization of the faith in full concordance with a Marxist framework of reference but distant from the gospel of Jesus Christ was not to keep evangelicals from recognizing its challenges. Padilla defined two main challenges: the need for an evaluation of the philosophical presuppositions of the evangelical faith, and the importance of seriously considering the situation where theology is being done. Padilla recognized that in many cases evangelical theological reflection had become marred by conservatism and conformism to the status quo. Furthermore, the harsh reality of the historical situation was a fact, and evangelical theology was obliged to make every effort to discern God's will and the demands of Christian discipleship in that situation. Since evangelicals tended to reject liberation theology as a valid proposal, Padilla asked: "Where then is evangelical theology proposing a solution, with the same eloquence, but also based more firmly on the Word of God?"[8] In a way, by asking this question, Padilla set the agenda for evangelical theological reflection in Latin America. The FTL was one of the groups that accepted the challenge.

---

7. C. René Padilla, "La Teología De La Liberación," *Pensamiento Cristiano* 20, no. 4 (Diciembre 1972): 171.

8. Ibid., 172.

FTL

The FTL (Fraternidad Teológica Latinoamericana; the Latin American Theological Fraternity, LATF) was defined as "a community of thinkers at the service of Christ and his church, convinced of the value of theological reflection regarding the being and doing of the church." It had three main objectives:

- To promote reflection around the gospel and its importance to people and society in Latin America. To stimulate the development of evangelical thought attentive to the Word of God and taking seriously the questions asked by life in Latin America, accepting for its reflection the normative character of the Bible as the Word written by God, and making every effort, under the direction of the Holy Spirit, to listen to the biblical message related to the particularities of our concrete situation.

- To become a platform of dialogue for thinkers who confess Jesus Christ as their Lord and God, and who are willing to reflect under the light of the Bible in order to build a bridge between the gospel and Latin American culture.

- To contribute towards the mission and life of the church of Christ in Latin America without intending to speak on behalf of the church nor to take on the position of theological voice for the evangelical people in the Latin American continent.

In order to achieve these goals, six areas of reflection were defined: biblical theology, ethics, ecclesiastical history and structure, apologetics, theological education, and pastoral ministry. The key was that any theological reflection in these areas should consider cultural specifics and the questions present in Latin America. It was a contextual reflection made from and for Latin America. This was the distinctive note during the Second International Theological Consultation of the FTL in Lima, Peru, 11–19 December 1972.

Educator and Pastor Emilio Antonio Núñez from El Salvador, for example, mentioned the need for a theologian to consider the ideologies that offered a definite solution to the problems Latin America was facing. He warned that those theologians tending to spiritualize the full eschatological biblical scheme were at a disadvantage compared with those putting forward a new order for Latin America. For Núñez, sound biblical hermeneutics together with the realities Latin American Christians experienced forced them to review their theological framework, especially regarding the messianic kingdom. "It seems that the time has come for a renewal of apocalyptic and millenarian elements within the Latin American evangelical church. Messianic hope has to do with heaven and earth, with individuals and society."[9]

Núñez recognized that the received teaching until that time, mainly from dispensationalism, highlighted the Jewish and future nature of the kingdom, without any concern for its present. For him, most missionaries and the leaders they trained for ministry were futurist and separatists, therefore unable to relate their teaching to Latin American culture, a problem even Núñez's generation was perpetuating. The majority of Latin American evangelicals, even Pentecostals, thus fell into apocalypticism, with a limited and feeble concept of the kingdom. They needed to properly identify the tension between the coming kingdom and the kingdom already here. Núñez's words carried weight since his context was dispensationalism. His analysis shows the maturity of a theologian who took a distance from the tradition he received and, without rejecting it altogether, evaluated it, highlighting its deficiencies.

Also in Lima, René Padilla reiterated what Núñez had said about the evangelical church in Latin America ignoring the present reality of the kingdom. Padilla explained that it was precisely through the church that the powers of the new age, brought forth by the Messiah, were present among the people. He said,

> It is urgent in Latin America to recognize the meaning of the "now" of the kingdom of God for all the life and mission of the church. A unilateral emphasis on evangelism, and on an evangelism conceived in terms of preaching the rudiments of repentance and faith, has resulted in an evangelical community marked by professionalism and often lacking the most basic signs of the kingdom, like communion (koinonia) and service (diakonia). Unfortunately the strategy some missions impose on the church in Latin America is inspired by an ecclesia-centric notion of evangelism identifying conversion to Christ as mentally accepting a doctrinal formula and as spiritual prowess with the ability to ideologically manipulate our neighbors. Theology in this part of the world has the task of forging a definition for the mission of the church from a Christ-centered viewpoint. It must

---

9. Emilio Antonio Núñez, "La Naturaleza Del Reino De Dios," paper presented at Fraternidad Teológica Latino Americana, II Consulta Teológica Internacional, Lima, 1972, 6.

be a definition which avoids the aberrations such missionary strategy has fallen into as the result of the conditioning capitalism has imposed over evangelical missiologists; a definition that does justice to biblical teaching regarding the church as a messianic community not looking for its glory but the Lord's glory.[10]

This led Padilla to conclude that a rediscovery of Christian hope was an essential need of Latin American evangelicals: "A hope answering the challenge of ideologies from left and right, with a program for a society where life is more humane. A hope radicalizing the ethical requirements of the gospel, shaking out of their bourgeois comfort a second and third generation of evangelicals who have forgotten the Christian meaning of poverty. Finally, a hope placing the mission of the church within the framework of God's purpose to form a new humanity."[11] Padilla proposed that it was time to redefine eschatology within Latin America's situation.

José Míguez Bonino said in Lima that in the Bible it was impossible to separate God's direct actions from human history. This was, according to Míguez, a problem with evangelical theology in Latin America: "Catholics and Protestants have lived mostly disconnected from any historical reference—I dare to say, from *general* history [i.e. history of the nations], because of our separation from the world, as well as from *special* history [i.e. history of the faith], because of the religious and otherworldly ways we have understood our faith (as doctrinal statement or emotional experience). When we become aware of such historical dimensions we do not know how to integrate them."[12]

Samuel Escobar explained that Anglo-Saxon Protestantism, the Protestantism which was most influential in Latin America, presented a fatal inability to live out its theology or practice truth to its ultimate consequences. Theological reflection in Latin America, Escobar added, was limited because of an incapacitating pragmatism. He identified within Latin American evangelicalism several traits of the so-called "radical reformation" of Anabaptism: "In the midst of a Christendom nurtured more by politics than by spirituality, evangelicals affirmed the *spiritual nature* of the kingdom of God. Amid a Constantinian Christianity with an official church, evangelicals

---

10. C. René Padilla, "La Iglesia y El Reino De Dios," paper presented at Fraternidad Teológica Latino Americana, II Consulta Teológica Internacional, Lima, 1972, 21–22.

11. Ibid., 27–28.

12. José Míguez Bonino, "Reino De Dios E Historia: Reflexiones Para Una Discusión Del Tema," paper presented at Fraternidad Teológica Latino Americana, II Consulta Teológica Internacional, Lima, 1972.

affirmed the *absolute separation* of the throne and the altar (pulpit)."[13] However, Anabaptism had lost the eschatological note. For example,

> Among the so-called evangelicals in North America, ethical radicalism is just not there anymore. Separation from the world is reduced to the better-known social taboos but with no significant challenge to the way of life of society in general. Although theoretically they do not want a merger between church and state, there is a vigorous disposition, whatever the cost, to keep the values, way of life, and privileges that come from the world. They fight any concession to socialism when capitalistic tradition is at stake, and at the same time they zealously protect a right to tax exemption, turning some ecclesiastical bodies into powerful financial corporations. They are suspicious of anyone who challenges by word or deed the legitimate authorities. Interest in prophecy has become a laboratory for what José Grau calls "fiction-eschatology" that intends to prove with numbers, exegetical juggling, and selective historical data that communists represent the Antichrist, the European Common Market is his ally, and the current pro-Israel attitude of some Western countries is spiritual foresight and a sign of God's favor over its national existence and foreign policies.[14]

Eschatology was crucial, especially in light of the Marxist challenge in the region. Escobar explained that it was "a proletariat messianism and the vision of a kingdom of bliss as result of a revolution" that fed Marxist militancy. The evangelical response of an apocalyptic vision, where the radical demands of the kingdom were put off, fit perfectly with the Marxist agenda which proposed a deterioration of the situation in order for a revolution to happen. Evangelicals believed that instead of being busy solving the urgent needs of the Latin American masses regarding bread, education, work, health, and dignity, what needed to be done was to strive to preach the gospel in order to hasten the *arrival* of such a kingdom. The connection between ethics and eschatology was lost. For Escobar, "something must be wrong among

---

13. Samuel Escobar, "El Reino De Dios, La Escatología y La Etica Social y Política En América Latina," paper presented at Fraternidad Teológica Latino Americana, II Consulta Teológica Internacional, Lima, 1972, 6.

14. Ibid., 9–10.

Christians when the children of darkness rob their hope. Even worse, when they are accused of turning it into opium."[15]

The urgent need to evaluate and clearly define evangelical eschatology led Escobar to propose four areas of exploration: ethics, mainly in areas such as peace and justice; critical thinking, teaching Christians to develop a critical view of the world; apologetics, to show Christians' contributions to society; and hope, to show how the kingdom can renew and change old ecclesiastical and political structures. To highlight the consequences of such eschatology, Escobar asked,

> Is it possible to serve a God who in so many ways manifests his peace and not to feel, at the same time, awareness of peace in national and international relations? Should we leave to others the hope of peace? Is it possible to believe what we just said and not to take interest in worker–employer relations? Is it possible not to sympathize with the struggle for a better and more humane treatment for the proletariat? When the conditions imposed by foreign capital for investment are "mistreatment of the workers" and "legislation to satisfy the fair expectations of investors," should only communists protest? Furthermore, when one is a Christian and an employer in these lands, is it enough to obey the letter of unjust laws?[16]

Escobar's words resembled what the CCLA had defined earlier in the century as the social agenda for evangelicals in Latin America. The same reality persisted and the same needs remained unattended by evangelical churches.

Argentinian Pentecostal pastor Juan Carlos Ortiz also wrote about the need to reconsider the evangelical message that was preached in Latin America, especially its ethical aspects. For Ortiz, the Scriptures did not divide the social from the spiritual, and consequently there was not a social gospel and another spiritual gospel. His experience exemplified this.

> In the fundamentalist evangelical church I belong to, we have lived under all the Bible verses that have to do with the glorious past of the apostolic era and the wonderful future up in heaven. But we have avoided any responsibility to solve the problems of here and now. Too little have we positioned ourselves in the

---

15. Ibid., 16–17.
16. Ibid., 18–19.

present. Preaching, hymns, and songs speak to us about how beautiful heaven will be. That there will not be any sadness, misery, sin, etc. However, such a gospel does not exist in the Scriptures. The immense truth of heaven and earth is true, when it is dovetailed with the truth of here on this earth and at this time.[17]

According to Ortiz, the gospel of the kingdom of God was one package – spiritual-economic-social-agrarian-health-etc. A gospel pushing only for spiritual things was as much a heresy as one that emphasized only the social aspects. The two were inseparable. The message needed to include the whole gospel, its offers and demands. It needed to be integral and complete. "We cannot save the 'little soul' of a person and leave him in his 'little house' of misery or abundance." The church needed to live the gospel of Jesus Christ in society; it needed to participate in its changing processes, not just observe them from a distance. "Yesterday, to cross our arms was helping the unjust system we suffer today in the distribution of wealth given by God. To cross our arms today means helping an unjust system of atheistic materialism which will deprive our children of their parents' faith." Ortiz proposed, then, an ecclesiology without religion, a Christ-centered church searching for the kingdom of God and its justice, where the condition for new people to become members was not simply that they raised their hands and were baptized, but that they decided to accept the demands of Jesus, denying themselves and taking up the cross, renouncing everything for the community's sake. There was a need for the re-evangelization of believers – a bold program coming from a Pentecostal pastor. Even though Ortiz was not related to the FTL, his analysis showed many similarities with those of the FTL.

For example, René Padilla said that the church in Latin America did not have its own theological reflection. To support his claim, Padilla drew attention to some specific areas: Christian literature made up only of translations; the repetition in sermons of imported ideas without any insertion into Latin American realities; the repetition of the theological formulas of the founding missions, professors (mostly foreign) and curricula of theological education, and hymnology. For Padilla, all of these factors pointed to a theological dependency, to a church without theology, or without any theological reflection doing justice to the Bible. He asked,

17. Juan Carlos Ortiz, "Definiciones Socio-Económicas De La Iglesia Para La Problemática Latinoamericana," *Pensamiento Cristiano* 19, no. 4 (1972).

What kind of gospel do we preach if our preaching is not nurtured by a serious study of the Word of God and our reflection on its significance for our concrete situation? Have we made the Christian faith really ours if we limit ourselves to repeating it according to formulas made in other latitudes? Can there be a really biblical evangelism – a presentation of the whole counsel of God – without theological reflection looking to comprehend the relevance of the gospel to the totality of human life in a defined historical context?[18]

There were three main consequences of theological dependency, according to Padilla: lack of incarnation of the gospel in Latin American culture; a church incapable of confronting current ideologies; and the loss of second and third generations of evangelicals. Padilla characterized as tragic the fact that, even after almost a century of continuous evangelical presence in Latin America, "the gospel still has a strange sound, or no sound at all, in connection with many of the aspirations and worries, problems and questions, values and customs of our life in Latin America." A church without theological reflection was at the mercy of whatever ideology might come round, and it did not have any criteria for critiquing and evaluating those ideologies. It was urgent, Padilla continued, to have a "theological armor to help us evaluate the various ways to interpret our situation (or to change it) without sacralizing any ideology, either from the left or from the right." He referred to ISAL as an example of the gospel being confused with political ideology and of theology not considering seriously the normative character of biblical revelation. In that case, God was transformed into an object easily manipulated by people and attached to strategies and programs that supposedly reflected his will. "The god who makes revolution an absolute is a false god: it is more a utopian *new man*, unreachable, a defaced person." Therefore, Padilla concluded that ISAL's theology was not an option for whoever wanted to be faithful to the gospel. Evangelical theology in Latin America should have three important characteristics: "to do justice to the totality of biblical witness, to take seriously our situation, and to be an incentive to fulfill Christian mission."[19]

---

18. C. René Padilla, "La Teología En Latinoamérica," *Pensamiento Cristiano* 19, no. 75 (1972): 207.

19. Ibid., 211–213.

Anglo-Saxon Clothing, Manifest Destiny, and Cultural Christianity

On other fronts people were analyzing missionary heritage as the background of the evangelical presence in Latin America. What Escobar had called the "Anglo-Saxon clothing" was being scrutinized and specified. Rubén Lores from Costa Rica, for instance, drew attention to the United States' political doctrine of "manifest destiny" as a key element in the historical and theological development of the churches initiated by North American missions in Latin America. Those churches, said Lores, "have received a *body* of attitudes, ethical stances, political postures, economic ideas, and relational loyalties that are more substantially related to the ideology of *manifest destiny* than to the Gospel of Christ."[20]

Missionary expansion developed mostly as a result of non-theological factors. For example, "missionary leaders enacted policies and strategies to take as much advantage as possible of the favourable situation that was offered to them by colonialism. What very few, if any, seem to realize, was that in a very real way the Gospel was being compromised by the conscious or unconscious legitimization of the political ambitions and exploitations of the colonial powers."[21] This resulted in new believers becoming "the best kind of supporters of the *status quo* that any ruler could expect," and "supporters of the *status quo* at the level of international relationships. Most missionary societies are based on imperialistic nations."[22]

Together with "manifest destiny," Lores included capitalism's ethics and economic theory as having been exported to the whole world by missionaries. Consequently, churches established by foreign missionaries and which "have been under foreign influence for too long are probably incapable of going back to a *tabula rasa* beginning in order to discover the true potentialities of the Gospel of Jesus Christ in terms of values and categories of their own culture."[23] Such a system was presented by missionaries as the only legitimate option for Christians in Latin America. Lores concluded by asking missionaries and

---

20. Rubén Lores, "Manifest Destiny and the Missionary Enterprise," *Study Encounter* 11, no. 1 (1975): 2. Lores defines manifest destiny as follows: "As it relates to the United States, 'manifest destiny' was the rebirth of the ancient idea that in any given period of history one nation or people exercises the imperium of civilization, culturally and politically. So, in a sense, this ideal expresses the notion that the 'decadent' European culture was being reborn in American soil."

21. Ibid., 8.

22. Ibid., 9.

23. Ibid., 11.

the agencies they represented to "understand the ambiguities of their calling and the way in which consciously or unconsciously this pervasive ideology of manifest destiny has made them more the ambassadors of Anglo-Saxon Christianity and the American way of life than of the Gospel of the Lord Jesus Christ."[24]

René Padilla presented a similar analysis at the International Congress for World Evangelization in Lausanne, Switzerland, 16–25 July 1974. Padilla defined what he called "cultural Christianity" as the "identification of Christianity with a culture or a cultural expression."[25] The main representation of cultural Christianity was the American way of life. To support this, Padilla quoted David Moberg saying: "We have equated 'Americanism' with Christianity to such an extent that we are tempted to believe that people in other cultures must adopt American institutional patterns when they are converted. We are led through natural psychological processes to an unconscious belief that the essence of our American Way of Life is basically, if not entirely, Christian."[26] Padilla said,

> The image of a Christian that has been projected by some forms of United States Christianity is that of a successful businessman who has found the formula for happiness, a formula he wants to share with others freely. The basic problem is that in a market of "free consumers" of religion in which the church has no possibility of maintaining its monopoly on religion, this Christianity has resorted to reducing its message to a minimum in order to make all men want to become Christians. The gospel thus becomes a type of merchandise the acquisition of which guarantees the consumer the highest values – success in life and personal happiness now and forever. The act of "accepting Christ" is the means to reach the ideal of the "good life" at no cost. The cross has lost its offense, since it simply points to the sacrifice of Jesus Christ for us but does not present a call to discipleship. The God of this type of Christianity is the God of "cheap grace," the God who constantly gives but never demands, the God fashioned

---

24. Ibid., 15.

25. C. René Padilla, "Evangelism and the World," in *Let the Earth Hear His Voice*, ed. J. D. Douglas (Minneapolis, MN: World Wide, 1975), 125.

26. From David O. Moberg, *The Great Reversal: Evangelism Versus Social Concern* (Philadelphia, PA: Lippincott, 1972), 42.

expressly for mass-man, who is controlled by the law of the least possible effort and seeks easy solutions; the God who gives his attention to those who will not reject him because they need him as an analgesic.[27]

Such a cultural Christianity used technology, reducing the message simply to a formula for success, mainly measured in numbers. It was the religious product of a civilization in which not even people escaped technology. In order to change the effects of such adaptation of Christianity to culture, Padilla proposed to recover the concept of Christ's sovereignty, because without it there was no repentance and salvation. He concluded, "The gospel, then, is a call not only to faith but also to repentance, to break with the world. And it is only in the extent to which we are free from this world that we are free to serve our fellow men."[28]

Puerto Rican Orlando Costas identified a bloc of nations, including the United States, as being largely responsible for the expansion of Christianity in Latin America. However, the history of international relationships included the fact of domination and exploitation of the southern republics. Costas argued that "the values undergirding the imperialistic philosophy and practice of these nations make their way into the church, distorting the gospel sometimes beyond recognition, and setting up what some of my Latin American friends would call ideological and/or cultural roadblocks to the understanding of biblical faith."[29] Missionaries from those countries were part of a syncretistic religious culture which presented values from their cultures of origin as Christian when they were definitely not Christian. Worse yet, added Costas, "these values have permeated the mental structure of the great majority of North Atlantic Christians and particularly their theological methodology." Furthermore,

> [Those values] have not only been used to serve as a theological justification of colonialism, and more recently neocolonialism, but have been the basis for a paternalistic relationship with national churches; a culturally alienating religiosity; an ethic of neutrality and noninvolvement; and an evangelism that is either totally divorced from the gut-issues of an oppressed

---

27. Padilla, "Evangelism and the World," 126.

28. Ibid., 127.

29. Orlando Costas, *The Church and Its Mission: A Shattering Critique from the Third World* (Wheaton, IL: Tyndale House, 1974), 13.

society or that has a one-sided orientation to the "beyond," or an evangelism that is reduced to social assistance (a "band-aid operation" as some would call it), paying little attention to the real causes of the problem (both spiritual and structural), and refusing to penetrate into the deeper dimensions of the gospel (life, death, guilt, reconciliation, etc.).[30]

In a similar analysis, José Míguez Bonino agreed with Lores about "manifest destiny" producing a Messiah complex within North American society and its missionary enterprise. Míguez identified several key cultural elements:

Missions and missionaries came to Latin America as – conscious or unconscious – expressions and agents of a world view in which the Protestant faith was integrated with a political philosophy (democracy in its American version), an economic system (free enterprise capitalism), a geological/historical project (the United States as champion and center of a "new world" of progress and freedom), and an ideology (the liberal creed of progress, education, and science).[31]

As a consequence of those influences, Protestant communities in Latin America grew in intimate relationship with interests and plans to expand the influence of the United States, helping to create an idealized and benevolent image of colonial powers. What was at stake was the very identity of evangelical churches in Latin America.

Protestant communities have been in many cases cultural enclaves which have remained foreign to the life of their countries, unconcerned and indifferent to the needs and problems of the world around them. Institutional dependence and an almost total missionary domination has in many cases kept these churches as little more than appendices of their overseas "headquarters" and fostered a dependent mentality. Their plans and programs have in many cases been merely a reflection or an implementation of the goals, slogans, and programs defined and launched in the United States and, as it was bound to be, they expressed

---

30. Ibid., 15.

31. José Míguez Bonino, "How Does United States' Presence Help, Hinder or Compromise Christian Mission in Latin America?," *Review and Expositor* 74, no. 2 (Spring 1977): 176.

the values, concerns, and ideology prevalent in the American churches, which in turn were closely related to those of the American society as a whole.[32]

Míguez encouraged Latin American churches to become aware of that dependency and to find ways to be renewed, strengthened, and encouraged, and to become a critical and positive factor in Latin America society.

What the above thinkers have in common is their awareness that the evangelical *package* from outside was a combination of cultural and religious elements and that it remained, for the most part, distant from the local situation in the Latin American countries. The question they raised seemed to be: How can we be authentic Christians in Latin America today? To answer this question, though, they did not ban interaction with foreign theological postures. For example, in 1973 the FTL organized a series of meetings in several countries with Carl Henry, a theologian from the United States, on the topic "Evangelical Responsibility in Current Theology." They also invited John Stott in 1974, Australian Bible scholar Leon Morris in 1976, and Michael Green from England in 1979. Furthermore, members of the FTL participated in various international theological meetings within the Lausanne Movement.[33]

The interaction and dialogue with theologians from other latitudes was not, in some cases, without difficulties. For instance, in his report of his visit to Latin America, Carl Henry commented that "some professors at Latin America Seminary in Costa Rica, one of the oldest evangelical seminaries whose leadership has in recent years been turned over to Latin Americans, espouse a compromise form of liberation theology, take a hard line critical of North American mission board influence, and support socialism as a preferred economic option and violence as a Christian possibility for social change."[34] He also said that Latin American evangelicals did not have a convincing alternative to socialism "as a framework of national hope for the Latin American masses, and [they] neglect the production of a creative theological literature."

---

32. Ibid., 178.

33. For a complete list of the FTL's activities see "Cronología De Actividades De La Fraternidad Teológica Latinoamericana," *Boletín Teológico* 27, no. 59–60 (Julio–Diciembre 1995).

34. Carl F. H. Henry, "Evangelical Leader Reports on Religion in Latin America," *Religious News Service*, 21 August 1973.

It did not take long for responses to Henry's comments to come in. Eighteen professors of the seminary in question wrote an open letter protesting against "the irresponsible and distorted reference to this institution." Henry should have realized that among the faculty there were different positions regarding the issues he mentioned. The letter also said,

> We recognize that it is difficult for some of our white North American evangelical brethren who live in a relatively free, democratic, and wealthy society to understand how Christians living in Latin America might prefer one of the socialist parties here to the military dictatorships and feudal oligarchies of the political right. In many countries, these parties provide the alternative to the present structures. Many Latin American evangelicals have at least as much difficulty understanding how so many North American brethren can continue to support Nixon and believe in capitalism after the Watergate debacle. We believe that Christians should do everything possible to facilitate and improve understanding and communication within the body of Christ – through well-informed, in-depth reporting – and not content themselves with simplistic, distorted, and inaccurate labeling. As an evangelical theological (not political!) institution, we affirm the right of certain brethren to support socialist parties, just as we affirm the right of other professors to vote Republican.[35]

Rubén Lores, president of the seminary, wrote a personal letter explaining that Henry's report "was incomplete" and that "he did not take time to discuss these issues with us and see them in the context of our ministry and the conditions of Latin America as a whole." Furthermore, Lores added, such negative reporting was exactly what the faculty at the seminary rejected, North American and Latin American professors together.[36]

Samuel Escobar, president of the FTL, also wrote a response to Henry. Escobar explained that Latin American theological reflection was being threatened by "fundamentalistic simplification with its sectarian, anti-cultural bias and its anti-communism." He wrote,

---

35. Seminario Bíblico Latinoamericano, "To Whom It May Concern," open letter, 26 September 1973.

36. Rubén Lores, "Carta Personal a Mr. Norman Rohrer," *Evangelical News Service* (21 September 1973).

Any informed observer of the Latin American situation knows that North American categories cannot be applied to a society that in some places has barely come out of the feudalistic structure it adopted when mediaeval Spain conquered it four and a half centuries ago. Words like "democracy" and "socialism" have to be qualified when an Anglo-Saxon uses them for Latin America. It must not be forgotten that the Anglo-Saxon world went through industrial revolution, Wesleyan revival, and labor movements of unquestionable Evangelical origins. Likewise, words like "violence" have to also be understood in the context of very unstable institutional life. There are countries in Latin America that have had more coups d'état than years of independent life. Probably many conservative Protestants who reject violence will applaud the violent overthrow of the democratically elected government in Chile.[37]

At the end, Escobar said there was a "growing weariness of police attitudes from persons and institutions in North America who have made themselves the watchdogs of orthodoxy around the world. These people sometimes are tempted to use institutional and financial pressure in order to impose a particular political or eschatological view."[38]

This episode was paradigmatic of what was happening. On one side, Latin Americans were defining their evangelical identity; on the other side, foreigners were looking in from outside in bewilderment. As mentioned above, the attraction liberation theologies had in academic circles around the world was such that many evangelicals were involved in those theologies. It was too difficult for outside observers to grasp the differences.

A New Theological Reflection

Besides the critical and analytical aspect regarding received theologies, constructive work was going on formulating theological proposals. Samuel Escobar called this a "new reflection," wanting both faithfulness to the

---

37. J. Samuel Escobar, "Evangelical Theology in Latin America," *EP News Service* (6 October 1973).

38. Ibid. For a more detailed account see Bruce Warren Robbins, "Contextualization in Costa Rican Theological Education Today: A History of the Seminario Biblico Latinoamericano, San Jose, Costa Rica, 1922–1900" (PhD dissertation, Southern Methodist University, 1991), 143–155.

evangelical heritage of the past and attention to the Latin American situation in the present. He explained,

> It is not an academic theology putting through the lab the last theories of some German or English thinkers and after a few modifications stamping them "Made in Latin America." It is a reflection born within evangelical communities of the most dynamic sector of Latin American Protestantism. These communities, which are growing through evangelism and have a high concept of mission in the world, are formed by people who come to the Bible not only with the lenses of the Bible scholar but also with the heart of an apostle and the burden of a missionary. In some sense, they have given themselves to the task of theological reflection being pressed by their presence in diverse sectors of Latin American society, pushed by their awareness of religious minority in a Christian continent, challenged by the social and cultural fermentation of a continent starting to become conscious of its particular Indo-European-African identity and searching for more independent forms of national life.[39]

Escobar identified three central themes of the new theological reflection: the kingdom of God, contextualization, and the mission of the people of God. There was continuity with previous reflection, but new language helped it to become more appropriate and richer for local theological production. For example, the term "kingdom of God" included "not only salvation but creation and God's sovereignty, the consummation of all things, and even the relationship between what God is doing among his people and, through them, human history." Contextualization, besides interpreting the Bible, had to do with obedience within the historical moment the Latin American church was living in. The mission of the church included *being* and *doing* church. Therefore, for Escobar, the new theological reflection was a proposal to widen and deepen evangelical discourse and not just substitute the old one with a new one.

> In reality, the new theological reflection has sprouted from a deep sense of mission and by going deeper into the Word of God trying to understand where it will lead us if we want to take it

---

39. Samuel Escobar, "La Teología Evangélica Hoy," *Pensamiento Cristiano* 24, no. 4 (Junio 1978): 232.

seriously within our current circumstances. Its "novelty" is based on the reconsideration of certain biblical themes in all their richness, because evangelical churches have grown and demand this task of discovering "the meat" for a generation not satisfied just with "the milk."[40]

To those who questioned the new theological reflection because it supposedly was replacing whatever was considered essential with secondary things and was running the risk of completely losing the revealed biblical message, Escobar answered that in the Bible we should not separate primary from secondary: to do so was like making a canon within the canon. For Latin Americans the whole Bible was God's Word. However, "a good part of it has remained unexplored, impoverishing the content of the faith and the quality of militancy. [That] might be due to inadequate hermeneutical clues or theological systems imposed by inertia or lack of alternatives."[41] Escobar concluded:

> The new theological reflection is intended to be, then, profoundly evangelical, that is, biblical and pertinent. It does not wish to lose the dimensions of its historical heritage but it wants the best of that heritage to dynamize its discourse and activities. For this reason it enters into a prophetic and reflective task: a prophetic task to reveal reductionisms, simplifications, and tergiversations which little by little have settled in the thought and being of evangelicals; also reflective, putting Truth into action, confronting the challenges of this world which push towards a renewal of the church and its message, as in better times of the people of God.[42]

Gonzalo Báez-Camargo divided the history of Latin American evangelical theological thought into three stages. First, there was the time of proselytization, when evangelicals considered that Protestantism should spread modern progress. That was also a time of rabid anti-Catholicism and Puritan morality. The second stage had three emphases: "to insist on the centrality of Christ for Christian life; the normative authority of the Bible as the supreme guide for faith, doctrine, and practice; and the visual demonstration

---

40. Ibid., 235.
41. Ibid.
42. Ibid., 237.

of what the other two emphases mean in the life of Protestants as individuals and churches as groups of people." It was the time when Protestantism demonstrated its social impact.[43] The last stage was the search for evangelical identity, starting with a clear definition of evangelical mission. Báez-Camargo asked: "Should we change the individual to change the world, or change the world to change the individual? In other words, whether the essential change that evangelical churches should promote is primarily that of structures or human beings." That was the task for theologians. Báez-Camargo warned, "If Protestantism in our lands stays faithful to its fundamental evangelical mission and does not let anything change its course, or if it does not let its message get devalued by strange infiltrations, it will undoubtedly continue its march."[44]

Pentecostals and Historical Churches

Argentinian Pentecostal Gabriel Vaccaro explained at the Assembly of Churches in Oaxtepec, Mexico, 1978, that there was a mutual suspicion between historical churches and Pentecostal ones. At the same time, some considered Pentecostals in Latin America to be supporters of capitalism and the status quo, while others labeled them "leftists" because they promoted justice and protested against the marginalization of anyone. Vaccaro explained,

> Pentecostals in Latin America are not for the status quo and even less for capitalism, and we insist against injustice towards people, but that should not give the idea that we are easily manipulated by ideologies from the left. Our position is clear, simple, and final: it comes out of the gospel of Jesus Christ. The message of our churches has been and is the encounter of people in their walk of life with Jesus Christ.[45]

Vaccaro's words might explain why Pentecostals were just starting to participate as actors at international gatherings and congresses where they had mostly been absent up to that time. Pentecostal churches could no longer remain at the margins of evangelical history in Latin America. They had much

---

43. Gonzalo Báez-Camargo, "El Futuro Del Protestantismo Latinoamericano," *Pensamiento Cristiano* 25, no. 2 (Diciembre 1978): 104–105.

44. Ibid., 108–09.

45. Gabriel O. Vaccaro, "Oaxtepec Desde Una Perspectiva Pentecostal," *Cuadernos de Teología* 5, no. 4 (1979): 291.

experience to share with other denominations. It was time to stop ignoring their important continental presence.

Another Pentecostal, also Argentinian, Ernesto Saracco, speaking at CLADE II in Lima,[46] summarized theological production by Latin American evangelicals as a search in three areas:

> First, a search for their identity, either holding tightly onto their heritage, often confusing it with the gospel; or rejecting it, with the danger of falling into the illusion of trying to live out a faith without any roots. Second, a search for ways to relate to the world and its practical consequences. Finally, a search for God. One day some thought they had found him hidden in their neighbor, others, living as a monk at church or comfortably in heaven.[47]

There was also a search for hermeneutics to read and interpret the Bible as Latin Americans. Saracco called evangelicals to recognize that the main problems with interpretation were not in the text but in the interpreter. He warned of the danger of evangelicals confusing the Word of God with their interpretations and the cultural trappings they imposed upon it. He mentioned that amid all the criticism of mixing the gospel with foreign cultures, it was also possible to mix it with Latin American culture: "Together, the attitude of the interpreter before God and his ecclesiastical and cultural tradition are factors which constantly condition the content and comprehension of the Word of God."[48] Here it was also imperative to recognize the need of the assistance of the Holy Spirit. However, Saracco warned,

> We must be careful not to fall into a hermeneutical fatalism tying up the Word so much to human situations in a way that attaches it to their destiny. We might say, using an expression Paul wrote in another context, but God's word is not chained (2 Tim 2:9). In reality, the Word of God is not in the sound doctrine of the evangelistic community, neither in its hermeneutics. Furthermore, it transcends and judges it. That's why the

---

46. CLADE was the Congreso Latinoamericano de Evangelización (Latin American Congress on Evangelism). For a short history of the CLADES see Samuel Escobar, "Los 'Clades' y La Misión De La Iglesia," *Iglesia y Misión* 67/68 (Enero–julio 1999): 20-4.

47. Norberto Saracco, "La Palabra y El Espíritu En La Comunidad Evangelizadora," in *América Latina y La Evangelización En Los Años 80: Un Congreso Auspiciado Por La Fraternidad Teológica Latinoamericana* (Lima: CLADE II, 1979), 173.

48. Ibid., 175.

evangelistic community should open itself up to be judged by the Word knowing that it does not have a monopoly over it or its interpretation. Of course, this goes against the grain for the triumphalist and self-sufficient mentality of most Latin American Protestantism which has perfectly packaged the whole revelation.[49]

It was absolutely necessary for evangelicals to understand the implications of the incarnation in order to fulfill their mission. This included at least four aspects: to consider the culture and worldview of society, to shake off every prerogative and all self-sufficiency, to carry the cross in contrast to accommodation with the status quo, and to opt for humanity and its full salvation.[50]

Saracco's and Vaccaro's contributions as Pentecostals were a watershed at that time. It was at Oaxtepec and CLADE II that Protestants and other evangelicals started to accept Pentecostals as mission partners. Previously, suspicion and even jealousy had determined their relationships with them. For example, Peter Savage talked of them as "churches equating their subjective experiences and dreams with the Revelation once given. This places the Word of God on a secondary plane of authority similar to the Mormon attitude to the Word of God."[51] As Vaccaro said: "The historical churches had for a long time underestimated our movement."[52] From then on it was absurd to keep excluding them, not only because Pentecostals had more members than all the other denominations combined, but also because Pentecostal voices started to articulate their faith in a way that made dialogue possible. It is noticeable also in Vaccaro's and Saracco's analyses that they provided a self-evaluation needed within a Pentecostal movement with almost eight decades of continuous presence in the continent. Not all Pentecostals were represented at Oaxtepec and Lima, but the fact that some were active protagonists meant that this was a converging moment for Latin American evangelicals.

---

49. Ibid.

50. Ibid., 177.

51. Personal memorandum to Clyde Taylor and Bruce Nichols, 17 March 1971.

52. Vaccaro, "Oaxtepec Desde Una Perspectiva Pentecostal," 290.

Women and Theology

However, we cannot say the same regarding female participation in Latin American theological forums up to the end of the seventies. Theological production was so far exclusively androcentric. During a meeting at CLADE II women asked the conveners for more active female participation from the podium. That had an effect at the following CLADE, but for the most part up to this point women were absent, with few exceptions – mostly in journals and evangelical magazines. It was only in the next decade that the contributions of Latin American women started to appear.

One of the first analyses of Latin American evangelical theological thought written by a woman was presented at the Ecumenical Dialogue of Third World Theologians in 1976. Beatriz Melano Couch, from Argentina, was a Protestant sympathetic to liberation theology. Melano started by explaining some important differences between Catholic and Protestant arrivals in Latin America.

> While the Roman Catholics exported mainly from Spain one church with one corpus of doctrine, one liturgy and cultural form, there are different kinds of "Protestantisms" imported from diverse countries of Europe (German Lutherans; Swiss, French, Hungarian, and Dutch Calvinists; Scotch Presbyterians; English Episcopalians; Welsh Methodists; Italian Waldensians), which represent waves of European immigration at the end of last century and the beginning of this one. To these different ethnic groups we must add those that came into being through the missionary enterprise coming from Europe and the United States and which represented the traditional and free churches and also the sects. All of these groups of immigrants and missionaries brought with them their own culture, their own church structure, doctrine, liturgy, morals, etc.[53]

Regarding the doctrines of those churches, Melano identified at least three approaches to mission and theology with a lot of crossover at any historical time. The first trend was that of what she called the "free churches and sects." Their main concern was the conversion of souls. Those churches stressed the

---

53. Beatriz Melano Couch, "New Visions of the Church in Latin America: A Protestant View," in *The Emergent Gospel: Theology from the Underside of History. Papers from the Ecumenical Dialogue of Third World Theologians, Dar es Salaam, August 5–12, 1976*, ed. Sergio Torres and Virginia Fabella (Maryknoll, NY: Orbis Books, 1978), 194.

otherworldliness of Christianity, maintaining a dualistic separation of world and church, body and soul, matter and spirit, evil and the kingdom of God (to come at the end of this evil age). Melano described this theology under four main areas:

1. The conversion of the soul as a change of life: this means a change in personal moral conduct. The change of heart implies that one also changes behavior. This has led to pietism and to legalism in ethics.

2. Church mission: this means mainly proselytism. Religion is not inherited: one must be converted. On a continent first evangelized with the sword and the cross, where popular religiosity was a mixture of Christian beliefs and superstitions, and where the people had little or no instruction in the meaning of the Christian faith, there was an insistence on the personal, rational, and emotional acceptance of Christ.

3. The relation between this approach and the Latin American culture: this means the importation of cultural forms foreign to the expressions of the people and therefore creates to a certain extent an *uprootedness* of the people from their own cultural background.

4. The liturgy: this is an expression of the mother church's liturgy, with the centrality of the sermon, which often becomes a lecture for the indoctrination of the people and a fervent polemic against the Roman Catholic Church with regard to its belief and practices.[54]

The second theological approach was, according to Melano, a "marriage of a certain kind of pietism with the social gospel." In this case the message was about changing not only hearts but also society: "The aim is the modernization of society according to the Christian values which are expressed politically in democracy, socially in the achievement of human rights, and economically in a system that respects the value of human beings, their dignity, and individual freedom." She described the main characteristic of this theological trend:

> In terms of church mission, this means not only the conversion of the soul but the creation of social living conditions that enable individuals to exercise their freedom and to develop their human potentials. So Christian responsibility is seen in terms of

---

54. Ibid., 195.

promoting just salaries, safe conditions, equal rights for labor, education for all, freedom of choice and of expression of the individual, caring for the needy, etc. In turn, this is expressed in the creation of institutions that embodied these ideals, such as hospitals, health centers, schools, Bible institutes, seminaries, centers for social welfare, etc.

This version of Protestantism was influenced by liberalism. Even though, Melano continued, Protestant liberalism and liberal philosophy coincided in several points, there were also significant differences. This version of Protestantism was critical of the semi-feudal society. It also promoted the modernization of society and the separation of church and state. But in the end, churches "accommodated themselves within an economic system: capitalism (supported by an individualistic philosophy); a political system: democracy; and a cultural aim: secularism (supported by pragmatism)."[55]

However, after World War II and the crisis of liberal ideas and liberal theologies, Latin American thinkers became aware of the inadequacy of their message to respond to their particular historical time. They had three main questions: "How can we be faithful to Jesus Christ in our time and at our own particular historical crossroads? What is the church's mission in the midst of economic and political oppression? What is the meaning of Christian hope for those who are kept marginalized by the rest of society through exploitation and discrimination?"[56] Melano described the seventies as the decade of more creativity in Protestant theological reflection. By the end of the decade the situation was one of polarization and conflict. On the one hand, "we still live under the impact of the dualistic theological approach, characterized by *otherworldliness* and the emphasis on the salvation of the soul and on individual morality; this view is associated with an aggressive conservative militancy in the political field." On the other hand, "sections of the church all through Latin America believe in the call for a revolutionary praxis."[57]

Third, Melano identified a group of *radical evangelicals* that in the seventies was trying to break conservative theological dualism and *otherworldliness* with serious analysis and immersion in Latin American situations.

---

55. Ibid., 196.
56. Ibid., 199.
57. Ibid., 211.

Their aim is to conscientize the most conservative Protestant elements in order to produce a renewal of the church; their point of departure is a rigorous biblical exegesis and they are moving toward a realistic understanding of the social, economic, political, and cultural situation of Latin America. Their position represents a new evangelical social ethics. They expose and denounce the structures of oppression and dependency and call for Christian commitment to bring about needed changes. For most of them the concrete political option for Latin America is a democratic form of socialism, yet they are very suspicious of the social class analysis used by theologians of liberation and strongly criticize it. They denounce it as neither scientific nor objective; they say that it represents a veiled Marxist ideology to be exposed and is as dangerous as the capitalist ideology that preconditions the hermeneutics of the conservative approach to theology.

Even though this group criticizes the hermeneutics and theology of the liberationists as well as their revolutionary commitment, they duly acknowledge the legitimacy of the effort of the Church and Society people (ISAL) to awaken the Protestant consciousness to the problematic of our continent.[58]

Those "radical evangelicals" were the FTL. For Melano, they represented a new and significant theological opening, and ignoring them would be evidence of "a lack of vision." Significantly, in her analysis, both liberationist and evangelical theologies were moving to a center: Christology, particularly "a new interpretation of the meaning of exile and suffering, of the cross and resurrection." In conclusion Melano proposed three tasks for theological production: "continual purification of our hermeneutical tools, to rethink some fundamental theological themes so as not to fall into reductionism but rather to embrace the totality of the biblical scope, and continue to have before us what can be called the *existential* dimension of liberation theology."[59]

Pastoralia

A year before CLADE II, 1978, Orlando Costas started *Pastoralia*, a journal for "pastors, lay leaders, seminarians, theology professors, directors of

---

58. Ibid., 213.
59. Ibid., 220–222.

denominations and Christian organizations, evangelists and missionaries" – that is, "all those brethren whose lives are preoccupied with the ways the mission of Jesus Christ in today's Latin America is taking shape, especially in and through evangelical churches."[60]

> It is, then, a journal which will focus on the pastoral task from a missiological perspective within the general context of Latin America, in light of the particular situation of the evangelical churches. We recognize that this particular context presents a challenge, because, traditionally, the pastoral task has been set in the perspective of the spiritual care of the congregation and the institutional maintenance of the church. We do not wish, not even for a second, to deny the close relationship between the pastoral task of those set apart for the spiritual care of believers and the administration of the local church. However, neither do we want to limit the pastoral task to certain functions carried out by an exclusive number of its members, independently of how much preparation they have had or how important their responsibilities might be.[61]

The multiplication of missiological options and the lack of serious and contextual pastoral literature created confusion about the mission of the church among lay pastors all over the continent. *Pastoralia* was designed to reach "the whole Latin American Christian people serving all evangelicals of our continent in an ecumenical spirit, being loyal to the Protestant Reformation and fully committed to our historical reality and the destiny of our people."[62] In a nutshell, that was the direction Latin American evangelicals were taking with their theological reflection. It was being done by Latin Americans for the Latin American churches, without forgetting their historical roots, promoting unity, and contextually committed to the realities in the continent.

---

60. Dirección, "Una Revista Para Una Nueva Situación," *Pastoralia* 1, no. 1 (1978): 1.
61. Ibid.
62. Ibid., 2.

5

Definition and Maturity

The seventies had been a busy decade for evangelicals doing theology in Latin America. They were active in many forums in and out of the region, as well as in dialogue with evangelicals from other continents concerning other theological proposals, and with local liberation theologies. It was also the decade when a clear break from received traditions was most evident. As Samuel Escobar said, "We were tired of the evangelical centers of power in North America telling us how to think, how to read, and what it meant to be evangelical; we decided it was time to start reflecting the faith as grown-ups and on our own."[1] Such a search for an indigenous theological expression was, however, "neither a free anti-Americanism nor a teenager's rebellion." Instead, Escobar explained,

> I understand mission and theology as a way of life which takes place in a community without any distinctions. Besides, I believe we should recognize the indebtedness Latin American evangelicals have toward Anglo-Saxon missionaries who brought the gospel. The problem is that our efforts to respond to the challenges of our environment, to think our faith within our particular context, have often been blocked by people or missionary organizations wanting us to limit ourselves to just repeating what they have learnt in their lands. Accusations of heresy and institutional squabbles come when we insist on our own way. Those people of missionary organizations do not appreciate indigenous efforts to think on our own; there is no sensibility to trying to understand the Latin American context. Most painfully, there are local caudillos who play this fundamentalist game because often

---

1. Escobar, "Heredero De La Reforma Radical," 64.

they are inside this paternalistic scheme and benefit from it. If translating and repeating like servants profits much and provides certain advantages, why bother trying to find indigeneity?[2]

Emilio Núñez found similar reactions to local theological production: "We already have an evangelical theology. There is no need for another one." This comment was coming from Latin Americans who were "afraid of any attempt to go beyond our forefathers in Biblical and theological research. To them, Evangelical theology is a finished product that admits no new forms of expression that would be more relevant to our society."[3] Núñez added,

> We need a Latin American theology, as Evangelicals in the United States of America need a theology to meet their own needs, and the spiritual and ethical needs of their own country. The Gospel brought to North America by the British, the Dutch, and other immigrants is contextualized in American reality. What American and European Evangelicals are doing, we Latin Americans are supposed to do.[4]

However, Núñez recognized that conservative evangelicals in Latin America were behind in theological work. He described evangelical theology as reactionary: "We did not take the initiative to do an Evangelical theology on the basis of Scriptures, in response to our social situation. We have been forced to enter into the theological arena by the social turmoil in which we live, and by the non-biblical, or anti-biblical answers that some theologians are giving to the problems of the Latin American people."[5] Here Núñez referred to liberation theologies as well as to "individualistic, dualistic, futuristic, and pessimistic" evangelical theologies. Regarding these he proclaimed,

> We are not called to do a rightist theology nor a leftist one; but a biblical and contextualized theology in response to the needs of the individual and to the challenges of our society. This theology has to be faithful to God's written revelation. It has to be concerned for the spiritual, physical, and material wellbeing of the people. It has to evaluate both the political left and the

---

2. Ibid.

3. Emilio Antonio Núñez C., *Doing Evangelical Theology in Latin America* (Portland, OR: Western Conservative Baptist Seminary, 1986), 1.

4. Ibid., 2.

5. Ibid., 3.

political right in the light of the Scriptures. It has to be critical of those theologies which are serving the purpose of a political system, instead of submitting themselves to the authority of the Word of God.[6]

What did that theology look like? According to Núñez the theological emphases needed in Latin America were:

> The teaching in both Testaments on the unity and dignity of the humanity of Christ and his ministry to people in physical and material need; the New Testament teaching on good works; the example of the first century Church in the area of social responsibility; the social implication of the Gospel in relation to the dignity of women; the nature and purpose of human government and our Christian behavior as members of the civil community; the biblical concept of labor and social justice; peace as the result of the practice of justice; love as the key word in our human relations; the present lordship of Christ over creation and history; his final triumph over the forces of evil in this world; the cosmic renovation as the final chapter in the redemptive program on earth.[7]

However, not everyone agreed with these assessments. For instance, Brazilian Lutheran Valdir Steuernagel said that "CLADE II by following the agenda of the LATF (Latin American Theological Fraternity [FTL]) did not satisfy the North American evangelical establishment, and a rupture with many conservative evangelicals in Latin America, especially those with closer ties to and/or financial dependency on the United States was inevitable."[8] It was not surprising that divisions among evangelicals surfaced more strongly at this time. They became greater in 1982: on one side, in Lima (11–18 November), ecumenical evangelicals founded CLAI (Consejo Latinoamericano de Iglesias), an organization with strong ties to the World Council of Churches; on the other side, in Panama (19–23 April), conservative evangelicals established CONELA (Confraternidad Evangélica Latinoamericana).

---

6. Ibid., 22.

7. Ibid., 56.

8. Valdir Steuernagel, "The Theology of Mission in Its Relation to Social Responsibility within the Lausanne Movement" (PhD dissertation, Lutheran School of Theology, 1988), 226.

CONELA and CLAI

Although the first informal meeting towards the formation of CONELA took place during the Consultation on World Evangelization organized by the Lausanne Committee in June 1980 in Pattaya, Thailand, the initial idea was born during CLADE II, Lima 1979, less than a year before Pattaya. One of the main promoters of CONELA was Argentinian Luis Palau, who said about CLADE II: "Incredibly, biblical evangelism was about the last thing anyone talked about during the conference. Much of the program stressed the temporal, rather than the spiritual. Many delegates complained about what they called the 'socio-political content' of the majority of messages."[9] Therefore, in Pattaya,

> Spontaneously, first twenty-eight and then forty people at the second meeting, we met and exchanged impressions on Latin American evangelical reality during this time in history and about the need, convenience, and possibility of forming a Latin American Evangelical Fellowship to express faithfully the feeling, thought, word, and life of the Evangelical Christian Church in Latin America which is mainly biblical, evangelistic, conservative, and faithful to the Bible. Because such an entity does not exist, other people, not always identified with this Church but sometimes even acting against it, have assumed the right to speak on its behalf, giving a distorted image of the Latin American evangelical reality.[10]

Why CONELA? What was the rationale for starting a new organization of evangelicals at that time? First, as alluded to by Palau, the participants of the impromptu meeting in Pattaya felt that some people had unilaterally taken upon themselves to represent Latin American evangelicals internationally, an action they did not recognize as legitimate. As we have seen, this was an old wound of disunity. They did not explain who they were talking about. Second, they wanted a fellowship with a clear and explicit rejection of violence, and committed to progress and respect for human rights. Third, "we need a fellowship which accepts as the only means of redemption the confrontation of humanity with Jesus Christ, Author and Perfecter of integral liberty."

---

9. Luis Palau and David Sanford, *Calling America and the Nations to Christ* (Nashville, TN: Thomas Nelson, 1994), 143.

10. Guillermo Conard, ed. *Los Documentos De Conela* (México D. F: CONELA, 1982), 3.

Here they defined 1 Corinthians 15:1–4 as the *raison d'être* and essence of the church. Fourth, there was a need to present a unified image or front instead of a unified plan of action. Fifth, "we need a fellowship to eliminate dualisms in orientation and information, and to take a permanent, firm, and definite position in theological, sociological, political, and moral issues in concordance with the Holy Scriptures and the interpretation adopted by our members."[11]

CONELA's founding meeting was a shared effort with the Lausanne Committee for World Evangelization, which helped mostly to raise funds. Also, CONELA adopted the Lausanne Covenant as its theological framework. CONELA defined nine objectives:

1. To be an entity to link, relate, and serve evangelicals.

2. To cultivate spiritual unity and mutual respect among the churches' leadership and among all Latin American evangelicals, respecting the autonomy of its members.

3. To promote evangelization and theological reflection from an evangelical perspective; and to promote the dynamics of integral growth of churches at the national, regional, continental, and worldwide levels.

4. To establish and maintain relationships with organizations and national and international entities in agreement with our theological position.

5. To manifest the reality of the evangelical presence, making known through media what God is doing in our continent and the whole world, and to inform churches of the relation to diverse schools of thought.

6. To promote a Christocentric biblical education within Latin American reality.

7. To expose and apply biblical criteria for the social participation of the church.

8. To responsibly safeguard respect for religious liberty in all the countries of Latin America.

9. To be the voice of Latin American evangelical thought.[12]

---

11. Ibid., 9.
12. Ibid., 13.

The final document, *Acta de Panamá*, was concise:

> We, participants in the Latin American Evangelical Consultation, held on April 19–23 of 1982 in the city of Panama, Republic of Panama, conscious of our responsibility as evangelical Christians to the millions of believers who make up the Church of our Lord in our continent, and faithful to the convictions of national denominations, organizations, and local congregations which have sent us, we testify that the evangelical Church in Latin America is biblical, Christ-centered, and in need of presenting a truly evangelical image; therefore:
>
> Being guided by the principles clearly stipulated in the Holy Scriptures – God's inspired Word, composed only of 66 books – we decide to form the Confraternidad Evangélica Latinoamericana.
>
> Since we believe it is indispensable to seriously continue the task of evangelization of our continent and the world according to the Lord's command in Matthew 28:18–20 and the example of the apostles (Acts 5:42), we invite all the brethren in Latin America and the Latino communities in North America who believe and share the same biblical faith, to unite in prayer and concrete expressions to help us achieve the goals we have proposed.
>
> We want to be a fellowship sharing the ideals and aims representing the people who sent us. With these convictions and under the guidance of the Holy Spirit,
>
> We approve this today.
>
> May our Lord help us to be faithful, to stand firm in the faith, and to exalt always the name of Jesus Christ.
>
> We promise to guard the faith that was once for all entrusted to the saints (Jude 3);
>
> We promise to be faithful to the Holy Scriptures (Josh 1:8);
>
> We promise to live in Him and for Him (Rom 14:8; 2 Cor 5:15).
>
> "To him who is able to keep you from falling and to present you before his glorious presence without fault and with great joy – to the only God our Savior be glory, majesty, power and

authority, through Jesus Christ our Lord, before all ages, now and forevermore! Amen" (Jude 24–25).[13]

CONELA had its first general assembly in Maracaibo, Venezuela, on 22–25 April 1986. There were ninety-five delegates from seventeen countries, plus a group of special guests "representing twenty-five millions of evangelical Christians." They defined CONELA as reaching the "evangelical, conservative and faithful-to-the-Bible majority." Therefore, they reiterated the decision to "maintain the biblical, conservative concept of the gospel, that is, the gospel according to the Holy Scriptures, for the eternal salvation of the sinner, by means of the blood sacrifice of our Lord Jesus Christ and his glorious resurrection, who by the Holy Spirit produces a new spiritual birth leading to a new life, resulting in material, physical, and social blessings."[14] CONELA took the role of guardian of the "authentic gospel in all Latin America," including the denunciation of "another gospel" which "magnifies temporal liberation of physical ailments, poverty, and certain political dictatorships, undermining spiritual liberty."[15] It would have been helpful if they had identified who exactly they were talking about.

In the end, the assembly defined four lines of action. The invitation was to the whole Latin American evangelical community to join CONELA in:

> The search for unity, fellowship, and service, as concrete signs of the Kingdom of God in us and among us.

> A serious reflection, based on the Scriptures and our evangelical theological heritage, on our Christian responsibility in a situation of damnation, hunger, misery, and injustice.

> The mission of being the salt and light of the earth, as indicators of the Path to Life in Jesus Christ, and propagators of his blessed Gospel at the eve of the twenty-first century.

> The contextualization of our message and Christian action so that Latin America can hear God's voice and perceive its redeeming presence, through our witness.[16]

---

13. Ibid., 46.

14. CONELA, *Declaración De Conela En Maracaibo* (Maracaibo, Venezuela: CONELA, 1986), 2.

15. Ibid., 3.

16. Ibid., 4.

CLAI (Consejo Latinoamericano de Iglesias) had been conceived at the meeting of ecumenical evangelicals in Oaxtepec, Mexico, in September 1978. It had four years' gestation before it was born in Lima, Peru, in November 1982, only a few months after CONELA was founded. One hundred and ten evangelical denominations and ten ecumenical and interdenominational organizations in Oaxtepec decided to go ahead and form CLAI, with the main purpose of promoting unity among the churches in order to encourage direct evangelical involvement in Latin American social reality. They considered topics such as power structures, marginalized populations, indigenous peoples, violations of human rights, ecology, and especially the difficult situation of the war in Nicaragua. The churches needed to present a united front to minister in these situations.

In Lima CLAI defined five main objectives:

1. To promote unity among the people of God in Latin America as an expression and sign of the unity of the Latin American people.

2. To manifest the unity that we already have in Christ, recognizing the richness represented in diverse traditions, confessions and expressions of our faith, reflection, teaching, proclamation and service, taking into account Latin American reality and identity.

3. To help its members discover their identity and commitment as Christians within Latin American reality in our search for an order of justice and fraternity.

4. To stimulate and support its members in their evangelistic task, as a sign of their faithfulness to Christ's commandment and his presence among Latin American people.

5. To promote theological and pastoral reflection and dialogue about the mission and Christian witness in the continent and the rest of the world.[17]

The final document of the Lima meeting started by recognizing the intrinsic value of human life, especially because Jesus became a human being. Salvation history was described as "the constant struggle of God with people for life to triumph over the forces of death." But it is through Jesus' death that we have real life. Such life cannot be separated from practicing justice;

---

17. CLAI, *Constitución y Reglamento Del Clai: Aprobado En La Asamblea Constitutiva, Noviembre 11 Al 18 De 1982, Lima, Perú* (Lima: CLAI, 1983).

therefore, the "biblical message is clear: wherever there is a human being who is impeded from living the whole of his humanity, there is a situation of sin." All spheres of human activity were to be characterized by justice and love in order for there to be *shalom* or total wellbeing.

However, the situation in the continent was far from reflecting "authentic humanity." There was the evidence of death in the Central American wars, many countries investing more in weapons, lack of education and health, and injustice in general.

> Justice, which is inherent to God's kingship, is undermined when our brethren disappear; when there are mothers mourning their children killed in their prime; when children, women, and the elderly are indiscriminately massacred; when our countries are full of political refugees and uprooted people. The brutal presence of torture, the bigger number of people who cannot find jobs, the alarming growing number of people who cannot read and write, the negation to huge sectors of the population of the minimal conditions to survive and of fundamental human rights, are perturbing manifestations of how injustice and lies deteriorate life in our continent.[18]

Hope was present when Christians promoted and defended human rights, became agents for justice – such as doctors and nurses helping refugees and those injured in war – spoke the truth, even risking their lives, and promoted unity and fraternal relationships: "CLAI wants to represent unity in mission, which is also unity in solidarity for justice. We desire unity in the search for truth, also promoting liberty and justice, the only way to love and be peacemakers in a continent divided by illegitimate interests."[19]

The formation of CONELA and CLAI received different interpretations, revealing circumstances that are not easily seen in their documents. While both organizations were still in process of formation, Peruvian Peter Savage, international coordinator of the FTL, asked what many were probably asking at that time: "What are the theological and missiological reasons for the Protestant world in Latin America having the luxury of two entities which

18. Pedro Arana Quiroz, ed. *Teología Del Camino: Documentos Presentados En Los Últimos Veinte Años Por Diferentes Comunidades Cristianas De América Latina* (Lima: Ediciones Presencia, 1987), 121.

19. Ibid., 123.

aim to create unity among 30 million Protestants in this subcontinent?"[20] In Oaxtepec in 1978, where CLAI was conceived, in spite of the discourse on unity, tensions arose because "delegates from the conservative churches felt offended by leftist analysis, concepts, and ideology." Savage mentioned that those conservatives at one point decided to leave the congress altogether but at the end they stayed to vote. The final vote for the formation of CLAI was as follows: 112 in favor, and 50 against: hardly unanimous. After Oaxtepec, the newly elected committee met in Puerto Rico and decided to become a regional organization of the World Council of Churches based in Geneva, Switzerland, "nullifying any hope of respect for theological plurality." Savage considered, then, that "CLAI so far is an elitist organization which does not reflect the voices, worries, and pain of the congregations in Latin America."[21]

Consequently, Savage described the formation of CONELA as a reaction of the conservative churches to the direction CLAI was taking. "CLAI did not know how to attract them, keep them, and be open to their preoccupations and battle lines." Savage therefore recommended to those working towards forming CONELA that the founding Panama meeting should include "theological diversity," as in Berlin, Lausanne, and Thailand. Also, CONELA should connect historically with the rich experience that had characterized the evangelical movement for over a century. Finally, there should be analysis of Latin America's problems, such as the "the seductions of a popular and consumeristic society, the seductions of popular magical religions, the seductions of status and power offered by contemporary and secular society, the diabolic seductions of the powers of this world, their style of action and addiction to power."[22] These were good recommendations which, judging by CONELA's documents from Panama, remained unaddressed.

A participant in Panama, Roger Velásquez from Nicaragua, defined CONELA's creation as separatist and exclusivist. It was based on a "presumed self-legitimacy." This spirit contradicted the intention of promoting unity among evangelicals. For Velásquez, in Panama theological reflection was limited, prejudiced, and unilateral.[23] The conference lacked serious reflection on the conditions in the continent, such as the "humiliating aspects of the latest vestiges of colonialism suffered not only by Argentina but also by

---

20. Peter Savage, "Editorial," *Boletín Teológico* 4, no. 2 (1981): 3.

21. Ibid., 9.

22. Ibid., 16.

23. Roger Velásquez, "Conela," *Pastoralia* 4, no. 8 (1982): 81.

many Latin American countries."[24] Velásquez also mentioned that CONELA adopted the Lausanne Covenant without taking time to discuss the need for contextualizing it so that it could apply to a continent "plagued with misery and oppression."

Velásquez questioned the motives for many international ministries based in the United States being represented in Panama. Were they adopting a Latin American identity or were they just looking to justify their agendas? The representatives of those organizations exerted a significant influence on CONELA. The claim that CONELA was a successor of the Panama Congress of 1916 was, according to Velásquez, an artificial jump. Then he asked,

> To insist that CONELA represents the majority of Protestant reality in Latin America demands a qualification. How many conservative churches in Latin America have knowledge of the Lausanne Covenant or at least have heard about it? It would be interesting to see how many churches will subscribe to it! And also, if CONELA really represents the majority of Protestant churches, how come only 185 delegates claim to have the right to speak on behalf of so many people?[25]

Velásquez ended by commenting that the adjective *evangélico*, which traditionally in Latin America was a synonym for Protestant, was used by CONELA mostly "to reflect the conservative, anti-liberal, and anti-ecumenical character of the Protestant church, a concept typical of foreign imports to Latin America."[26]

Regarding the formation of CLAI, Samuel Escobar observed that there was an expectation to include a bigger number of local churches to prevent "a bureaucratic elite" running the organization. However, that did not happen "in spite of the good intentions. Both the funds and the hired personnel were mostly from ecumenical entities and people closely related to the WCC."[27] Escobar used four criteria to evaluate both organizations, CONELA and CLAI: their doctrinal statements, attitudes toward the Catholic Church, ecclesiastical politics, and attitudes toward Latin American reality.

CLAI's doctrinal statement was brief:

---

24. Ibid., 82.

25. Ibid. CLAI also claimed to be in direct line with Panama 1916.

26. Ibid., 83.

27. Samuel Escobar, "Los Movimientos De Cooperación Evangélica En América Latina," *Misión* 5, no. 3–4 (1986): 107.

The churches and movements that make up CLAI are those that recognize Jesus Christ as the Lord and Savior according to the Holy Scriptures and in unity try to fulfill their common vocation and mission for the glory of God the Father, the Son, and the Holy Spirit.[28]

Escobar evaluated this statement as incomplete since "it said nothing about the authority, salvation, and the way to interpret the Bible, for example – essential issues for evangelicals because those issues differentiate them from Rome or modern liberalism. This statement is insufficient for evangelism and pastoral ministry in a Roman Catholic continent."[29] As for CONELA, even though it adopted the Lausanne Covenant as its doctrinal statement, "neither in the formation process, nor during the founding meeting" was "a serious study of it . . . done." However, CONELA did set out in its founding document that it accepted a Bible with sixty-six books only, a clear position against the Catholic canon. For Escobar, CONELA's official position was to keep some of its members from cooperating with the Catholic Church. CLAI, on the contrary, showed from its beginning a close relationship with the Roman Catholic hierarchy and programs.

Both organizations experienced tensions between the churches and para-ecclesiastical groups. The bottom line Escobar said, was financial: "We cannot deny that one of the reasons to proclaim themselves as 'representative' is the ability to raise funds from wealthier churches or from the ecumenical or evangelical organizations of the North-Atlantic world." Neither group had given financial statements to reveal how much they really depended on foreign or local funds.[30]

Escobar pointed to polarization regarding the positions of both organizations towards Latin American reality: "a conservative line from the right in CONELA and one that is revolutionary and from the left in CLAI" – a simplification but nonetheless helpful for understanding the situation. Escobar ended his analysis saying,

Neither CONELA nor CLAI have yet demonstrated enough respect for evangelical truth and clarity, in my opinion. The Lausanne Covenant CONELA invokes is, without any doubt, an evangelical document. But it does not seem to be the basic

---

28. Ibid., 108.
29. Ibid.
30. Ibid., 109.

criterion guiding CONELA's actions. Also CONELA claims to be in line with the Evangelical Conference in Panama 1916. But the rush during its organization, the lack of serious study of the bases, and the narrow criterion for the invitations are contrary to the spirit of Panama 1916. Thus, even though CONELA invokes an evangelical document and an evangelical past, its missionary practice shows the same faults and the same politics we cannot admit in CLAI. Time will tell whether there is an alternative of unity and evangelical cooperation. Every conscientious evangelical should pray for this and keep watch.[31]

Brazilian Valdir Steuernagel had a similar analysis of the situation:

While CONELA was born to offer evangelicals in Latin America a representative forum, it was conceived from the beginning as an opposition to the Latin American Council of Churches (CLAI). Furthermore, it was articulated in opposition to the emphasis that had been stressed by the LATF [Latin American Theological Fraternity; FTL] from the beginning: an authentic Latin American church, facing the task of proclaiming the gospel of Jesus Christ in the environment of the suffering, tragic, and culturally rich Latin American situation. At the root of the tensions within Latin American evangelicalism is the tension that has characterized the history of the Lausanne Movement: what is the gospel of Jesus Christ all about? Is it possible to proclaim this gospel without relating it to the entire context in which it is announced? If this gospel is truly preached and accepted, how will this fact impact the entire context of life, and how will the emerging church articulate and fulfill its Christian mission in that very context?[32]

It seemed that there were other factors that prompted the formation of CONELA. North American anthropologist and author David Stoll, for instance, mentioned that conservative Latin American evangelicals disliked the strong financial dependence of CLAI on the World Council of Churches and "they were offended by what they felt were radical political

31. Ibid., 110.
32. Steuernagel, "Theology of Mission in Its Relation to Social Responsibility," 226.

pronouncements. Here, they feared, was another front for the WCC to misrepresent them."[33] Stoll explained,

> But CONELA was not just a reaction to the organizing efforts of ecumenical Protestants. It also expressed a division among evangelicals claiming to uphold the Lausanne Covenant. This was apparent from the very germ of the new body, in 1980, at the Billy Graham-financed conference in Pattaya, Thailand. The men who set up the first organizing session for CONELA wished to keep out, not just clearly defined ecumenical Protestants, who were few at Pattaya, but the larger number of evangelicals who wished to remain in dialogue with them. That meant excluding evangelicals pledged to upholding the Lausanne Covenant, in particular several of the best-known members of the Latin American Theological Fraternity [FTL]. CONELA's leadership proved to have few members of the fraternity, which declined to affiliate either with it or CLAI, in the vain hope of serving as a bridge between the two.[34]

Both the FTL and CONELA claimed to be heirs of Lausanne, and both consequently adopted the Lausanne Covenant as their basic document. Why, then, this rift? The following year, 1980, at the Consultation on World Evangelization,

> Forty of us Latin American representatives gathered spontaneously to study the creation of an entity that could open communication channels between leaders, churches, and service organizations across Latin America. We formed an ad hoc committee under the name CONELA with a mandate to call a continent-wide meeting by early 1982. Some 200 distinguished Latin American evangelical leaders met in Panama that April, and CONELA was officially launched. At that time it was hard to overemphasize the importance of CONELA's task. Leftist ideologies were penetrating the Latin American church, and there was no united defense of the biblical gospel, nor offensive

---

33. David Stoll, *Is Latin America Turning Protestant? The Politics of Evangelical Growth* (Berkeley and Los Angeles: University of California Press, 1990), 133.

34. Ibid.

as to how Christians should apply biblical principles in their churches.[35]

According to an external observer, CONELA's purpose included "being liaison among Latin American evangelicals, the fostering of spiritual unity, evangelism, theological reflection and church growth, and the exposition of Biblical principles regarding the Church's participation in society."[36] However, one might ask what kind of unity CONELA was promoting since "CONELA's statutes prohibit member groups from having relations with either the World Council of Churches or the International Council of Christian Churches."[37] Also, some conservative churches were supporting CLAI, giving the impression that CONELA was unnecessary. Besides that, there seemed to be a huge overlap with what the FTL was already doing. Whatever the reasons behind starting CONELA, it gives us an idea of the complexity of the evangelical situation in Latin America during the eighties. There were many things on the table, but every group had a different agenda, which did not include dining together.

W. Dayton Roberts, vice president of Latin America Mission, also commented on CLAI and CONELA. He showed that the issue also affected organizations involved in Christian ministry in the region. Roberts asked: "Specifically, where does the LAM stand with respect to CLAI (the Latin American Council of Churches in formation)? And to CONELA (Consultation of Evangelicals in Latin America), its conservative counterpart?" His answer: "We are waiting to see."[38] He said that CLAI presumed to represent the entire evangelical community of the continent, including para-ecclesiastical agencies. However, in spite of a practical structure open to diversity, "there is little evidence (1) that the bulk of the evangelical groupings will move behind the CLAI banner, or (2) that CLAI is prepared to speak for any points of view other than the one held by the powerful minority of ecumenical inclination which is guiding its affairs."[39]

---

35. W. Harold Fuller, *People of the Mandate: The Story of the World Evangelical Fellowship* (Grand Rapids, MI: Baker, 1996). Foreword by Luis Palau, xii.

36. Paul E. Pretiz, "Conela Raises Its Flag in Panama," *Latin American Evangelist*, Sep–Oct 1982, 19.

37. "Latin American Evangelicals Unite," *Evangelical Missions Quarterly* 19, no. 1 (1983): 66. See Conard, *Los Documentos De Conela*, 18.

38. W. Dayton Roberts, *Protestant Cooperation in Latin America. Background Briefing Paper 13* (Coral Gables, FL: Latin America Mission, 1981), 5.

39. Ibid.

To be very specific, CLAI in its Oaxtepec statements and elsewhere has assumed that the entire evangelical community for which it tries to speak shares a liberation theology, a collectivized and politicized concept of salvation, and a socioeconomic outlook often at variance with historic evangelicalism in Latin America as well as with the current convictions of a majority of the constituent denominations which CLAI today claims to represent. Until CLAI is prepared to acknowledge the existence of other points of view and to allow them tolerant expression in the documents of the council, as well as in the selection of its leadership, its claims to plurality are unconvincing.[40]

Supporting CONELA also raised several difficulties for Roberts. He gave some other information about the meeting in Pattaya: "although it professes to have adopted the Lausanne Pact as its basic doctrinal statement, it was born at a caucus of Latin Americans (and some aggressive North Americans!) in Thailand which other Latin Americans – who also subscribed to the Lausanne Pact and who were participating in the Thailand conference – would not attend, because the original purpose of the caucus was to protest the presence of a respected WCC executive from Uruguay. Many of the Latins did not share the exclusivist orientation of the caucus' conveners."[41] Quite an un-Lausanne attitude indeed!

CONELA's declarations on social ethics came short of what the Lausanne Covenant said, and, for Roberts, these statements seemed "to be more *laissez-faire* than Christ Himself, and CONELA's ostensible neutrality in things sociopolitical ends up by endorsing the status quo." In the end, Roberts said,

By pulling up short of the Lausanne Pact, CONELA seems to want to highlight its more reactionary stance and to divorce itself from CLAI's position. The major difference between CLAI and CONELA, then, is not one of soteriology nor of loyalty to the Scriptures – both would claim to acknowledge Jesus Christ as Savior and the Word of God as their supreme authority – it is a difference in social ethics. This difference is symbolized in the persons of the presidents of the two organizing-executive committees. The president of CONELA is a rock-ribbed

---

40. Ibid., 6.
41. Ibid.

conservative. The president of CLAI is a liberation bishop. It is not an unimportant discrepancy, by any means. But one wonders whether Christian fellowship should be proscribed by it. On the other hand, if the two movements are basically missiological agencies, they have every right to exist side by side and to concentrate on the particular objectives embodied in their respective postures.[42]

Needless to say, these events set the stage for a rocky decade and any hope for unity vanished. Meanwhile, during the late seventies and all through the eighties, the FTL was active in several international theological meetings: within the Lausanne Movement, the Pasadena Consultation on the Homogeneous Unit Principle (1977), the Willowbank Consultation of the Gospel and Culture (1978), Consultation on Simple Lifestyle (1980), Consultation on World Evangelization (1980) and the Consultation on the Relationship between Evangelism and Social Responsibility (1982); a meeting with the World Evangelical Fellowship and the World Council of Churches on the use of the Bible in theology (1976), a conference of Third World theologians in Korea (1982), the conference Context and Hermeneutics in the Americas (1983), and the Third Conference of Evangelical Theologians from the Third World (1987).

Multidirectional Dialogue

Latin American theological reflection in the seventies and eighties was described in this way: "The preferred theological theme was Christology, with emphasis on the historical Jesus in the context of the theology of the kingdom of God, and later in the context of an explicit Trinitarian theology. This theme became not only the point of departure to do theology and to reflect theologically, but also the criteria for theology, mission, ethics, and spirituality."[43] C. René Padilla, for instance, revisiting Latin American evangelical Christology, described it as "docetic": "It affirms Christ's transforming power in relation to the individual, but is totally unable to relate

---

42. Ibid., 7.

43. David Del Salto, "The Promise of a Trinitarian Christology for the Latin American Evangelical Church" (PhD dissertation, Lutheran School of Theology, 2008), 209.

the gospel to social ethics and social life."[44] We remember that Mackay, Justo González, José Míguez, and others had developed the same idea. Considering the Gospels as reliable historical documents, Padilla called evangelicals to take seriously Jesus' humanity and its ethical implications: "Unless the humanity of Jesus is given full weight, no real link can be established between his mission and that of his followers."[45]

> The basic question for Christians in Latin America relates to the way in which faith in Jesus is to be lived out in their concrete situation. Because the Word became flesh, they cannot but affirm history as the context in which God is fulfilling his redemptive will. The historicity of Jesus leaves no room for a dualism in which the soul is separated from the body, or for a message exclusively concerned with salvation beyond death, or for a church that isolates itself from society to become a ghetto.[46]

According to Padilla, evangelicals in Latin America should urgently consider their context of "religious oppression and legalism, injustice and poverty, wealth and power." Also, the Latin American evangelical church needed to understand the cross of Christ and its power in order to become God's servant in a dehumanizing and violent environment.

In his response to Padilla, Emilio Antonio Núñez agreed that the religious ideas about Jesus, both Roman Catholic and evangelical, were not completely biblical. Núñez then remarked,

> My biggest question as a Latin American preacher and teacher is how to recover in my own theological thinking and teaching the humanity of Christ without falling into the trap of another ideology. One of the reasons we inherited a Christology that understands only the deity of Christ is that many missionaries who came to Latin America came out of the liberal–conservative controversy in North America. In their apologetics, they were trying to defend the deity of Christ, to answer the liberal

---

44. C. René Padilla, "Toward a Contextual Theology from Latin America," in *Conflict and Context: Hermeneutics in the Americas. A Report on the Context and Hermeneutics in the Americas Conference Sponsored by Theological Students Fellowship and the Latin American Theological Fraternity, Tyayacapan, Mexico, November 24–29, 1983*, ed. Mark Branson and C. René Padilla (Grand Rapids, MI: Eerdmans, 1986), 83.

45. Ibid., 84.

46. Ibid., 90.

challenge. The apologetics I was taught in a Bible school forty years ago emphasized Christ's deity. Now we come to realize that that Christology and apologetics are under the influence of a particular ideology. But it is too easy to leave one extreme only to move into another. Now I am supposed to preach the historical Jesus, the Jesus who took sides with the poor.

After the Second World War there was a strong anticommunist sentiment in evangelical circles in North America and Latin America. To be a real evangelical, a genuine evangelical, one was supposed to be faithful to the policies of the US State Department and the Pentagon. Evangelicals were supposed to defend capitalism. But now we are confronted by another challenge. To be a genuine, authentic evangelical, we are supposed to defend a particular form of socialism. In earlier days, I was asked to wear Uncle Sam's hat. Now, I am asked to wear Che Guevara's beret.[47]

Núñez's words well express the tensions and issues that evangelicals were facing at that time. His quest was sincere and it led him to write a book on these questions.[48] Núñez described the historical and social context of liberation theologies, their methodology and fundamental themes. He also proposed a theological response to these theologies. For Núñez, evangelical theology in Latin America needed to be "*biblical* in its foundations, *ecclesiastical* in its close relationship to the community of faith, *pastoral* in its attempt to be an orientating voice for the people of God, *contextual* with regard to that which is social and cultural, and *missionary* in its purpose to reach with the gospel those who are not Christians."[49] Among conservative evangelicals there was a general disdain for theology in favor of pragmatic action. But Núñez called evangelicals to "sit down to study the Word of God exegetically, not only in order to prove and defend our theology, but especially to discover what the biblical text has to say to us about the critical situation in which we live." He added,

---

47. Emilio Antonio Núñez, "Response to Padilla," in Padilla, "Toward a Contextual Theology from Latin America," 96.

48. Emilio Antonio Núñez C, *Liberation Theology*, trans. Paul E. Sywulka (Chicago, IL: Moody Press, 1985).

49. Ibid., 280.

On the other hand it is very easy to run from our social problems by taking refuge in a meticulous exegetical exercise that does not produce a theology for the here and now of our people. We can feel very comfortable wrapped up in the study of remote biblical cultures while we turn our backs to the crude reality surrounding us. We may also take refuge in the future and become eschatologists who say little or nothing about the present reality that troubles the Latin American people. By escaping to the past or to the future, we draw a theological arch over the distressing problems of Latin America. If there is a reference to those problems it is superficial, not deep.[50]

Latin American theology, according to Núñez, needed to find in the Bible answers for the fundamental questions people were asking outside of the church. Interpreters of the Bible had to be careful not to attribute another meaning to the text than that which it already had, since "there is no need to distort the Scripture in order to answer the questions of our countrymen."

The Bible abounds with teachings about the dignity of the human being (including both sexes); liberty and slavery; personal and social justice; private property; wealth and poverty; labor relations; peace and war; family responsibilities and privileges; the origin and nature of the State; the duties and limitations of civil power; civic duties of the Christian; Christian philanthropy (good works as fruits of salvation); and human relationships within the family, in the community of faith, in the civil order, and on the international scene.[51]

Núñez proposed that, besides hearing the gospel, Latin Americans needed to see it in the lives of Christians. He said: "Our theological response to the Word of God and to the great problems of Latin America should be backed by an authentic Christian praxis." Then, in prophetic fashion, Núñez made an appeal to evangelicals:

In Latin America there are evangelical churches that run the risk of becoming classists, indifferent to the great majorities who suffer the most deplorable results of our social and economic underdevelopment. It seems like the middle class, which

50. Ibid., 281.
51. Ibid., 286.

has struggled to reach that height, easily becomes devoted to preserving its achievements and even to improving them by climbing one more step up the social ladder, all the while turning its back on the less privileged classes. The churches that emerge from that social mobility can easily forget the demands of Christian discipleship and the example of the Lord Jesus, who had compassion on the multitudes who were scattered and mistreated like sheep without a shepherd.[52]

Núñez's words contrasted with CONELA's feeble commitment at its Theological Consultation on Social Responsibility, Panama, in September 1983. If the final document reflects the tenor of the meeting, it did not really say anything specific about the topic. Its recommendations are so general that it succeeded in avoiding any real plan of action:

> That multidisciplinary meetings be organized for evangelical leaders at local, regional, and international level to continue with the study of the following topics: Liberty and liberation; social service and social action; church participation in the political process; prophetic ministry of the church; wealth and poverty; and other similar problems.

> That the institutions of theological education give more emphasis to the topic of social responsibility and hold national and international consultations for institutes and seminaries.

> That publication and reading of literature at different levels be stimulated to guide Christians about their social responsibility.

> That local churches involve their graduates in projects of social responsibility.[53]

CONELA said it was influenced by the previous international gatherings dealing with the issue of evangelism and social responsibility: Wheaton 1966, Bogotá 1969, Lausanne 1974, Lima 1979, Grand Rapids 1982, and Wheaton 1983. There was plenty of analysis and practical ideas in the final reports of all those conferences that CONELA could have used at its Panama meeting in 1983. For example, the Lausanne Committee for World Evangelization

---

52. Ibid., 289.

53. "Confraternidad Evangélica Latinoamericana Conela. Informe De La Consulta Teológica Sobre La Responsabilidad Social," *Misión* 3, no. 2 (1984): 75–76.

published the final document of the International Consultation on the Relationship between Evangelism and Social Responsibility, Grand Rapids 1982.[54] Some members of CONELA and others of the FTL participated in the discussions led by John Stott. The document explicitly says,

> Social activity not only follows evangelism as its consequence and aim, and precedes it as its bridge, but also accompanies it as its partner. They are like the two blades of a pair of scissors or the two wings of a bird. This partnership is clearly seen in the public ministry of Jesus, who not only preached the gospel but fed the hungry and healed the sick. In his ministry, kerygma (proclamation) and diakonia (service) went hand in hand. His words explained his works, and his works dramatized his words. Both were expressions of his compassion for people, and both should be of ours. Both also issue from the lordship of Jesus, for he sends us out into the world both to preach and to serve. If we proclaim the Good News of God's love, we must manifest his love in caring for the needy. Indeed, so close is this link between proclaiming and serving, that they actually overlap.
>
> This is not to say that they should be identified with each other, for evangelism is not social responsibility, nor is social responsibility evangelism. Yet, each involves the other.
>
> To proclaim Jesus as Lord and Saviour (evangelism) has social implications, since it summons people to repent of social as well as personal sins, and to live a new life of righteousness and peace in the new society which challenges the old.
>
> To give food to the hungry (social responsibility) has evangelistic implications, since good works of love, if done in the name of Christ, are a demonstration and commendation of the gospel.
>
> It has been said, therefore, that evangelism, even when it does not have a primarily social intention, nevertheless has a social dimension, while social responsibility, even when it does not have a primarily evangelistic intention, nevertheless has an evangelistic dimension.

---

54. Lausanne Committee for World Evangelization (LCWE), *Grand Rapids Report: Evangelism and Social Responsibility: An Evangelical Commitment.* Lausanne Occasional Papers No. 21 (Wheaton, IL: LCWE and WEF, 1982).

Thus, evangelism and social responsibility, while distinct from one another, are integrally related in our proclamation of and obedience to the gospel. The partnership is, in reality, a marriage.[55]

Grand Rapids 1982 defined social service as "Relieving human need. Philanthropic activity. Seeking to minister to individuals and families. Works of mercy." Social action was defined as "Removing the causes of human need. Political and economic activity. Seeking to transform the structures of society. The quest for justice."[56] It was recognized, however, that the distinctions between the two are often unclear and that they overlap in many practical instances. The document concluded,

> We agree that alongside personal evangelism there should be personal social service. Individual Christians should be involved in both, according to their opportunities, gifts, and callings.
>
> What about social action of a political kind, in distinction to social service of a philanthropic kind? Does social action belong to the mission of the church as church, or is it the prerogative of individual believers who make up the church, and of groups?
>
> We have no doubt about individuals and groups. The church should encourage its members to become conscientious citizens, to take the initiative to found and operate social programmes, to inform themselves about political issues, and to advocate or dissent according to their conscience.
>
> Since individual action is usually limited in its effects, however, Christians should also be encouraged to form or join groups and movements which concern themselves with specific needs in society, undertake research into social issues, and organize appropriate action. We welcome the existence and activity of such groups, for they supplement the church's work in many important areas. Christians should also be encouraged to participate responsibly in the political party of their choice, their labour union(s) or business association(s), and similar movements. Whenever possible, they should form a Christian

---

55. Ibid., 8.
56. Ibid., 16.

group within them, and/or start or join a Christian party, union, or movement, in order to develop specifically Christian policies.[57]

For René Padilla, this report was a landmark for the comprehension of Christian mission in the world. "If, as this document says, evangelism and social responsibility are as closely united as in marriage, it is obvious that the priority of evangelization mentioned in the Lausanne Covenant does not mean evangelism has to be considered more important than its partner all the time everywhere. If it is, something is really wrong with this marriage!"[58] Maybe that was CONELA's confusion. For them, evangelism and social responsibility were not even dating!

The final document of the Wheaton '83 conference expanded the practical applications on the issue of evangelism and social responsibility of the church.[59] CONELA had enough material in that document to apply to this question.

> Christ's followers, therefore, are called, in one way or another, not to conform to the values of society but to transform them (Rom 12:1–2; Eph 5:8–14). This calling flows from our confession that God loves the world and that the earth belongs to Him. It is true that Satan is active in the world, even claiming it to be his (Luke 4:5–7). He is, however, a usurper, having no property rights here. All authority in heaven and on earth has been given to Christ Jesus (Matt 28:18; Col 1:15–20). Although His Lordship is not yet acknowledged by all (Heb 2:8) He is the ruler of the kings of the earth (Rev 1:5), King of kings and Lord of lords (Rev 19:16). In faith we confess that the old order is passing away; the new order has already begun (2 Cor 5:17; Eph 2:7–10; Matt 12:18; Luke 7:21–23).[60]

Wheaton '83 used the word "transformation" instead of "development" to describe "the change from a condition of human existence contrary to God's purpose to one in which people are able to enjoy fullness of life in harmony with God."

---

57. Ibid., 17.

58. C. René Padilla, "Evangelización y Responsabilidad Social: De Wheaton '66 a Wheaton '83," *Misión* 4, no. 3 (1985): 88.

59. Lausanne Committee for World Evangelization (LCWE), *Transformation: The Church in Response to Human Need* (Wheaton, IL: LCWE, 1983).

60. Ibid., 2.

We have come to see that the goal of transformation is best described by the biblical vision of the Kingdom of God. This new way of being human in submission to the Lord of all has many facets. In particular, it means striving to bring peace among individuals, races, and nations by overcoming prejudices, fears, and preconceived ideas about others. It means sharing basic resources like food, water, the means of healing, and knowledge. It also means working for a greater participation of people in the decisions which affect their lives, making possible an equal receiving from others and giving of themselves. Finally, it means growing up into Christ in all things as a body of people dependent upon the work of the Holy Spirit and upon each other.[61]

Ministering to the poor should not be limited to acts of mercy but should also include changing evil structures that maintain poverty. Wheaton '83 encouraged believers to "combine both in our ministry and be willing to suffer the consequences." Economic and political actions go together with evangelism. Therefore, churches must get involved in society to confront evil and social injustice, including public protests. For Padilla, Wheaton '83 completed the process of forming an evangelical social conscience: "It made evident that for a considerable number of evangelicals evangelism cannot be divorced from a significant commitment to the people and their concrete needs."[62]

Theological Agendas

Similar ideas were included in the theological agenda Samuel Escobar delineated at the beginning of the 1980s. Escobar defined four major areas for theology: hermeneutics, contextualization, Christology, and ecclesiology.[63] Even though Escobar had in mind the FTL when writing this agenda, it reflected the theological situation within the evangelical churches. The main thrust in Escobar's theological agenda was to evaluate received models in light of the complex Latin American situation and challenges, and to

---

61. Ibid., 3.

62. Padilla, "Evangelización y Responsabilidad Social," 89.

63. J. Samuel Escobar, "La Agenda Teológica Para El Futuro," *Boletín Teológico* 4, no. 2 (1981).

develop a biblical and theological response that would help evangelicals in their mission.

It was this agenda that Escobar expanded in his book on liberation theology. While rejecting the Marxist analysis and element in that theology, he recognized that the way many Catholics were serving the needy in difficult situations and with great sacrifice was a wake-up call for the evangelical conscience. Escobar's warning was that "it would be tragic if only for fear of the excesses of a liberation theology which puts Marxist praxis in first place, evangelicals opted for indifference, for a non-critical support of oppressive and corrupt regimes, and for abandoning the glorious evangelical heritage that sees the gospel as a factor for change." He also said, "It would be tragic if in responding to these new situations evangelicals became conservative or defenders of an unjust social order both national and international. For the evangelical churches and communities rooted in our lands, that is the challenge liberation theology presents, and we need to take it seriously."[64] Then Escobar explained,

> Evangelical praxis is Christ-centered and it is defined from the gospel. We should not be intimidated by those people who, starting from a Marxist conception of praxis and a materialistic and dialectic view of history, only consider as praxis whatever is meaningful politically according to their ideological perspective. Evangelical praxis is to know Jesus Christ and that knowledge is expressed by doing good works. Worship and ethics go together in the Old and New Testaments. Evangelical praxis is daily life at home and in the wider sphere of civil community. Faith should lead to praxis under any social or political circumstances. It is not only those people whose actions have public or political repercussions or who have intentions to change structures who have praxis. The simple lives of believers are the practice of the kingdom of God which is producing its effect in Peru or Russia, in the United States or Cuba, in China or South Africa.[65]

After more than a decade of coordinating the FTL, Peruvian Peter Savage also proposed a road map for evangelicals doing theology in Latin America. Savage was explaining the characteristics of theological work the FTL had

---

64. Escobar, *La Fe Evangélica*, 182.
65. Ibid., 191.

explored during those years. Savage described theology as a Christian vocation for those with God's call and gifts for such a work. Theologians were people who developed a theological and biblical worldview. They interacted with social sciences but did not easily accept their conclusions; neither did they set them at the same level as the Bible. Theology was part of the mission of the church and it was for the church. Theology should not be done at a desk, but rather "from the dust of the battle in which the church is involved, in the smog of the problems that confound it, amid the pains which create the angst of life in society."[66] Theologians were aware of the guidance of the Holy Spirit and were totally immersed in their historical context.

Savage listed ten concerns in a theological agenda:

- a definition of evangelical hermeneutics
- a historical conscience and the kingdom of God
- the place of the poor in the mission of the church and in evangelical hermeneutics
- a recovery of the biblical doctrine of sin as opposed to legalism and privatization
- a clear definition of Christian salvation and liberation
- a biblical view of human beings and the new humanity in Christ
- evangelical Christology
- ecclesiology
- the relationship between church and state
- global interdependence

Savage had in mind not only the challenges of liberation theology and the need for evangelicals to dialogue with it, but also those of imported evangelical theologies and programs. In a way, this agenda reflected much of what was already being done, but it also marked a route for the years to come.

Emilio Antonio Núñez added several nuances to Savage's theological agenda in a "Letter for Young Theologians."[67] The church, said Núñez, would always need theologians in order to grow spiritually and in its mission. But theology should be "forged in the anvil of Christian ministry" and was not just a matter for academic specialists with no relationship with the Christian community. For Núñez,

---

66. Peter Savage, "El Quehacer Teológico En El Contexto Latinoamericano," *Boletín Teológico* 5, no. 1 (1982): 6.

67. Emilio Antonio Núñez C., "Carta a Jóvenes Teólogos," *Boletín Teológico* 5, no. 1 (1982).

Anyone called to dig deep into theology has a theological mentality: his mind is attracted irresistibly by theology. That does not mean he is less or more intelligent than others. But his interest in theological issues is noticeable and grows daily. He has an insatiable curiosity. He is never satisfied with acquired knowledge. Books are his favorite hobby. He reads tirelessly. A researching spirit dominates him. He is not convinced by pat and superficial answers. He always wants to get to the heart of the issue, away from any rhetorical glitter. He is self-disciplined in his search for truth. He is systematic and scrupulous in this passionate quest. He does not count the cost of his vocation. He lives for and towards it. That is his service to God. While others crave the applause of multitudes, he consecrates himself to his silent task of a Christian thinker. He knows that when the applauses fades away ideas will continue triumphantly, because the Word of the Lord will remain forever (1 Pet 1:25).[68]

Thus, according to Núñez, a theologian is someone for whom the Bible is the ultimate authority, and who finds in it the certitude needed when challenged by other ideas. He follows the example of his Master walking among his people, being sensitive to their tragedies. "He has brains, but does not lack a heart; he is abundant in tears but he does not avoid action. His theology comes forth not only at a desk but also in close relationship with human beings, in the daily struggle for life."[69] Theology is done in the context of the Christian community, but the theologian should avoid any theological provincialism and nationalism. Theology is more than theory; it should become incarnate in the life of the believer. In Núñez's words: "It is orthopraxis and not only orthodoxy." There should not be a dichotomy between theology and ecclesiastical praxis. Pastors, evangelists, counselors, and other ministers needed theology to be effective. The existence of such a dichotomy explained, for Núñez, the "theological underdevelopment" of Latin American evangelicals.

In one of his later works, Gonzalo Báez-Camargo explained the need for a Latin American theology that would integrate individual conversion and regeneration with social involvement and improvement. In his words,

---

68. Ibid., 154.
69. Ibid., 155.

Some say they are so busy saving souls, one by one, that they do not have any time to fight for the elimination of economic and social injustices. Others claim to be so involved in reforming society that they do not have any room to worry about the regeneration of individuals. Some have committed themselves exclusively to fishing people out of the sewage and do nothing to make it disappear, and do not even realize many others are falling into it. Others try to get rid of it without caring that many people are drowning in it. How is it possible that neither group has seen or understood that both things are necessary and that both have to be done?[70]

To separate spiritual needs from physical ones was, according to Báez-Camargo, not only a false but mostly a pagan assumption. Such a notion was a hindrance to evangelical work and had reduced evangelization to the "spiritual" realm. Therefore, Báez-Camargo called the church to consider human beings as whole units: "the mission of the church has to do with whole human beings, not with disincarnated spirits."[71]

For Padilla, Núñez, Savage, Escobar, and Báez-Camargo, Latin American evangelical theology was a developing process. It was rolling forward, and there was no way to stop it. Their comments help us to see that by the early 1980s evangelicals were taking their theological task seriously. But they also made it clear that there was much yet to do. Years of theological dependency had created a culture that was hard to change. Denominational and evangelical politics were pushing strongly to keep the situation unchanged. But the mavericks and theological iconoclasts wanted nothing to do with it anymore. They had tasted theological maturity and had started to enjoy it. The tug-of-war was not over, but that was not going to deter them from pulling even harder in the direction of an authentic Latin American evangelical theology.

Misión

About the same time Savage's theological agenda was presented, 1982, a new evangelical magazine started: Misión, directed by René Padilla. It was a magazine for Christian readers presenting different themes from an

---

70. Gonzalo Báez-Camargo, *Genio y Espíritu Del Metodismo Wesleyano* (México: Casa Unida de Publicaciones, 1981), 58.

71. Ibid., 61.

evangelical perspective. Furthermore it was "Made in Latin America" by Latin Americans, with occasional contributions by authors from other continents living in Latin America. It was a magazine centered on the life and mission of the church – in other words, it was a missiological magazine. *Misión* was committed to evangelism as defined in section four of the Lausanne Covenant: "the proclamation of the historical, biblical Christ as Saviour and Lord, with a view to persuading people to come to him personally and so be reconciled to God." However, as Padilla explained, the Lausanne Covenant made it clear that evangelism was inseparable from political and social action, discipleship, and the unity of the church. Padilla stated,

> If evangelism is inseparable from social and political action, we evangelicals cannot close our eyes before the drama our people live. According to data from the United Nations, for example, 75% of children in El Salvador suffer malnutrition, 67% of peasant women give birth without any medical attention, 60% of the land is owned by 2% of the population, illiteracy is higher than 50%, 90% of Salvadorians earn less than $100 a year. Throughout our continent's width and length there is hunger and lack of clothing, sickness and ignorance, exploitation and unemployment, violence and oppression, injustice and abuse of power. What is our role in the midst of this tragic situation towards those to whom we take the name of Jesus? What shape should the mission take if it is to be faithful to the gospel as well as pertinent?[72]

Regarding the relationship of evangelism and discipleship, Padilla exhorted evangelicals not just to fill church buildings but to be sure that believers showed through their lives the values of the kingdom of God. He asked: "What does it mean to be a witness of Jesus Christ in the world of business, social media, science, arts, labour struggles, and politics? Which lifestyle incarnates the values of the Kingdom in the midst of a society dominated not by hunger and thirst for justice, but by an insatiable wish to have in order to be?" Finally, Padilla commented on the relationship between evangelism and unity. Considering the formation of CONELA and CLAI that year, he expressed the need to open the channels of communication between different sectors of the church. Then he asked: "How can we live

---

72. C. René Padilla, "El Nacimiento De Una Revista," *Misión* 1, no. 1 (1982): 6.

Christian unity in our environment so that Jesus' prayer is fulfilled, 'That they be completely united so that the world may believe that you have sent me'?"[73]

The first issue of *Misión* included a report of a consultation convened by Latin America Mission to understand the context for Christian mission in the region during the 1980s.[74] In the political arena, militarism, instability, and intervention from the United States would continue. A balance between energy use, ecology, and economic growth was necessary but in many countries it was not present, with negative consequences for the population. Latin America was experiencing a depredation of natural resources fueled by unchecked consumerism. Economically, the rich were getting richer, and the poor, poorer. Also, Latin America was continue to be technologically dependent. The population would reach the 600 million mark, with a heavy urban concentration, creating bigger problems of housing, education, sewage, transportation, and public health.

> Concerning the situation of the gospel in the Third World, particularly within the Spanish and Portuguese speaking countries, the consultation found motives for hope. Large sectors of the people show evidence of a vibrant faith in Jesus Christ, a growing phenomenon in Latin America. But it was also concerned about certain tendencies towards "popular religiosity" and the centralized control inside the Catholic community, together with the lack of missionary vision and a total absence of awareness of the consequent lifestyle of the evangelical church, a church that is growing rapidly.[75]

The lifestyle of most evangelicals was selfish and consumerist, reflecting middle-class values. Other persistent problems were the crisis of theological education, loss of family values, lack of missionary interest, and passive pietism without social concern. However, the three largest challenges for evangelicals in the 1980s were political extremism, the charismatic movement, and otherworldly spirituality. The report ended on a hopeful note: "a more mature pietism pregnant with evangelistic vitality, and a bigger commitment to social justice and service could be the biggest blessing for a continent in conflict."[76]

---

73. Ibid.

74. W. Dayton Roberts, "América Latina En La Década De Los 80," *Misión* 1, no. 1 (1982).

75. Ibid., 10.

76. Ibid., 12.

Third World Theologies

Latin American evangelical theology was not an isolated phenomenon in the 1980s. It was part of a strong development of "Third World theologies." Padilla called it a "theological explosion."[77] Several representatives of FTL participated in the meeting of Third World theologians in Seoul, Korea, from 27 August to 5 September 1982.[78] For Padilla, the meeting resulted in three conclusions. First, Third World theologies should not be a mere replica of European or North American theologies. Christians anywhere have the right to think freely and with their particular style, without feeling the pressure to conform to molds cast somewhere else. Second, theology should maintain a strong tie with the particular historical context, and its main function is to foster Christian obedience. Third, theology should be faithful to the Bible. Padilla quoted here the Seoul Declaration: "We have concertedly committed ourselves to building our theology on the inspired and infallible Word of God, under the authority of our Lord Jesus Christ, through the illumination of the Holy Spirit." The agenda proposed at Seoul for Latin America was:

> Those of us in Latin America will have to forge theology from within a context in which the social, economic, and political structures are in a state of disarray, unable to close the gap between the rich and the poor, and to solve the problems created by economic and technological dependence. Theology will have to give priority to problems related to justice and peace, the control of the arms race, the evangelistic implications of demographic and urban growth, the pathetic conditions of aboriginal peoples and other ethnic groups, the missiological challenge of popular religiosity and syncretism, the emergence of biblical and ecclesial renewal movements in and outside the Roman Catholic Church, and the quest for Christian unity among Protestants of all persuasions.[79]

Theologians from FTL were also active participants at the consultations of the International Fellowship of Evangelical Mission Theologians in Bangkok, Thailand (1982), Tlayacapan, Mexico (1984), Nairobi, Kenya

---

77. C. René Padilla, "La Explosión Teológica En El Tercer Mundo," *Misión* 4, no. 1 (1982).

78. "The Seoul Declaration: Toward an Evangelical Theology for the Third World," *International Bulletin of Missionary Research* 7, no. 2 (1983).

79. Ibid., 65.

(1987), and Osijek, in the former Yugoslavia (1991). Besides the heavy international program, there was an equally intense regional production: Jarabacoa, Dominican Republic (1983), a consultation regarding Christians and Political Participation; Quito, Ecuador (1985), New Alternatives for Theological Education; Huampani, Peru (1987), a consultation with Christian agencies on Integral Transformation; Santiago, Chile (1988), Christian Faith and Social Sciences; Medellin, Colombia (1988), International Consultation on Liberation Theology; Valle de Bravo, Mexico (1988), Urban Mission; Buenos Aires, Argentina (1990), Christians Facing Political Totalitarianisms; Santiago, Chile (1990), Christians Facing Economic Dependence and Foreign Debt in Latin America; Lima, Peru (1990), Christians and Violence in Latin America; São Paulo, Brazil (1990), the Gospel and the Question of Poverty; Quito, Ecuador (1990), Theology and Life, commemorating the twentieth anniversary of the FTL; and Buenos Aires, Argentina (1991), Second Consultation on Evangelical Political Participation in Latin America. All this activity had its culmination at CLADE III, Quito, Ecuador, from 24 August to 4 September 1992: The Whole Gospel for All People from Latin America.[80]

The paper read by Argentinian Pentecostal Norberto Saracco at the meeting in Bangkok (1982) showed the direction Latin American evangelical theological reflection was taking.[81] Saracco explained the "Galilean option" of Jesus, a hermeneutical key to reading the Gospels which was developed within the FTL.[82] Jesus chose Galilee intentionally as the special and preferred context for his ministry. "His Galilean option would have disappointed the expectations of the religious of his era, and also of those interested groups who wanted to have a monopoly on the Messiah."[83] Saracco explained that at the time of Jesus, Galilee was a forgotten and despised province, with a mixed population and "abundance of orphans, widows, poor, and unemployed." Things were different, though, in Jerusalem, the religious center of the land.

---

80. "Cronología De Actividades De La Fraternidad Teológica Latinoamericana"; Rolando Gutiérrez-Cortéz, "La Propuesta Teológica De La FTL," *Boletín Teológico* 20, no. 32 (1988).

81. Norberto Saracco, "The Liberating Options of Jesus," in *Sharing Jesus in the Two Thirds World: Evangelical Christologies from the Contexts of Poverty, Powerlessness and Religious Pluralism*, ed. Vinay Samuel and Chris Sugden (Bangalore, India: Partnership in Mission Asia, 1983). Other Latin Americans who participated in Bangkok with papers were: Orlando Costas (Puerto Rico), René Padilla (Argentina), Rolando Gutiérrez-Cortéz (Mexico), and Key Yuasa (Brazil).

82. Samuel Escobar attributes to Orlando Costas the first definition of the "Galilean option"; Samuel Escobar, "The Legacy of Orlando Costas," *International Bulletin of Missionary Research* 25, no. 2 (2001): 55.

83. Saracco, "The Liberating Options of Jesus," 50.

People in Jerusalem enjoyed a privileged status. There was a social and economic conflict between Jerusalem and the provinces, especially Galilee. In light of his preference for Galilee, Jesus' ministry had two emphases: "His response to immediate needs (sickness, poverty), and his identification with the expectations of the neediest."[84]

At the time of the crucifixion, continued Saracco, the confrontation between the messianic expectations represented by Jesus the Galilean and those of the religious elites in Jerusalem reached its climax.

> In this situation, Jesus became a threat to the Jewish aristocracy and the people of Jerusalem. Some saw their structure of power in jeopardy. Others were afraid that their source of sustenance would diminish. Because of this, representatives of the Sanhedrin and anonymous elements of the inhabitants of Jerusalem joined their voices against Jesus. The critical activity of Jesus in front of the Temple (Mark 11:15ff), and his preaching against it, constituted a serious threat to the benefits and privileges of the priestly aristocracy. In his Galilean option, Jesus identified and unmasked the center of oppression which was hidden behind the religious order, rather than the Roman empire. The common affirmation, that the people who received Jesus triumphantly are the same who one week later crucify him, is incorrect. In reality, they were two groups who represented opposite poles of society.
>
> In the Galilean option, Jesus liberated God, the gospel, and the mission from the clutch of an alienating religiosity. It is in opposition to all ideologies of faith, which tend to sustain and maintain dehumanizing relationships. Mission here has a universal projection in the context of a people who struggle and suffer for their total liberation.[85]

Jesus challenged the ideological use of the law by his actions in favor of the "sick and defeated, the poor and the stranger, the children, the women, and sinners," people who were treated by the religious authorities as "humans of a second category." About the cross, Saracco asked, "what did Jesus do to deserve such an end, and what meaning does his life and death have for us?"[86]

---

84. Ibid., 52.
85. Ibid., 53.
86. Ibid., 59.

The options Jesus chose were an indirect provocation of the dehumanizing political and religious structures of his time. Therefore,

> The options of Jesus challenge us to live our faith in such a way that it descends from the subjective plane to historical works. Such an attitude would be marked by the vulnerability and precariousness of our humanity. At the same time, however, it should be a sign of hope and salvation. We make this option, fully conscious that the conflict with the power of evil places us always in the perspective of the cross. Nevertheless, our faith and hope is in him who arose and waits for us always in Galilee.[87]

Saracco's presentation reflected the strong christological content of the theological agenda during those years. It was biblical in its source and avoided the Docetism of previous proposals. It was contextual without imposing any predetermined meaning on the text. Saracco and other Latin American theologians were responding biblically to the methodological and hermeneutical challenges of liberation theologies and, at the same time, arriving at similar ethical implications for Christian life and commitment. As Orlando Costas said, also in Bangkok, about the papers presented at the conference: "Unlike European theology most of them have stressed the importance of repossessing and recovering the historicity of Jesus of Nazareth as a fundamental starting point for building a Christology from the world of the oppressed."[88] Therefore, Costas concluded, at Bangkok,

> Being a conference of theologians from the world of the poor, the powerless and the oppressed, we do not pretend to produce in it definite polished statements. We come by and large from ministries that allow little time for systematic reflection and offer limited research facilities. We have come, nevertheless, full of courage, hoping to be able to render a service to the church-in-mission in the Two-Thirds World. Our final product is not to be judged by the traditional standards of mainstream western theology, though we recognize that we have learnt many good things from it. Rather, the success of the Conference will be

---

87. Ibid., 60.

88. Orlando Costas, "Proclaiming Christ in the Two Thirds World," in *Sharing Jesus in the Two Thirds World: Evangelical Christologies from the Contexts of Poverty, Powerlessness and Religious Pluralism*, ed. Vinay Samuel and Chris Sugden (Bangalore, India: Partnership in Mission Asia, 1982), 11.

judged in time by whether it helps the church of the oppressed in general and its evangelical variant in particular to proclaim Jesus Christ more faithfully, to communicate his Word more effectively, and to represent him more authentically in the Two-Thirds World.[89]

Costas' comments, even though they were specific about the conference in Bangkok, could equally be applied to the theological production of Latin American evangelicals. It came from the context of poverty and oppression; it was not academic in the rigorous North Atlantic sense; it did not follow North Atlantic agendas but maintained a dialogue with foreign theologies; and it was intended to serve the evangelical community in its mission. The effectiveness of such theology was better reflected in the lives of the Christians than in how many bookshelves it filled.

Dialogue with Foreign Theological and Missiological Agendas

Church Growth (CG) theory was developed in the United States and exported to the world. Fred Smith, a US missionary in Ecuador and a graduate from the School of Church Growth at the Fuller Seminary in Pasadena, California, wrote an article for *Misión* explaining the main tenets of CG theory, especially its biblical bases. Using the book of Acts, Smith defined fifteen principles of CG. Two Latin Americans responded to Smith's article: Samuel Escobar and Emilio Antonio Núñez. This was just one of the many conversations about this topic.[90]

Smith traced the origin of CG to Donald McGavran's book *The Bridges of God* (1955); afterwards the movement developed, attracting other missiologists from the United States. It was, according to Smith, a school of thought which "has been of much benefit around the world, helping churches to recognize their duty to grow and know how to fulfill it."[91] For Smith, the church grows when there is cooperation between the actions of the Holy Spirit and human obedience. People need to be sensitive to the Holy Spirit's guidance and wise, using their spiritual gifts to bring more members to the

---

89. Ibid., 15.

90. For another discussion on Church Growth see Costas, *The Church and Its Mission*. Also, C. René Padilla, "La Unidad De La Iglesia y El Principio De La Unidades Homgéneas," *Misión* 2, no. 3 (1983).

91. Fred Smith, "Algunos Principios Del Iglecrecimiento En Los Hechos De Los Apóstoles," *Misión* 8, no. 1 (1989): 6.

churches. Christians need to develop a ministry philosophy to create in the congregation the right environment for growth. Churches need to define goals, to pray fervently, and to be sure the whole congregation supports the plan to grow. They also need to define whether the population is receptive or resistant to the gospel: "To know if a people group is receptive or not to the gospel helps to invest time and limited resources. If it is receptive then everything should be done to reach it with the gospel as long as that favorable disposition is present; however, before a resistant group it would be better to go somewhere else and find a group ready to receive the gospel."[92]

Smith also defined the concept of homogeneous units, key in CG theory. The main thrust of this concept is that "people like to become Christians without crossing any racial, linguistic, or class barriers." According to Smith, church history showed that churches grow faster if they keep believers within one sector of the population. Even though Smith recognized that was not the optimal situation, he saw it as just a fact of this fallen world. Since, according to Smith, from the beginning in the book of Acts divisions were part of the church, he asked, "Are we going to close our eyes to this fact and pretend it does not exist? Or, are we going to recognize it as it is, a sin which follows us even today, and work within these limitations of social and cultural barriers?" He explained that such divisions actually started in Genesis 10 at the Tower of Babel. Smith said,

> I agree with the ideal of one church without any kinds of barriers. But we will never have it. Of course, there are heterogeneous churches, but they are the exception not the rule, and they exist only in some places (mostly urban) and under certain conditions. This principle is not necessary for a church to grow, but under some circumstances it will favor growth. For example: in the south of the United States it is better to have a church for black people and another one for white people, even within the same denomination. Forming a church composed of both groups would not be successful. Maybe some people would say that such churches exist, but they are the exception not the rule. What I am not doing here is promoting division within God's body; because, after conversion, any Christian has to recognize that within the body of Christ there are no social or racial divisions and all are equal in God's eyes. But, on this side of heaven, there

---

92. Ibid., 9.

will always be economic, social, linguistic, and other barriers. Whoever wants to start a new church needs to take this truth into account: everyone likes to be Christian without crossing any racial, linguistic, or class barriers. If they forget this principle, the church might grow, but not as when it is observed.[93]

Smith continued by talking about three Ps: presence, proclamation, and persuasion. Besides this he defined teamwork, watching for CG opportunities, the public testimony of the church, and strategic places to locate the church. He found all of these principles in the book of Acts.

The first to respond to Smith's article, Samuel Escobar, defined CG theory as reflecting "the evangelistic zeal, the missionary interest, the voluntary lay activism, and the entrepreneur spirit characteristic of a sector of conservative Protestantism in North America. This theory also reflects some traits of United States culture: a passion for statistics, application of anthropology and sociology to life, a pragmatic tendency more interested in *method* than *content*, and the criteria of *investing to profit* and *competing to prove who is the best*, typical of the capitalist economy."[94] Escobar compared CG to the imperial missionary theories of Spain in the sixteenth century and England in the nineteenth century. All reflected the culture of their countries of origin.

Granting that there was a possible biblical base for most of Smith's points, Escobar pointed out two which were impossible to base on the Bible: receptivity/resistance, and homogeneous units. However, Escobar highlighted that many of the principles Smith listed in his article had been part of Latin American evangelical history within both historical and Pentecostal churches. Churches in Latin America had experienced substantial growth even before CG became known in the region. However, the two points Escobar contested were more sociological than biblical. Escobar said,

> Regarding receptivity/resistance, the verses [mentioned by Smith] narrate cases of resistance to the gospel. But not one of them says that when met with resistance the apostles went to look for a more receptive place. The only case among the ones mentioned by the author is Acts 13:46, where because of the jealousy and rebellion of the Jews (v. 45), Paul and Barnabas decided to go to the Gentiles. We know from the rest of Acts and

---

93. Ibid., 10.

94. Samuel Escobar, "El Crecimiento De La Iglesia En América Latina y La Teoría De 'Iglecrecimiento': Comentarios Sobre El Artículo De Fred Smith," *Misión* 8, no. 1 (1989): 15.

the New Testament that the reason for going to the Gentiles was not only or primarily Jewish resistance, but the special calling Paul had to the Gentile world. Furthermore, in other situations when the Jews resisted (Acts 4:18) the apostles expressed their intention to continue evangelizing, albeit with suffering.[95]

According to Escobar, a practical application of the receptivity/resistance theory resulted in the fact that, in spite of all the talk in the United States about "unreached peoples," most missionaries went to places with a previous history of Christianity and therefore it was much easier to live and work. "The principle formulated by North American theory is that of the least effort and investment producing a *profit*. It is not the apostolic and biblical principle to go to unreached places (Rom 15:20–21). *Church Growth theory says nothing about the place of suffering in mission, a principle that is present in every page of the book of Acts.*"[96]

"Functional," "mechanistic," and "segregationist" was how Escobar described the idea of homogeneous units of CG. Such ideology, found behind racial separation in the United States and apartheid in South Africa, was being justified biblically by CG. However, the New Testament church was precisely the negation of such segregation. Granting that racism was also present in Latin America, Escobar said "it would be a tragedy and shame for the gospel if missionaries with a racist mentality came now to reproduce ecclesiastical models like those in the south of the United States."[97] The problem with the application of this idea that Escobar pinpointed was the accommodation of the gospel to the culture and customs of a particular group, leaving out entire sections of the biblical message confronting them. For instance, he mentioned a Peruvian landholder who told Escobar when they met at church: "I was a Catholic before, but since the priests started talking about Land Reform I came to this church, because I found out there are people of my class here and a spiritual and pure gospel is preached without raising any social issues." Escobar added: "It is interesting that the author of the article says nothing about the social impact of evangelism, a principle clearly demonstrated in the book of Acts."[98]

---

95. Ibid., 17.
96. Ibid., 18.
97. Ibid., 19.
98. Ibid.

Escobar concluded by recognizing the church's need to grow, and that CG had brought new motivation for it; however, there were several red flags regarding the CG theory:

> Ideas conducing to reduce the gospel to a minimum in order to have in the flock the maximum number of people, or to evangelize causing the minimum possible social change, have characterized nominal Christianity in Latin America. Since the sixteenth century we have suffered the moral, social and spiritual prostration of this type of Christianity. We do not now need a new North American version of the same. Latin American evangelicals have a rich experience and the Word of God. From it they can extract a much better orientation and better norms than the ones from certain sociological and anthropological theories riddled with injustices and contradictions.[99]

Emilio Antonio Núñez commented point by point on Smith's article on CG. Growth in the New Testament was the result of God's action and human obedience. But which was the best model for CG? Núñez disagreed that there was only one model. "Of course, the safest is to follow the New Testament's principles instead of prioritizing those of a contemporary system, even if it seems to be novel."[100] Regarding Smith's comments on the power of the Holy Spirit and demonic activity, Núñez warned evangelicals about getting so obsessed with Satan that they lost their focus on Christ. It was not that Satan and his activity were not real; but, as Núñez said, "we should ask if we see such opposition only in individual sin or if we perceive it also in the power structures that oppress humanity. Do we see them in the forces of the anti-kingdom, man's kingdom that is the kingdom without God?"[101]

Núñez agreed with Smith that church members should be involved in ministry. Núñez's questions had to do with the type of member CG was suggesting:

> In the current situation in Latin America, what do we understand by faithful and fruitful members? Traditional evangelicals formed according to the ideals of the North American middle-class church? Or evangelicals who are conscious of their historical,

---

99. Ibid.

100. Emilio Antonio Núñez C., "Crecimiento Numérico Versus Crecimiento Integral: Comentarios Sobre El Artículo De Fred Smith," *Misión* 8, no. 1 (1989): 22.

101. Ibid., 23.

cultural, and social reality, who also care for the economic and social predicament of the majority, without taking refuge in an individualistic, dualistic, and futuristic gospel? We ought to recover for ourselves in the Scriptures the whole gospel, for all human beings and for the whole human being. That's what we mean when we talk about integral church growth: quantitative and qualitative, for the soul and the body, for spiritual as well as material needs, for the present and eternity.[102]

Regarding the need for churches to define goals, Núñez agreed only that the goals should emphasize not only numerical growth but also discipleship. However, most of Núñez's comments had to do with the receptivity/resistance and the homogeneous unit principles.

There is no indication that the apostles preached only to receptive people. That we need strategies to best use our resources and opportunities is clear and irrefutable. But to abandon entire groups of people in the hands of the prince of this world to work in places or countries with promises of easy and immediate results, does not seem to go with the spirit of the New Testament. There are fields ready to harvest; but there are also fields waiting for the sowing which demands dedication, hard work, and even sacrifice.

Forty-five years ago, when this writer started in the ministry of the gospel, there were not thousands of immediate conversions as a result of evangelistic efforts, but the Lord was preparing the soil for what today is considered an evangelical explosion in these countries. Should evangelicals have abandoned Central America to preach in places with more receptivity? What can we say about the pioneers of the gospel in Central America and the meager results they achieved, meager from the point of view of modern theories of church growth?[103]

Núñez recognized that group affinity may help with pre-evangelism, but he explained that the gospel liberates people from their racial and social prejudices: "Of course it is easier to accept a gospel which strengthens our racial and cultural pride than the message of authentic Christian discipleship."

---

102. Ibid., 24.
103. Ibid.

The idea that people like to become Christian without crossing barriers might be realistic, but was it biblical? Núñez answered with a resounding "no." That was not Jesus' example because he "did not form a church for fishermen and another one for tax collectors." Neither was it Paul's example, who mentioned that in Corinth, for instance, there were rich and poor members in the same congregation. Nevertheless, these problems with the receptivity/resistance and the homogeneous unit principles "should not be an excuse for us not to strive towards an integral growth of the church. Such growth includes, indubitably, a numerical one."[104]

Female Theologians

By the mid-eighties women were becoming more involved in theological reflection. For example, twenty-eight women from nine Latin American and Caribbean countries met in Buenos Aires, Argentina, from 31 October to 4 November 1985, to talk about Latin American theology from a feminine perspective.[105] The meeting was sponsored by the Ecumenical Association of Third World Theologians. According to Elsa Tamez:

> In the Buenos Aires meeting, we did not focus exclusively on society's negative attitudes toward women. We simply addressed these problems as they are experienced by all women; we wanted to concentrate on the progress of women's achievements, as well as women's contributions to Latin American theology. Nevertheless, we did take up the themes of violence against women, sexual violence, women's disadvantage in the work place, and others. Cora Ferro spoke briefly about the church's view of women as inferior beings as reflected in the Eco Católico, the official paper of the Roman Catholic Church in Costa Rica. Aracely de Rochietti presented us with several issues including the Protestant churches' internal debt toward women. María José Rosado talked with us about the important role of nuns and their difficulties as women pastors; Graciela Uribe elaborated on this theme. In the first half of her presentation, María Clara Bingemer dug at the theological roots of discrimination against

---

104. Ibid., 25.

105. For the presentations and final document of this meeting see Elsa Tamez, ed. *Through Her Eyes: Women's Theology from Latin America* (Maryknoll, NY: Orbis Books, 1989).

women. Working toward the same end, Alida Verhoeven rejected language, images, and symbols which excluded the life, experience, and thought of women, youth, peoples, and nations of other races and skin colors.[106]

The final statement of the meeting described women's theological activity as unifying, communitarian and relational, contextual and concrete, militant, marked by a sense of humor, joy, and celebration, filled with a spirituality of hope, free, and oriented toward refashioning women's history. Also, the participants defined various tasks for theological reflection:

> To seek a synthesis in our ongoing formation between cultural values – those practices aimed at changing the situation – and theories that operate on different levels of human life.

> To pay attention to the theological experience and reflection that is taking place in base-level groups, especially by women, to take on this experience and to allow ourselves to be challenged by it in the process of a mutual enrichment, while also making our contribution.

> To systematize and transmit our experience and reflection.

> To seek, from this theological perspective, common paths with men, helping them to see the strength and tenderness that are part of the common task of bringing forth and nourishing the life of the new person – woman/man – and the new society.[107]

CLADE III

Women were also active presenters and participants at the Third Latin American Congress on Evangelism, Quito, Ecuador, 24 August to 4 September 1992 (CLADE III). At the inaugural meeting of CLADE III, René Padilla gave four characteristics of the theological task in Latin America: communal, spiritual, contextual, and missiological. It had to be *communal* to avoid the system in which a few contributed while the majority just listened passively. Furthermore, "the goal of theology is not the construction of a doctrinal system which follows tightly the laws of logic, but discerning God's will for

---

106. Ibid., 3.
107. Ibid., 153.

practical life. It has to do more with the wisdom whose beginning is the fear of the Lord than with academic excellence. It demands, therefore, besides the capacity to reason, a spirit of prayer and openness to the Holy Spirit's direction."[108] That was what made the theological task *spiritual*.

Theology also needed to be a *contextual* task, based on God's revelation in Jesus Christ and oriented toward the incarnation of the Bible in Latin American reality. It had to be biblical, not only because it used the Bible but because "it focuses on the life and mission of the church in today's world from the perspective of a theology rooted in the Scriptures and in dialogue with the sciences which help us to read the socioeconomic, political, and cultural situation in Latin America, the continent where the Lord has called us to proclaim and live the gospel."[109] It was, finally, a *missiological* task. Padilla explained,

> It takes for granted that at the center of the mission is the proclamation of Jesus Christ as Lord, whose sovereignty extends over all creation. Consequently, it looks not only to geographical extension and numerical growth of the church, but to the complete fulfillment of God's purpose for every aspect of human life, in its personal and social dimension. Our goal to evangelize is not merely for our congregations to have more members, but for God's will to be done "on earth as it is in heaven." The focus of our reflection is evangelism, but not evangelism per se, but in close relationship with integral mission, the mission of the Kingdom of God and his justice.[110]

The presentation of Argentinian Baptist Pablo Deiros at CLADE III on forgiveness had all four characteristics Padilla mentioned. Deiros found that in Latin America, even though evangelicals had proclaimed forgiveness of sins, "as it happens to most of the theological content of the Latin American evangelical faith, it has not always found an explicit expression. That is so because for the majority of Latin American evangelicals, theology is something alive, more oriented to experiencing the faith than to its grammar. It is not that faith has not been verbalized, but it has not been done in the

---

108. CLADE III, *Clade III: Tercer Congreso Latinoamericano De Evangelización, Quito 1992: Todo El Evangelio Para Todos Los Pueblos Desde América Latina* (Buenos Aires: Fraternidad Teológica Latinoamericana, 1993), 7.

109. Ibid.

110. Ibid.

traditional way we find in other cultures, especially European."[111] However, from the onset, evangelicals preached the gospel of forgiveness, only they were not aware of its full scope and reach. Initially forgiveness was understood exclusively as personal and individualistic. Deiros asked, "What does the gospel of forgiveness mean in Latin America today in light of the particular internal and external circumstances of our communities of evangelical faith? And also, how should we proclaim the gospel of forgiveness in Latin America today?"[112]

Forgiveness was imperative in a continent with a long history of hate, local and national revolts, and political instability. The predominant idea was "not forgetting nor forgiving." Deiros described Latin American history as "generation after generation reviving old hostilities and animosities." Then he described the context:

> In a continent torn apart by fratricidal fights, class conflicts, and sectarian clashes; in a land ransacked by the stooges of the current chiefs together with the petty causes of the powerful elites; in countries where personal ambitions and interests have been arbitrarily imposed above the rights and needs of the masses, it is imperative to proclaim that there is forgiveness. To the peoples who have been bled dry and still have open wounds; to men and women that every day suffer the martyrdom of marginality, poverty, and dehumanization, we have to announce that there is forgiveness, that pain should not last forever, that hope for an order with justice and peace is fed from the forgiveness given and received in Jesus (Isa 61:1–3). To thousands of human beings trapped within a punitive and fatalistic religiosity, with a remote and never-satisfied god, with an insecure soteriology and arbitrary hamartiology, we evangelicals must announce to them that there is forgiveness in Jesus' blood. That because of God's love showed in the expiatory death of Christ, in spite of our personal and collective sins, individual and structural ones, we can be forgiven (Rom 5:8).[113]

However, the cross and its effects were also interpreted individualistically and futuristically for life beyond the grave with little or no effect on life today.

---

111. Ibid., 72.

112. Ibid., 73.

113. Ibid., 74.

Latin America was in need of a complete gospel of forgiveness to free people from any sacramentalism, even the evangelical type. Deiros explained,

> We must confess that we have made our institutions, worship practices, spiritual gifts, and even the biblical sacraments to operate as spurious substitutes of the only and basic redemptive act for the forgiveness of our sins, the death of Jesus Christ on the cross. Which gospel are we proclaiming? Is it the gospel of a wrongly understood biblical fundamentalism? Perhaps it is the gospel of the gift of tongues? Maybe the gospel of an efficient organization? Most probably it is the gospel of a secularized Christianity more in tune with the kingdoms of this world than with the kingdom of God. "We preach Christ crucified" (1 Cor 1:23; 2:2). Latin America today needs this to be our gospel.[114]

Deiros concluded that Latin America demanded an adequate *soteriology* but even more an authentic *kyriology* (Jesus as Lord over everything). Interestingly, Deiros reiterated the importance of a Christology without docetic influence. Docetism seemed to be a lingering tendency, one hard to break away from, that kept coming up as a major obstacle for evangelicals.

Also at CLADE III Brazilian Pentecostal pastor Ricardo Gondim compared the theologies and churches started by faith-mission organizations with the theologies and practices of Pentecostals. Regarding the former, Gondim described them as having the "one-dimensional discourse of the missionary to save souls only in the spiritual dimension, often with a strong dose of colonialism despising local culture, and severing itself from any concrete relevance."[115] He added,

> Such evangelistic practice pushed the church away from any project with social, political, or historical pertinence. Growth of the main evangelical trends became merely quantitative, and the church, even though it was present in society, stayed at the margin of the formative processes of Latin American culture. Because critical reflection does not blossom in closed systems, the inhibiting factor of fundamentalism did not venture to do theology, but limited itself to translating it. Fundamentalist proposals within the missionary project inhibited any possibility

---

114. Ibid., 76.
115. Ibid., 174.

of thinking of the Gospel as the transforming power of history. A pre-millennial emphasis jettisoned any initiative to rescue social values.[116]

Consequently, evangelicals in Latin America had preached a disengaged message and became irrelevant to society in general. When talking about Pentecostalism, Gondim evaluated it as the most significant religious movement in Latin America and the segment of Protestantism which adapted much faster to Latin America. However, Gondim considered that Latin American Pentecostalism was based on an "experimental subjectivism." He said,

> While Pentecostalism in North America struggled to identify itself with fundamentalism and its best-known trends (from verbal inspiration of the Bible to pre-millennialism), in Latin America there was a tendency towards separation from that pattern at the cost of a huge theological fragility and a clear vulnerability to syncretism. A great part of Latin American Pentecostalism succumbed to a mystification of even the Bible and allegorizing paragraphs that were supposed to be read, at least, following the grammatical-historical method of interpretation. Experience became the main criteria for truth elevating subjectivism above God's truth objectively revealed in the Scriptures. Such emphasis made Pentecostalism vulnerable to arrogant practices, often producing emotional catharsis artificially manipulated, making people confused about the meaning of power.[117]

Gondim also pointed to the centralized Pentecostal leadership that had little accountability: "Dictatorship degrades the exercise of criticism, delays modernization, and inhibits creativity."[118] He called Pentecostalism to evaluate its structural makeup; otherwise, even though it would attract many followers, it would continue making no impact in society – a harsh but much-needed evaluation of his tradition.

Another doctrinal trend Gondim identified within Pentecostalism was the so-called "prosperity movement" or "movement of positive thinking," which originated in the United States in the sixties and seventies. Although

---

116. Ibid.
117. Ibid., 176.
118. Ibid., 177.

it seemed to move initially in the right direction, most classical Pentecostal denominations in North America – Assemblies of God, Foursquare Gospel, and Church of God – rejected "not only the emphases of this movement but also its theological premises. After its initial success, the movement started to rip apart mainly because of its irresponsible promises of perfect health, guaranteed divine healing, and the urgency for all believers to show external signs of wealth."[119] However, as Gondim explained, it was after its demise in the North that this movement was exported to the South.

> The main dilemmas prosperity theology brought to the Latin America community were: (a) its Gnostic perception of knowledge; (b) its Christology; (c) its anthropology; (d) the negation of a theology of the Church as an empathic community towards human suffering.
>
> Without tranquility to face pain, without any reflection within the bourgeois evangelical population on poverty, and without a priestly vocation of suffering as a calling of the church, prosperity theology was seen as an escape for the middle class, which always wanted to ascend socially but resisted descending due to the swift impoverishment of the continent. The gospel of power was impoverished by materialistic consumerism clothed in biblical doctrine.[120]

Pentecostalism's Growth

A similar view of new trends within Pentecostalism came from Carmelo Alvarez, a Puerto Rican minister with the Church of Christ. Alvarez referred to the prosperity movement as an alternative to indigenous Pentecostalism. He described the main characteristics of this new offshoot of Pentecostalism:

> Exorcism and prosperity are its central elements. Energetic, charismatic leaders exhort huge gatherings. Continuous worship services are held in old cinemas and auditoriums. The public meetings are conceived more as public spectacles than as community worship. The hymns, sermons, and exhortations are a kind of therapy for the suffering masses. When the leader comes

119. Ibid., 178.
120. Ibid.

on stage enough enthusiasm has already been created to generate an almost hysterical explosion of emotion in the congregation. Observers have noted that the flexible bond which results from this shared emotion demands little personal commitment, and is a welcomed alternative to the pain, needs, and conflicts the participants must confront daily. Faced with daily crises, people prefer a moment of ecstasy, with this vibrant and untamed Jesus, to the silences and existential vacuum of daily life.[121]

Alvarez evaluated the use of the Bible by these new movements as fetish and magical: "rarely is the Bible studied since the central acts are healing and liberation." Also, the pastor becomes the moral agent with messianic authority, especially in finances. Alvarez explained that such a kind of Pentecostalism "offers economic benefits to the pastors, incorporating them into the *religious marketplace*, and converting the church into a commercial venture."[122]

Presbyterian Leonildo Silveira Campos from Brazil called prosperity-oriented Pentecostalism the "third wave," which started in the 1970s, coinciding with "an unprecedented economic crisis set off by the international petroleum crisis, and worsened by the inability of the Brazilian military dictatorship to solve the basic problems of the poorest people."[123] Silveira Campos identified several tendencies within this wave of Pentecostalism. Regarding ecclesiology, third-wave Pentecostalism "adopted the image of the auditorium, a *supermarket* where religious products – or their ingredients – are on display for all to help themselves. This Pentecostalism shaped its own ritual, turned pastors into indispensable authorities, eliminated representative congregational forms of government, and placed everything in the hands of the charismatic (in the Weberian sense) leaders."[124] People went to their religious meetings to forget their miseries and find "optimism, hope, and dreams of utopia."

---

121. Carmelo Alvarez, "Historic Panorama of Pentecostalism in Latin America and the Caribbean," in *In the Power of the Spirit: The Pentecostal Challenge to Historic Churches in Latin America*, ed. Benjamín F. Gutierrez and Dennis A. Smith (Mexico City: AIPRAL; Guatemala: CELEP; Louisville, KY: Presbyterian Church [USA], 1996), 35.

122. Ibid., 36.

123. Leonildo Silveira Campos, "Why Historic Churches Are Declining and Pentecostal Churches Are Growing in Brazil: A Sociological Perspective," in *In the Power of the Spirit: The Pentecostal Challenge to Historic Churches in Latin America*, ed. Benjamín F. Gutierrez and Dennis A. Smith (Mexico City: AIPRAL; Guatemala: CELEP; Louisville, KY: Presbyterian Church [USA], 1996), 71.

124. Ibid., 88.

In terms of theology, doctrines that were important for historic Protestantism have been discarded. The principle of sola scriptura has been weakened by the adoption of individual revelation and the magical-therapeutic use of the Bible. The doctrines of sola gratia and sola fide have been limited by the idea of personal effort and sacrifice and the use of emotions to confirm salvation and God's revelation. The universal priesthood has been maintained; however, the charismatic leader is seen as the intermediary in relations between the sacred and the profane, and the individual's participation has become merely decorative, lost in the wholesale nature of Pentecostal worship.[125]

Prayer and worship in third-wave Pentecostalism became money-centered. The gospel of prosperity overshadowed even eschatological hope. For Silveira Campos these churches created new sacraments; for example, the Universal Church of the Kingdom of God in Brazil had "introduced bread with water, the blessed rose, the anointed oil, the blessed salt, and many other ways to make visible an invisible grace." Third-wave Pentecostalism redefined demonology, angelology, and anthropology into a concept of *spiritual warfare* where God and the devil are in a continuous struggle. Silveira Campos explained that, regarding ethics, third-wave Pentecostalism "abandoned the rigorous demands on personal behavior that were previously required, and adopted a lighter style, leaving to the individual the responsibility to balance his or her desires with a minimum of discipline." Such a move produced a hedonistic and more fluid religiosity. The result was what Silveira Campos described as "a religious practice that expressed more continuity than rupture with a popular culture loaded with pre-Columbian traits."[126]

At the Consultation with Pentecostal Churches convened by the Comisión Evangélica Pentecostal Latinoamericana (CEPLA; Latin American Evangelical Pentecostal Commission) and the World Council of Churches in 1994, Latin American Pentecostalism was described in this way:

It is essentially a popular movement among the poorest sectors of society that responds to the spiritual needs of the people. Pentecostal faith offers an intimate personal relationship between the believer and God. The Pentecostal Christian encounters the

125. Ibid.
126. Ibid., 89.

power of the Spirit in his or her daily life and feels compelled to share the experience of God's presence with others. Evangelism is done in a direct, personal way, and with a sense of urgency. Popular indigenous Pentecostalism is rooted in the culture of the people. It has a strong sense of community. The faith is personal but not individual; it is lived out and celebrated in the worshipping and serving community. Celebration, care for the neighbour, and solidarity with the needy go hand in hand, holding the spiritual and the social together. The Pentecostal message can be a powerful agent of healing and reconciliation in broken communities. The social commitment of these churches of the poor is a source of hope in the midst of hopelessness.[127]

The consultation recognized the need to improve biblical and theological training in light of leadership shortcomings. Also, it was necessary to place safeguards to reduce the "scandal of division," because "the priority of proclaiming the good news is often perverted to become sheer competition for filling the church." They also recognized that in many Pentecostal churches women felt treated as inferior to men, and in order to be effective in evangelism that issue had to be addressed.

Peruvian Pentecostal pastor Bernardo Campos considered the Pentecostal movement as "one of the most important religious experiences" of the twentieth century. However, as Campos explained, Pentecostalism was a movement and not a denomination or a religious organization. Campos defined four major characteristics of Pentecostalism: a movement of spirituality, a movement of protest, a popular movement, and a movement of social change.

According to Pentecostal's self-understanding, Pentecostalism is not a simple socio-religious phenomenon, or the result of political and religious expansion of North American financial capitalism. For Pentecostals, Pentecostalism is the religion and faith consequence of the action of God through his Holy Spirit, which was poured out at Pentecost in the first century of the Christian history (Acts 2 – 4; Luke 24:49; Joel 2:27–32) and expanded from East to West. As a movement, Pentecostalism transcends the exclusive ecclesial boundaries and presents itself

---

127. WCC, *Consultation with Pentecostal Churches. Lima, Peru, 14 to 19 November 1994* (Geneva: World Council of Churches, 1994), 8.

within Christianity as a divine action through various religious practices of a certain kind.

From a theological point of view, Pentecostalism, in Latin America and elsewhere, is a religious experience of the divine. As a religious experience, it represents a ritualized enlargement of the original Pentecost event (Acts 2, 10, 19), with the aim and aspiration to express the very substance of Christianity – in this case the foundational Pentecostalism – in the fervour of a spirituality that seeks to repeat the primitive Christian life, which functions as a foundational myth. What is significant about this behaviour is that, as a movement of spirituality, Pentecostalism is a creator of identities. To be Pentecostal, just as to be Catholic, or Protestant, is a manner of being in society. As a spiritual movement, Pentecostalism is not confined by class or ideological boundaries, nor is it bound by geography or religious traditions. Pentecostalism has the capacity to permeate diverse and frequently clashing social classes, and to pass through radically opposed historical processes. In Latin America, where religion is a decisive factor and secularization usually takes the form of a social protest, the Pentecostal movement has produced a social impact and has adopted cultural forms which threaten to tear down the religious hegemony of the Catholic Church.[128]

For Campos, Latin American Pentecostals were becoming more involved in civil society. Therefore, the movement could not any longer be characterized as socially idle: "We see that Pentecostalism is coming of age; more and more we are becoming aware that we must be subjects and protagonists of our own history."[129] Furthermore, Campos explained the rapid growth of Pentecostal churches not only in terms of numbers but also because it provided the space where "the affirmation of an inclusive and pluralistic national identity and the search for alternative ways of democratic life are made possible; it is also an essential factor of social transformation."[130]

The final declaration of the Consultation of Pentecostals in Lima recognized the need to "strengthen the ecumenism of the Spirit moving in us for the transformation of women and men, society and creation in God's

---

128. Ibid., 18.
129. Ibid., 19.
130. Ibid., 20.

great purpose of reconciling and gathering in all things in Christ Jesus."[131] It also said:

> In the atmosphere of fellowship and Christian love we reflected on Pentecostal identity, spirituality, evangelism, social commitment, women's participation, unity, cooperation, and dialogue.
>
> We believe that evangelism is a way of life to be cultivated in the light of the Great Commission. The believers are mostly poor and, moved by the power of God, they become active agents of God, working so that all may taste of Christ's Spirit. Our witness to the gospel is also expressed through social commitment to those in great need. Often these actions are carried out only with the resources of the Holy Spirit and do not necessarily involve money. We understand Pentecostal witness as a commitment to solidarity, creating community and unity on a basis of living service to the poorest of the earth.[132]

The proposed agenda was quite comprehensive. It included a North–South dialogue with other Pentecostal organizations, dialogue with the Catholic Church, the enabling of women's involvement and active participation in the ecumenical movement, work with indigenous groups, development of youth work, the expansion of CEPLA to reach other Pentecostals, and dialogue on mission and evangelism. CEPLA also had a meeting – Jubilee, the Feast of the Spirit – in Havana, Cuba, 23–28 September 1998. The main goal of the meeting was to "create an awareness in our Pentecostal churches for a more active participation, with the Spirit's help, in the transformation of our present order which dehumanizes us all, men and women equally."[133]

At the Havana meeting, Bernardo Campos described the development of Pentecostalism in Latin America in three periods depending on the dynamic with the Catholic Church: rejection, assimilation, and distance. According to Campos, those periods corresponded to three historic tendencies: implantation Pentecostalism (1909–1930), fermenting Pentecostalism (1930–1959), and expansion Pentecostalism (1960–). During the first period, Pentecostalism was clearly anti-Catholic:

---

131. Ibid., 35.

132. Ibid.

133. CEPLA, *Jubileo, La Fiesta Del Espíritu: Identidad y Misión Del Pentecostalismo Latinoamericano* (Quito, Ecuador: Consejo Latinoamericano de Iglesias CLAI, 1999), vi.

In their criticism of Romanism, the first Pentecostals did not distinguish any tendencies within Roman Catholicism, not only because they did not know them, although Pentecostals were united in their view of the pagan world, but also because in many countries in Latin America the tendencies of Roman Catholicism were not well defined. Paganism was, for any traditional Pentecostal, a synonym of Catholicism and vice versa. The Catholic Church seemed according to their schemes a visible sign of idolatry, the incarnation of sin in society, and it was represented with a Bible concordance as the Beast of Revelation, the Great Prostitute, or Babylon the Great –a long list of condemnations that by and large justified its evangelization.[134]

The second developmental period for Pentecostalism was characterized by the opening of Bible institutes to train local leaders and a massive arrival of missionaries "without any clear political line and medium theological education," primarily to become teachers at the Bible institutes. It was also the beginning of industrialization in the region, with great numbers of peasants moving to the urban centers and filling the Pentecostal churches. Pentecostalism then became the "spiritual power of the poor." Campos mentioned that by 1940, one in every four Protestants was a Pentecostal. Pentecostals studied popular Catholicism, better understanding its different tendencies, and sharpening their evangelistic tools.

The "Constantinization" of Pentecostalism was the main trait of the third stage. Campos said: "Chile and Guatemala mean for Latin American Pentecostalism the seal of an alliance with military regimes."[135]

In this period of its history, Pentecostalism, as for Protestantism during the Independence, was the only force capable of shaking the religious monopoly of Christendom Catholicism and the New Christendom [movements within Catholicism]. Chile and Brazil, two different fronts, were the typical cases of Pentecostal Constantinization where the Roman Catholic Church was forced to take action to counteract it and when the United States did not miss the opportunity for political proselytism.

---

134. Bernardo Campos, *Experiencia Del Espíritu: Claves Para Una Interpretación Del Pentecostalismo* (Quito, Ecuador: CLAI, 2002), 4.

135. Ibid., 8.

Also, Pentecostal catechesis was politicized. The Pentecostal missionary and the pastor, both leaders with opinions in the name of the true gospel or complete gospel, promoted from the pulpit and from their radio programs an anti-communism crusade.[136]

However, new and younger generations of Pentecostals supported social and political changes in the region, causing conflict with traditional Pentecostals. For Campos, that was the main reason why some Pentecostal churches worked closely with CLAI while others joined CONELA. The former were open to ecumenical work and ecclesiastical renewal. On the other side,

> Pentecostals of a conservative mentality joined CONELA. Following the theology and ideology of the empire, and dominated by missionary leaders that were emerging onto the Latin American scene after having lost hegemony from 1929 to 1949, many Pentecostal leaders saw in CONELA the materialization of their aspirations. Eager for social advancement and embedded within the capitalistic mentality of social prestige, they strived towards a Pentecostalization of the planet and served as channels of dispersion of United States neo-conservatism. Some of the most successful Latin American preachers, naively but conscientiously, became imitators of North American evangelicalism. Such a servile mentality, in any case, did not have any scruples about making strategic alliances with ultra-conservative Catholicism.[137]

Campos described third-stage Pentecostalism as divided but still strong, and considered as a religious and political threat by Catholicism. In spite of a significant revival in Catholic practices, such as the ecclesial base communities and an openness to a wider distribution of the Bible, new generations of Pentecostals were not in dialogue with Catholics. Campos favored such partnership but, for it to happen, a new Pentecostal mentality was needed to further any concerted action.[138]

---

136. Ibid., 9.
137. Ibid., 10.
138. Ibid., 11.

Alvarez, Silveira, and Campos have left a sharp analysis of their Pentecostal tradition and development. They, together with other Pentecostals in different forums, represent the growth of Pentecostalism not only in numbers but mostly in understanding of their role in Latin American society. Within Pentecostalism there has been a lot of wiggle room for experiments and innovations, bringing tension between new developments and proposals and traditional Pentecostalism and historical churches. But, as we have seen, Pentecostalism and polemics go together in the region.

The organizers of the Panama Congress in 1916 never imagined that their vision of an evangelical Latin American church, relevant to society and fully native, was going to look as the church did at the end of the century. The average evangelical Christian in Latin America at the turn of the century was represented by a woman from a poor neighborhood, with little education and a big family, going to church meetings almost every night of the week, being a leader of the congregation, and expecting a series of miracles in her family and in her own person. A few more years would have to pass for the gospel to make it through the class structure and reach the higher strata of Latin American society. Latin Americans have entered the twenty-first century fully confident in the promise that not even the gates of Hades will defeat the advance of the gospel. Maranatha!

Conclusion

It has been believed that Latin American evangelical theology started late in the twentieth century, around the sixth decade. Earlier contextual developments with a definite interest in clear local theological thought were mostly unknown. However, from the onset of the century thinkers took on the challenge to theologically address the conditions and questions of the region. Several factors worked against the circulation and popularization of such contextual theologies, such as the negative influence of the massive missionary influx in the first half of the century, most having separatist and futuristic doctrinal schemes and successfully spreading them through their hundreds of Bible institutes. Most of these pre-packed theologies stunted any possibility of indigenous development. In addition, the denominational divisions fueled by foreign finances were imported to the region. Soon the theology of the group with the largest budget became orthodoxy, while theologies with less funding were declared heretical. Whoever had the money set the rules and doctrines, blocking any autochthonous theological thought most of the time. Finally, historical events – the Cold War, for example – aroused suspicion and disunity. This explains in part why, in the twentieth century, Latin American evangelicals developed several strands of theological thought with almost no interaction between them. Other than on a few occasions when one group criticized another, such as evangelicals and ISAL, each group worked unperturbed by what others were doing.

Evangelical theology in Latin America during the twentieth century should not, and cannot, be defined solely as an academic and scholastic activity done in the corridors of seminaries. It was, rather, a rich theological discussion carried out in publications, sermons, denominational and local bulletins, conferences, and through other similar means. However, the distribution of this dialogue was limited by slow communication and a lack of technological means to make it available to a wider public and for later generations. Most of it remained local for a limited public. A good chunk of the theology was lost and forgotten because it was never printed or preserved in other ways. Researchers today can access only the tip of the theological iceberg.

Latin American evangelical theology was in dialogue with the rest of the world throughout the twentieth century. Developments in theological thought in Europe and North America were on the table, not as historical relics, but as real partners in the conversation. Many Latin Americans considered foreign theologies to be examples of contextual work. These theologies were scrutinized and adapted whenever possible. However, what to do with foreign theological systems has been a point of contention among various Latin Americans.

Evangelical theologians in Latin America were also forced to engage with Roman Catholic theologies. As the latecomers and the minority religious option, evangelicals needed to fight against direct social and political persecution, especially in the early part of the century. It is hard for outsiders to understand how the predominant religion affected the identity and mission of evangelicals. They had to show why there was a need for their presence. They had to demonstrate that they were not secret agents of foreign powers involved in a conspiracy to appropriate the region's raw materials, nor were they the criminals and outlaws the religious hierarchy claimed they were. They approached Catholic theologies with different strategies. Most of this dialogue was antagonistic and difficult. Only during the last decades of the century, when evangelicals became a significant percentage of the population, did they start to ignore the religious establishment. But their theological evaluation of the Catholic Church as the enemy of the faith and of the need for all Catholics to convert has not changed one iota. Most evangelical theologians have not compromised their allegiance to their faith on the altar of religious toleration. The history of mutual rejection and direct persecution is hard to forget. The supposed institutional *aggiornamento* of the Catholic Church after Vatican II never materialized into a more fraternal relationship. Latin Americans are suspicious of highly publicized encounters between evangelicals and Catholics in other latitudes. For many Latin American evangelicals, those meetings are treason. This trait of evangelical identity in Latin America is hard to understand and is almost never perceived by North Americans and Europeans.

If the impression has been given that the development of evangelical theology in Latin America has been local, chaotic, unpredictable, polarizing, and divisive, that is because it has indeed been so. Besides a few of the concerted efforts of ISAL and the FTL to break down denominational and ideological barriers, most developments in theological thought have been constrained by traditional ecclesiastical camps. Suspicion and lack of trust has made unity difficult if not impossible. This has been, and still is, the biggest weakness and limitation of Latin American evangelical theological development. We wonder how things might have been different had the evangelicals worked more intentionally toward coming together for the sake of the gospel and putting aside their inherited differences. This remains one of the greatest challenges evangelicals face for the future.

Early theological dependency has been partially overcome. However, this has not translated into a general acceptance and application of local theologies. For example, North American "health and wealth" theologies, together with the New Apostolic Movement, distributed efficiently by satellite TV to all corners of the region, have spread swiftly. The "megachurch" movement, with its managerial model, has brought an ecclesiology that fits better with the predominant capitalist system than with the kingdom of God. The reasons behind the disregard for autochthonous theologies are complex, and more research is needed to uncover the reasons why Latin American evangelical theology is the theology of just a few. Nonetheless, we can venture a few answers.

Theological education in the region has been, for the most part, a copy of what is done in the United States. Curricula, the philosophy of education, and most of the programs have been modeled after North American seminaries. Even today, most of the textbooks are translations mostly from English. Only a handful of seminaries and Bible institutes have included some Latin American authors. The problem is that most of the translated texts are taught with little effort to contextualize their content. This has continued theoretical dependency on theologies from other latitudes. Latin America needs educators who will design contextual theological programs suited to its needs.

Since Latin American evangelical theologies in the sixties and seventies developed in parallel to liberation theologies many people confuse them. Historically, those were difficult days during the Cold War and the negative political situation affected and infected fraternal relationships among evangelicals in the region. ISAL's radicalization and alienation from the churches and the divided response from FTL members to liberation theologies gave the impression that what evangelicals were doing theologically was just another strand of liberation theology and therefore it had to be rejected altogether. This international mingling was, as has been explained, clearly seen in the discussion around the formation of CONELA and CLAI. It did not help that most denominations were established by missionaries with politically conservative views who were not able to see the differences between what was being done by liberation theologians on the one side and evangelicals on the other. For those missionaries, and the leaders they trained, both theology schools were one and the same. Such confusion and subsequent rejection of what evangelicals were doing theologically has remained, even though the political framework that inspired it has become obsolete.

There is also the cultural element that considers the lifestyle and products from the North as intrinsically better than their local counterparts. North American and European cultures are well known in Latin America through the media. For most people, their goal in life is to imitate them as closely as possible. For example, the younger generations prefer to learn the languages of the North instead of the native languages. With a few exceptions, artists and musicians from the North are known better than local ones. The same can be said for theologians and local theologies. Many Latin Americans are not even aware that these autochthonous theologies exist.

In spite of new and faster communications it is still difficult to distribute publications and books within the region. The existing market conditions make it cumbersome and expensive to ship boxes even between neighboring countries. Many businesses use one of the largest Latin American cities, Miami, as their point of delivery because it is easier and financially more convenient. This makes it difficult, not to mention more expensive, for publishing houses printing books by Latin American theologians to make them more visible throughout Latin America. Recent efforts have helped with this but inefficient postal systems and outdated carriers continue to be used. Publishers need to find ways to get around these difficulties so that their productions reach more customers.

Amazingly, amid these and other hurdles, Latin American evangelicals remain active in finding the biblical message for the church and the continent. Some of the issues of the twentieth century are still current – such as poverty, corruption, social inequality, racism, and lack of opportunities for the majority. There are also new challenges that need to be addressed theologically: environmental stewardship, new ecclesiologies, gender issues, bioethical advancements, immigration, and political refugees and displacement. This goes together with redefining what it means to be the people of the Kingdom in Latin America today. Theology in Latin America has been missiological and it should continue being so. Only then will Latin American evangelicals have something relevant to say to their context and to the world.

Bibliography

Alvarez, Carmelo. "Historic Panorama of Pentecostalism in Latin America and the Caribbean." In *In the Power of the Spirit: The Pentecostal Challenge to Historic Churches in Latin America*, edited by Benjamín F. Gutiérrez and Dennis A. Smith, 29–40. Mexico City: AIPRAL; Guatemala: CELEP; Louisville, KY: Presbyterian Church (USA), 1996.

Arana Quiroz, Pedro. "La Revelación De Dios y La Teología En Latinoamérica." In *El Debate Contemporáneo Sobre La Biblia*, edited by Peter Savage, 37–78. Barcelona: Ediciones Evangélicas Europeas, 1972.

———, ed. *Teología Del Camino: Documentos Presentados En Los Últimos Veinte Años Por Diferentes Comunidades Cristianas De América Latina*. Lima: Ediciones Presencia, 1987.

Assmann, Hugo. "The Christian Contribution to the Liberation of Latin America" ["El Aporte Cristiano Al Proceso De Liberación De América Latina"]. In *Anticipation* 9 (Oct. 1971). Translated by Paul Abrecht.

———. *Theology for a Nomad Church*. Maryknoll, NY: Orbis Books, 1975.

Báez-Camargo, Gonzalo. "The Earliest Protestant Missionary Venture in Latin America." *Church History* 21, no. 2 (1952): 135–145.

———. "El Futuro Del Protestantismo Latinoamericano." *Pensamiento Cristiano* 25, no. 2 (Diciembre 1978): 101–109.

———. *Genio y Espíritu Del Metodismo Wesleyano*. Mexico: Casa Unida de Publicaciones, 1981.

———. *Hacia La Renovación Religiosa En Hispano-América: Resumen E Interpretación Del Congreso Evangélico Hispano-Americano De La Habana*. Mexico City: Casa Unida de Publicaciones, 1930.

Barth, Markus. "What Is the Gospel?" *International Review of Mission* 53, no. 3 (1964): 441–448.

Braga, Erasmo. *Pan-Americanismo: Aspecto Religioso. Una Relación E Interpretación Del Congreso De Acción Cristiana En La América Latina Celebrado En Panamá Los 10 a 19 De Febrero De 1916*. Translated by Eduardo Monteverde. New York, NY: Sociedad para la Educación Misionera en los Estados Unidos y el Canadá, 1917.

Bucafusco, Luis P. "Impresiones Personales Sobre La III Cela." In *Deudores Al Mundo, III Conferencia Evangélica (CELA)*, 13–16. Montevideo: UNELAM, 1969.

CAM. *The Central American Bulletin* 22, no. 1 (1916).

CAM. "Origin and Purpose of the Mission." *The Central American Bulletin* 3, no. 2 (1897): 2.

Campos, Bernardo. *Experiencia Del Espíritu: Claves Para Una Interpretación Del Pentecostalismo*. Quito, Ecuador: CLAI, 2002.

Castillo-Cárdenas, Gonzalo. "El Cristianismo Evangélico En América Latina." *Cuadernos Teológicos* 2, no. 5 (1964): 61–65.

Castro, Emilio. "Evangelism in Latin America." *International Review of Mission* 53, no. 4 (1964): 452–56.

———. *Un Pueblo Peregrino: Reflexiones Sobre La Misión De La Iglesia En El Mundo Actual*. Buenos Aires: La Aurora, 1966.

CELA I. *El Cristianismo Evangélico En América Latina. Informes y Resoluciones De La Primera Conferencia Evangélica Latinoamericana, 18 Al 30 De Julio De 1949, Buenos Aires, Argentina*. Buenos Aires: La Aurora, 1949.

CELA II. *Cristo La Esperanza Para América Latina: Ponencias-Informes-Comentarios De La Segunda Conferencia Evangélica Latinoamericana, 20 De Julio a 6 De Agosto De 1961, Lima, Perú*. Buenos Aires: Confederación Evangélica del Río de la Plata, 1962.

CEPLA. *Jubileo, La Fiesta Del Espíritu: Identidad y Misión Del Pentecostalismo Latinoamericano*. Quito, Ecuador: Consejo Latinoamericano de Iglesias CLAI, 1999.

CLADE III. *Clade III: Tercer Congreso Latinoamericano De Evangelización, Quito 1992: Todo El Evangelio Para Todos Los Pueblos Desde América Latina*. Buenos Aires: Fraternidad Teológica Latinoamericana, 1993.

CLAI. *Constitución y Reglamento Del Clai: Aprobado En La Asamblea Constitutiva, Noviembre 11 Al 18 De 1982, Lima, Perú*. Lima: CLAI, 1983.

Committee on Cooperation in Latin America (CCLA). *Christian Work in Latin America*. Vol. 3, *Cooperation and the Promotion of Unity, the Training and Efficiency of Missionaries, the Devotional Addresses, the Popular Addresses*. New York, NY: Missionary Education Movement of the United States and Canada, 1917.

———. *Christian Work in Latin America*. Vol. 2, *Literature, Women's Work, the Church in the Field, the Home Base*. New York, NY: Missionary Education Movement of the United States and Canada, 1917.

———. *Christian Work in Latin America*, Vol. 1, *Survey and Occupation, Message and Method, Education*. New York, NY: Missionary Education Movement of the United States and Canada, 1917.

———. *Regional Conferences in Latin America*. New York, NY: Missionary Education Movement, 1917.

Conard, Guillermo, ed. *Los Documentos De Conela*. Mexico City: CONELA, 1982.

CONELA. *Declaración De Conela En Maracaibo*. Maracaibo, Venezuela: CONELA, 1986.

"Confraternidad Evangélica Latinoamericana Conela. Informe De La Consulta Teológica Sobre La Responsabilidad Social." *Misión* 3, no. 2 (1984): 75–76.

Conteris, Hiber. "El Rol De La Iglesia En El Cambio Social De América Latina." *Cristianismo y Sociedad* 3, no. 7 (1965): 53–60.

Conway, Martin. "A Permanent Argument." *International Review of Mission* 53, no. 4 (1964): 449–451.

Costas, Orlando. *The Church and Its Mission: A Shattering Critique from the Third World*. Wheaton, IL: Tyndale House, 1974.

———. "Proclaiming Christ in the Two Thirds World." In *Sharing Jesus in the Two Thirds World: Evangelical Christologies from the Contexts of Poverty, Powerlessness and Religious Pluralism*, edited by Vinay Samuel and Chris Sugden, 1–15. Bangalore, India: Partnership in Mission Asia, 1982.

"Cronología De Actividades De La Fraternidad Teológica Latinoamericana." *Boletín Teológico* 27, no. 59–60 (Julio–Diciembre 1995): 26–33.

De Santa Ana, Julio. *Good News to the Poor: The Challenge of the Poor in the History of the Church*. Maryknoll, NY: Orbis Books, 1979.

———. *Is There Hope for the Third World?* Amsterdam: VU Boekhandel/ Uitgeverij, 1988.

———. *Protestantismo, Cultura y Sociedad: Problemas y Perspectivas De La Fe Evangélica En América Latina*. Buenos Aires: La Aurora, 1970.

———. *Separation Without Hope? Essays on the Relation between the Church and the Poor during the Industrial Revolution and the Western Colonial Expansion*. Maryknoll, NY: Orbis Books, 1980.

———. *Sustainability and Globalization*. Geneva: WCC Publications, 1998.

———. *Through the Third World Towards One World*. Amsterdam: Vrije Universiteit, 1990.

———. *Towards a Church of the Poor: The Work of an Ecumenical Group on the Church and the Poor*. Maryknoll, NY: Orbis Books, 1981.

Dekker, James C. "North American Protestant Theology: Impact on Central America." *Evangelical Review of Theology* 9, no. 3 (July 1985): 378–392.

Del Salto, David. "The Promise of a Trinitarian Christology for the Latin American Evangelical Church." PhD dissertation, Lutheran School of Theology, 2008.

Dirección. "Una Revista Para Una Nueva Situación." *Pastoralia* 1, no. 1 (1978): 1–3.

"Editorial." *Cuadernos Teológicos* 1, no. 1 (1950).

Escobar, Samuel. J. "El Contenido Bíblico y El Ropaje Anglosajón En La Teología Latinoamericana." In *El Debate Contemporáneo Sobre La Biblia*, edited by Peter Savage, 17–36. Barcelona: Ediciones Evangélicas Europeas, 1972.

———. "El Crecimiento De La Iglesia En América Latina y La Teoría De 'Iglecrecimiento': Comentarios Sobre El Artículo De Fred Smith." *Misión* 8, no. 1 (1989): 15–19.

———. "El Reino De Dios, La Escatología y La Etica Social y Política En América Latina." Paper presented at Fraternidad Teológica Latino Americana, II Consulta Teológica Internacional, Lima, 1972.

————. *En Busca De Cristo En América Latina*. Buenos Aires: Kairos, 2012.

————. "Evangelical Theology in Latin America." *EP News Service* (6 October 1973).

————. "Heredero De La Reforma Radical." In *Hacia Una Teología Latinoamericana: Ensayos En Honor a Pedro Savage*, edited by C. René Padilla, 51–71. San José, Costa Rica: Editorial Caribe, 1984.

————. "La Agenda Teológica Para El Futuro." *Boletín Teológico* 4, no. 2 (1981): 1.

————. *La Fe Evangélica y Las Teologías De La Liberación*. El Paso: Casa Bautista de Publicaciones, 1987.

————. "La Nueva Generación Evangélica." *Pensamiento Cristiano* (1969): 188–193.

————. "La Teología Evangélica Hoy." *Pensamiento Cristiano* 24, no. 4 (Junio 1978): 232–237.

————. "The Legacy of John Alexander Mackay." *International Bulletin of Missionary Research* 16 (1992): 116–118, 120–122.

————. "The Legacy of Orlando Costas." *International Bulletin of Missionary Research* 25, no. 2 (2001): 50–56.

————. "Los 'Clades' y La Misión De La Iglesia." *Iglesia y Misión* 67/68 (Enero–julio 1999): 20–24.

————. "Los Movimientos De Cooperación Evangélica En América Latina." *Misión* 5, no. 3–4 (1986): 103–111.

————. "¿Somos Fundamentalistas?" *Pensamiento Cristiano* 13 (1966): 88–96.

Estrello, Francisco E. "El Cristianismo De Hoy y De Mañana En El Mundo." *Luminar* 9, no. 4 (1945): 48–62.

Ferris, George Irwin, Jr. "Protestantism in Nicaragua: Its Historical Roots and Influences Affecting Its Growth." Dissertation, Temple University, 1981.

Fuller, W. Harold. *People of the Mandate: The Story of the World Evangelical Fellowship*. Grand Rapids, MI: Baker, 1996.

Gaxiola, Manuel Jesús. "The Pentecostal Ministry." *International Review of Mission* 66, no. 261 (1 January 1977): 57–63.

Gonzáles, Justo L. *Revolución y Encarnación*. Vol. 1, Colección Universitas. Río Piedras, Puerto Rico: Librería La Reforma, 1965.

Gringoire, Pedro. "Presentación." *Luminar* 1, no. 1 (1936): 1–6.

Gutiérrez, Gustavo. *A Theology of Liberation: History, Politics and Salvation*. Translated by Sister Caridad Inda and John Eagleson. Maryknoll, NY: Orbis Books, 1973.

Gutiérrez-Cortéz, Rolando. "La Propuesta Teológica De La FTL." *Boletín Teológico* 20, no. 32 (1988): 329–340.

Hall, Daniel Enrique. "The Protestant Movement." In *As Protestant Latin America Sees It*, edited by Milton Stauffer, 85–104. New York, NY: Student Volunteer Movement for Foreign Missions, 1927.

Hayward, Victor E. W. "Call to Witness." *International Review of Mission* 54, no. 2 (1965): 189–192.

———. "Call to Witness – But What Kind of Witness?" *International Review of Mission* 53, no. 2 (1964): 201–208.

Henry, Carl F. H. "Evangelical Leader Reports on Religion in Latin America." *Religious News Service*. 21 August 1973.

———. *Evangelical Responsibility in Contemporary Theology*. Grand Rapids, MI: Eerdmans, 1957.

Inman, Samuel G. *New Churches in Old Lands: Thoughts Concerning the Evangelical Movement in Hispanic America, Especially in View of Discussions Related to the Havana Congress*. [n.p.] 1929.

———. *Ventures in Inter-American Friendship*. New York, NY: Missionary Movement of the United States and Canada, 1925.

ISAL. *América Hoy: Acción De Dios y Responsabilidad Del Hombre*. Montevideo: Iglesia y Sociedad en América Latina, 1966.

———. "Bases Para Una Estrategia y Programa De Isal. IV Asamblea Continental, Julio 1971. Ñaña, Perú." In *América Latina: Movilización Popular y Fe Cristiana*, edited by Rafael Tomás Carvajal et al., 137–172. Montevideo: ISAL, 1971.

———. *Encuentro y Desafío: La Acción Cristiana Evangélica Latinoamericana Ante La Cambiante Situación Social, Política y Económica*. Montevideo: ISAL, 1961.

———. "II Consulta Latinoamericana De Iglesia y Sociedad 'El Tabo': Chile, Enero 12–21, 1966." *Cristianismo y Sociedad* 4, no. 9–10 (1966): 83–102.

———. "III Consulta Latinoamericana De Isal." *Carta de Isal* 1, no. 1 (Abril 1968): 1–4.

"Latin American Evangelicals Unite." *Evangelical Missions Quarterly* 19, no. 1 (1983): 65–66.

Lausanne Committee for World Evangelization (LCWE). *Grand Rapids Report: Evangelism and Social Responsibility: An Evangelical Commitment*. Lausanne Occasional Papers No. 21. Wheaton, IL: LCWE and WEF, 1982.

———. *Transformation: The Church in Response to Human Need*. Wheaton, IL: LCWE, 1983.

Liggett, Thomas J. *Latin America: A Challenge to Protestantism*. Rio Piedras, Puerto Rico: Evangelical Seminary of Puerto Rico, 1959.

Lores, Rubén. "Carta Personal a Mr. Norman Rohrer." *Evangelical News Service*. 21 September 1973.

———. "Manifest Destiny and the Missionary Enterprise." *Study Encounter* 11, no. 1 (1975): 1–16.

Mackay, John A. "Latin America and Revolution I: The New Mood in Society and Culture." *Christian Century* 46, no. 17 (1965): 1409–1412.

———. *The Other Spanish Christ: A Study in the Spiritual History of Spain and South America*. New York, NY: Macmillan, 1933.

———. *A Preface to Christian Theology*. New York, NY: Macmillan, 1941.

———. *That Other America*. New York, NY: Friendship Press, 1935.

Mclean, James H. "Theology and Citizenship in Latin America: An Appraisal." *Theology Today* 2, no. 2 (1945): 214–229.

Melano Couch, Beatriz. "New Visions of the Church in Latin America: A Protestant View." In *The Emergent Gospel: Theology from the Underside of History. Papers from the Ecumenical Dialogue of Third World Theologians, Dar es Salaam, August 5–12, 1976*, edited by Sergio Torres and Virginia Fabella, 193–226. Maryknoll, NY: Orbis Books, 1978.

Mergal Llera, Angel Manuel. *Arte Cristiano De La Predicación*. Mexico: Comité de la Literatura de la Asociación de Iglesias Evangélicas de Puerto Rico, 1951.

Míguez Bonino, José. "How Does United States' Presence Help, Hinder or Compromise Christian Mission in Latin America?" *Review and Expositor* 74, no. 2 (Spring 1977): 173–182.

———. "Nuestro Mensaje." In CELA II, *Cristo La Esperanza Para América Latina: Ponencias-Informes-Comentarios De La Segunda Conferencia Evangélica Latinoamericana, 20 De Julio a 6 De Agosto De 1961, Lima, Perú*. Buenos Aires: Confederación Evangélica del Río de la Plata, 1962.

———. "Protestantism's Contribution to Latin America." *Lutheran Quarterly* 22, no. 1 (February 1970): 92–98.

———. "Reino De Dios E Historia: Reflexiones Para Una Discusión Del Tema." Paper presented at Fraternidad Teológica Latino Americana, II Consulta Teológica Internacional, Lima, 1972.

Moberg, David O. *The Great Reversal: Evangelism Versus Social Concern*. Philadelphia, PA: Lippincott, 1972.

Navarro Monzó, Julio. *The Religious Problem in Latin American Culture*. Montevideo: Young Men's Christian Association, 1925.

Neely, Alan. "Protestant Antecedents of the Latin American Theology of Liberation." PhD dissertation, American University, 1977.

Núñez C., Emilio Antonio. "Carta a Jóvenes Teólogos." *Boletín Teológico* 5, no. 1 (1982): 152–158.

———. "Crecimiento Numérico Versus Crecimiento Integral: Comentarios Sobre El Artículo De Fred Smith." *Misión* 8, no. 1 (1989): 20–25.

———. *Doing Evangelical Theology in Latin America*. Portland, OR: Western Conservative Baptist Seminary, 1986.

———. "La Naturaleza Del Reino De Dios." Paper presented at Fraternidad Teológica Latino Americana, II Consulta Teológica Internacional, Lima, 1972.

———. *Liberation Theology*. Translated by Paul E. Sywulka. Chicago, IL: Moody Press, 1985.

Odell, Luis L. "Junta Latinoamericana De Iglesia y Sociedad (Jlais): Origen, Definición, Objetivos." *Cristianismo y Sociedad* 1, no. 2 (1963): Insert.

Orellana, Luis. *El Fuego y La Nieve: Historia De Movimiento Pentecostal En Chile: 1909-1932*. Concepción, Chile: Centro Evangélico de Estudios Pentecostales (CELEP), 2006.

Orrego, Antenor. "El Destino Trascendente De América." *Luminar* 1, no. 4 (1937): 57–67.

Ortiz, Juan Carlos. "Definiciones Socio-Económicas De La Iglesia Para La Problemática Latinoamericana." *Pensamiento Cristiano* 19, no. 4 (1972).

Padilla, C. René. "El Nacimiento De Una Revista." *Misión* 1, no. 1 (1982): 5–6.

————. "Evangelism and the World." In *Let the Earth Hear His Voice*, edited by J. D. Douglas, 116–133. Minneapolis, MN: World Wide, 1975.

————. "Evangelización y Responsabilidad Social: De Wheaton '66 a Wheaton '83." *Misión* 4, no. 3 (1985): 83–90.

————. "La Autoridad De La Biblia En La Teología Latinoamericana." In *El Debate Contemporáneo Sobre La Biblia*, edited by Peter Savage, 121–153. Barcelona: Ediciones Evangélicas Europeas, 1972.

————. "La Explosión Teológica En El Tercer Mundo." *Misión* 4, no. 1 (1982): 30–31.

————. "La Iglesia y El Reino De Dios." Paper presented at Fraternidad Teológica Latino Americana, II Consulta Teológica Internacional, Lima, 1972.

————. "La Teología De La Liberación." *Pensamiento Cristiano* 20, no. 4 (Diciembre 1972): 170–172.

————. "La Teología En Latinoamérica." *Pensamiento Cristiano* 19, no. 75 (1972): 205–213.

————. "La Unidad De La Iglesia y El Principio De La Unidades Homgéneas." *Misión* 2, no. 3 (1983): 13–19, 38–42.

————. "Toward a Contextual Theology from Latin America." In *Conflict and Context: Hermeneutics in the Americas. A Report on the Context and Hermeneutics in the Americas Conference Sponsored by Theological Students Fellowship and the Latin American Theological Fraternity, Tyayacapan, Mexico, November 24-29, 1983*, edited by Mark Branson and C. René Padilla, 81–91. Grand Rapids, MI: Eerdmans, 1986.

Padilla, Washington. *La Iglesia y Los Dioses Modernos: Historia Del Protestantismo En El Ecuador*. Biblioteca De Ciencias Sociales, Volumen 23. Quito, Ecuador: Corporación Editora Nacional, 1989.

Palau, Luis, and David Sanford. *Calling America and the Nations to Christ*. Nashville, TN: Thomas Nelson, 1994.

Panorama Iberoamericano, 1962. Huampaní: II Congreso de Comunicaciones Evangélicas, 1962.

Pretiz, Paul E. "Conela Raises Its Flag in Panama." *Latin American Evangelist*, Sep–Oct 1982.

Redacción. "Cristo y Las Iglesias Cristianas." *La Nueva Democracia* 1, no. 3 (1920): 2–3.

———. "Nuestro Saludo y Nuestro Programa." *La Nueva Democracia* 1, no. 1 (1920): 2–3.

———. "¿Por Qué Rechazan Muchos La Religión?" *La Nueva Democracia* 1, no. 2 (1920): 3–4.

Rembao, Alberto. "The Presence of Protestantism in Latin America." *International Review of Missions* 21, no. 1 (1948): 57–70.

Richard, Pablo. *The Church Born by the Force of God in Central America*. New York, NY: New York Circus Publications, 1985.

———. *Death of Christendoms, Birth of the Church: Historical Analysis and Theological Interpretation of the Church in Latin America*. Maryknoll, NY: Orbis Books, 1987.

Robbins, Bruce Warren. "Contextualization in Costa Rican Theological Education Today: A History of the Seminario Biblico Latinoamericano, San José, Costa Rica, 1922–1990." PhD dissertation, Southern Methodist University, 1991.

Roberts, W. Dayton. "América Latina En La Década De Los 80." *Misión* 1, no. 1 (1982): 9–12.

———. "The Legacy of R. Kenneth Strachan." *Occasional Bulletin of Missionary Research* 3, no. 1 (1979): 2–6.

———. *Protestant Cooperation in Latin America. Background Briefing Paper 13*. Coral Gables, FL: Latin America Mission, 1981.

———. *Strachan of Costa Rica: Missionary Insights and Strategies*. Grand Rapids, MI: Eerdmans, 1971.

Rodríguez, Gabino. "The Evangelical Churches." In *As Protestant Latin America Sees It*, edited by Milton Stauffer, 105–123. New York, NY: Student Volunteer Movement for Foreign Missions, 1927.

Salinas, Daniel. *Latin American Evangelical Theology in the 1970s: The Golden Decade*. Leiden: Brill, 2009.

Sandeen, Ernest R. "Toward a Historical Interpretation of the Origins of Fundamentalism." *Church History* 36, no. 1 (1967): 66–83.

Santiago, Angel Daniel. "Contextual Theology and Revolutionary Transformation: The Missiology of M. Richard Shaull, 1942–2002." ThM thesis, Princeton Theological Seminary, 2000.

Saracco, Norberto. "La Palabra y El Espíritu En La Comunidad Evangelizadora." In *América Latina y La Evangelización En Los Años 80: Un Congreso Auspiciado Por La Fraternidad Teológica Latinoamericana*, 171–181. Lima: CLADE II, 1979.

———. "The Liberating Options of Jesus." In *Sharing Jesus in the Two Thirds World: Evangelical Christologies from the Contexts of Poverty, Powerlessness and Religious Pluralism*, edited by Vinay Samuel and Chris Sugden, 49–60. Bangalore, India: Partnership in Mission Asia, 1983.

Savage, Peter. "Editorial." *Boletín Teológico* 4, no. 2 (1981): 3–19.

———. "El Quehacer Teológico En El Contexto Latinoamericano." *Boletín Teológico* 5, no. 1 (1982): 3–29.

———, ed. *El Debate Contemporáneo Sobre La Biblia*. Barcelona: Ediciones Evangélicas Europeas, 1972.

Scofield, C. I., ed. *The Holy Bible Containing the Old and New Testaments, Authorized Version, with a New System of Connected Topical References to All the Greater Themes of Scripture, with Annotations, Revised Marginal Renderings, Summaries, Definitions, Chronology, and Index*. New York, NY: Oxford University Press, 1917.

Seminario Bíblico Latinoamericano. "To Whom It May Concern." Open letter, 26 September 1973.

"The Seoul Declaration: Toward an Evangelical Theology for the Third World." *International Bulletin of Missionary Research* 7, no. 2 (1983): 64–65.

Silveira Campos, Leonildo. "Why Historic Churches Are Declining and Pentecostal Churches Are Growing in Brazil: A Sociological Perspective." In *In the Power of the Spirit: The Pentecostal Challenge to Historic Churches in Latin America*, edited by Benjamín F. Gutiérrez and Dennis A. Smith, 65–94. Mexico City: AIPRAL; Guatemala: CELEP; Louisville, KY: Presbyterian Church (USA), 1996.

Smith, Fred. "Algunos Principios Del Iglecrecimiento En Los Hechos De Los Apóstoles." *Misión* 8, no. 1 (1989): 6–13.

Sosa, Adam F. "Algunas Consideraciones Sobre La Actual Posición Teológica De Los Evangélicos Latinoamericanos." *Cuadernos Teológicos* 9, no. 2 (1960): 151–61.

Speer, Robert E. *Missions in South America*. New York, NY: Board of Foreign Missions of the Presbyterian Church in the USA, 1909.

———. *South American Problems*. New York, NY: Student Volunteer Movement for Foreign Missions, 1912.

Speer, Robert E., Samuel G. Inman, and Frank K. Sanders, eds. *Christian Work in South America: Official Report of the Congress on Christian Work in South America, at Montevideo, Uruguay, April 1925*. Vol. 2, *Church and the Community, Religious Education, Literature, Relations Between Foreign and National Workers, Special Religious Problems, Cooperation and Unity*. New York and Chicago: Fleming H. Revell, 1925.

———, eds. *Christian Work in South America: Official Report of the Congress on Christian Work in South America, at Montevideo, Uruguay, April 1925*. Vol. 1, *Unoccupied Fields, Indians, Education, Evangelism, Social Movements, Health Industry*. New York and Chicago: Fleming H. Revell, 1925.

Steuernagel, Valdir. "The Theology of Mission in Its Relation to Social Responsibility within the Lausanne Movement." PhD dissertation, Lutheran School of Theology, 1988.

Stoll, David. *Is Latin America Turning Protestant? The Politics of Evangelical Growth.* Berkeley and Los Angeles: University of California Press, 1990.

Strachan, Kenneth. "Call to Witness." *International Review of Mission* 53, no. 2 (1964): 191–200.

———. "A Further Comment." *International Review of Mission* 53, no. 2 (1964): 209–215.

———. *The Inescapable Calling: The Missionary Task of the Church of Christ in the Light of Contemporary Challenge and Opportunity.* Grand Rapids, MI: Eerdmans, 1968.

Svelmoe, Bill. "Evangelism Only? Theory Versus Practice in the Early Faith Missions." *Missiology: An International Review* 31, no. 2 (2003): 195–206.

Tamez, Elsa, ed. *Through Her Eyes: Women's Theology from Latin America.* Maryknoll, NY: Orbis Books, 1989.

Terlep, Alan Thomas. "Inventing the Rapture: The Formation of American Dispensationalism, 1850–1875." Dissertation, University of Chicago, 2010.

Vaccaro, Gabriel O. "Oaxtepec Desde Una Perspectiva Pentecostal." *Cuadernos de Teología* 5, no. 4 (1979): 289–292.

Varetto, Juan C. *Bosquejos Para Sermones.* Buenos Aires: Editorial Evangélica Bautista, 1955.

———. *Cuatro Conversaciones Familiares Sobre Samson.* Buenos Aires: Editorial Evangélica Bautista, 1952.

———. *Diego Thomson, Apóstol De La Instrucción Pública E Iniciador De La Obra Evangélica En La América Latina.* Buenos Aires: Imprenta Evangélica, 1918.

———. *Discursos Evangélicos.* Buenos Aires: Junta Bautista de Publicaciones, 1919.

———. *El Apóstol Del Plata, Juan F. Thomson.* Buenos Aires: La Aurora, 1943.

———. *Federic Crowe En Guatemala.* Buenos Aires: Junta Bautista de Publicaciones, 1940.

———. *Héroes y Mártires De La Obra Misionera Desde Los Apóstoles Hasta Nuestros Días.* Buenos Aires: Convención Evangélica Bautista, 1934.

———. *Hostilidad Del Clero a La Independencia Americana.* Buenos Aires: Imprenta Metodista, 1922.

———. *La Marcha Del Cristianismo: Desde Los Apóstoles Hasta Los Valdenses.* Buenos Aires: Junta de Publicaciones de la Convención Evangélica Bautista, 1973.

———. *La Reforma Religiosa Del Siglo XVI.* Buenos Aires: Junta de Publicaciones de la Convención Evangélica Bautista, 1949.

———. *Las Biblias En Castellano.* Buenos Aires: Junta de Publicaciones de la Convención Evangélica Bautista, 1925.

———. *Los Hechos De Los Apóstoles Explicado*. Buenos Aires: Editorial Evangélica Bautista, 1952.

———. *Refutación Del Adventismo*. Buenos Aires: Junta de Publicaciones de la Convención Evangélica Bautista, 1948.

———. *Rogerio Williams: Héroe De La Libertad Religiosa*. Buenos Aires: Junta de Publicaciones de la Convención Evangélica Bautista, 1921.

———. *Separación De La Iglesia y El Estado*. Buenos Aires: Junta de Publicaciones de la Convención Evangélica Bautista de las Repúblicas del Plata, 1927.

———. *Una Conversación Familiar Con Los Que Quieren Bautizarse*. Santiago: Wilson, 1950.

Various. *Gonzalo Báez-Camargo: Una Vida Al Descubierto*. Mexico City: Centro de Comunicación Cultural (CUPSA A.C.), 1985.

Velásquez, Roger. "Conela." *Pastoralia* 4, no. 8 (1982): 78–83.

WCC. *Consultation with Pentecostal Churches. Lima, Peru, 14 to 19 November 1994*. Geneva: World Council of Churches, 1994.

Index

A

Alvarez, Carmelo 172, 173
American way of life 62
Arana, Pedro 50, 56, 94, 133

B

Báez-Camargo, Gonzalo 4, 21, 23, 24,
  35, 42, 43, 46, 50, 117, 153
Braga, Erasmo 25, 35, 41
Bruce, F. F. 57, 114, 119

C

CAM 25, 28
Campos, Bernardo 175, 176, 177, 178,
  179, 180
Capitalism 80, 103, 108, 111, 113, 117,
  122, 143, 175
Castro, Emilio 50, 68, 92
Catholic Church 4, 6, 7, 8, 9, 10, 14, 31,
  33, 61, 65, 74, 99, 135, 136, 156,
  166, 176, 177, 178, 182
CCLA 5, 9, 10, 13, 14, 15, 16, 21, 28,
  29, 35, 37, 39, 42, 43, 46, 51, 52,
  53, 78, 96, 105
CELA 50, 51, 52, 53, 57, 58, 71, 72, 73,
  74, 77, 90
Central American Mission 25
Certeza 56, 57
Christology 14, 16, 19, 36, 46, 61, 72,
  74, 123, 141, 142, 149, 151, 159,
  170, 172
Church Growth 160
CLADE 118, 119, 120, 123, 127, 128,
  157, 167, 168, 170
CLAI 127, 128, 132, 133, 134, 135, 136,
  137, 138, 139, 140, 154, 177, 178,
  179, 183

Clifford, Alejandro 56
Cold War 55, 181, 183
Committee on Cooperation for Latin
  America 13, 37
Communism 55
CONELA 127, 128, 129, 131, 132, 133,
  134, 135, 136, 137, 138, 139, 140,
  145, 148, 154, 179, 183
Conteris, Hiber 81, 82
Contextualization 115, 131, 149
Costas, Orlando 110, 123, 157, 159,
  160
Cristianismo y Sociedad 79, 81, 82, 83
Cuadernos Teológicos 57, 58, 80

D

Darby, John 25, 26
Deiros, Pablo 168, 169, 170
de Santa Ana, Julio 87, 90, 195
Dispensationalism 4, 26, 28, 102
Docetism 74, 75, 159, 170

E

Ebionism 75
Ecclesiology 14, 36, 78, 106, 149, 151,
  173, 183
Ecumenical 10, 50, 53, 57, 58, 69, 124,
  127, 132, 135, 136, 138, 139, 177,
  179
Eschatology 104
Escobar, Samuel 36, 38, 50, 56, 57, 61,
  62, 63, 64, 86, 92, 93, 94, 103,
  104, 105, 108, 113, 114, 115, 116,
  118, 125, 126, 135, 136, 149, 150,
  153, 157, 160, 162, 163, 164

Ethics 17, 28, 50, 58, 94, 101, 104, 105, 108, 121, 123, 140, 141, 142, 150, 174

Evangelism 6, 13, 19, 20, 21, 28, 29, 35, 48, 50, 57, 58, 59, 60, 65, 66, 68, 70, 71, 78, 80, 81, 84, 85, 95, 102, 107, 110, 111, 115, 128, 136, 139, 145, 146, 147, 148, 149, 154, 163, 165, 168, 175, 177

Evangelism in Depth 65

F

Faith Missions 28, 29, 42, 61

FTL 90, 92, 96, 100, 101, 106, 112, 113, 123, 127, 133, 137, 138, 139, 141, 146, 149, 150, 156, 157, 182, 183

Fundamentalism 26, 61, 62, 63, 64, 87, 88, 93, 170, 171

G

Galilean option 157

Gaxiola, Manuel J. 97, 98, 99

Gondim, Ricardo 170, 171, 172

González, Justo L. 75, 76

Green, Michael 112

Gutiérrez, Gustavo 97, 99, 100, 157

Guy Inman, Samuel 21

H

Hall, Daniel E. 31, 34

Havana 13, 20, 21, 23, 24, 43, 177

Hayward, Victor 66, 67, 68, 69

Henry, Carl 62, 112, 113

Hermeneutics 27, 88, 101, 118, 123, 141, 142, 143, 149, 15

I

Incarnation 69, 72, 73, 75, 76, 88, 107, 119, 168, 178

Industrialization 33, 71, 178

Inman, Samuel G. 15, 16, 17, 22, 23, 24, 37, 39, 41, 83

Integral Mission 63, 168

ISAL 76, 77, 78, 79, 80, 81, 82, 83, 84, 85, 86, 87, 89, 90, 94, 107, 123, 181, 182, 183

K

Kingdom of God 13, 52, 62, 63, 75, 85, 102, 103, 106, 115, 121, 131, 141, 149, 150, 151, 154, 168, 170, 174, 183

L

La Nueva Democracia 25, 35, 37, 38, 40, 41, 42

Latin America Mission 65, 139, 155

Lausanne Committee 128, 129, 145, 146, 148

Lausanne Covenant 129, 135, 136, 138, 140, 148, 154

Lausanne Movement 112, 137

Liberalism 61, 62

Liberation theology 1, 97, 98, 99, 100, 112, 120, 123, 140, 150, 151, 183

Liggett, Thomas 60, 61

Lores, Rubén 108, 111, 113

Luminar 42, 43, 44, 46

M

Mackay, John A. 3, 9, 34, 35, 36, 37, 46, 47, 48, 49, 50, 71, 74, 75

Manifest Destiny 108

Marxism 98

Marxist 56, 65, 71, 100, 104, 123, 150

Marx, Karl 76

McGavran, Donald 160

Melano, Beatriz 120, 121, 122, 123

Mergal, Angel M. 42, 52, 55, 58

Míguez Bonino, José 50, 72, 92, 103, 111

Misión 92, 118, 135, 145, 148, 153, 154, 155, 156, 160, 162, 164, 177

Montevideo 3, 15, 16, 17, 19, 20, 22, 23, 24, 77, 79, 86, 91

Moraes, Benjamín 71
Morris, Leon 112

N

Navarro Monzó, Julio 3, 23, 25, 35
Núñez, Emilio A. 101, 102, 126, 127,
    142, 143, 144, 145, 151, 152, 153,
    160, 164, 165, 166

O

Oaxtepec 117, 119, 123, 132, 134, 140
Odell, Luis 78, 79
Ortiz, Juan C. 105, 106

P

Packer, James 57
Padilla, C. René 50, 56, 94, 95, 99, 100,
    102, 103, 106, 107, 109, 110, 141,
    142, 143, 148, 149, 153, 154, 156,
    157, 160, 167, 168
Padilla, Washington 63, 191, 195
Palau, Luis 128, 139
Panama 1916 5, 31, 63, 64, 135, 137
pan-Americanism 22
Pastoralia 123, 124, 134, 187, 195
Paternalism 91
Pensamiento Cristiano 56, 57, 61, 100,
    106, 107, 115, 117
Pentecostal 14, 15, 28, 29, 53, 81, 84,
    97, 99, 105, 106, 117, 118, 119,
    157, 162, 170, 171, 172, 173, 174,
    175, 176, 177, 178, 179, 180
Pentecostalism 5, 84, 171, 172, 173,
    174, 175, 176, 177, 178, 179, 180,
Pentecostals 5, 14, 15, 98, 99, 102, 117,
    119, 170, 174, 175, 176, 177, 178,
    179, 180
Pietism 59, 93, 95, 121, 155
Powell, David 56
Praxis 100, 122, 144, 150, 152
Prosperity Theology 172

R

Reformation 23, 59, 61, 87, 94, 124
Rembao, Alberto 25, 38, 41, 42, 53
Revolution 3, 13, 55, 56, 74, 76, 77, 81,
    82, 83, 85, 94, 104, 107, 114
Revolutionary 40, 42, 74, 76, 100, 122,
    123, 136
Roberts, Dayton 41, 69, 139, 140, 155
Rodríguez, Gabino 32, 33, 34, 36
Rojas, Ricardo 46

S

Saracco, Ernesto 118, 119, 157
Saracco, Norberto 157
Savage, Peter 50, 57, 93, 94, 95, 96, 119,
    125, 133, 134, 150, 151, 153
Scofield, C. I. 25, 26, 28, 29
Silveira Campos, Leonildo 173, 174
Smith, Fred 160, 161, 162, 164, 173
Social Gospel 13, 18, 33, 62, 87, 105,
    121
Socialism 55, 104, 112, 114, 123, 143
Social justice 39, 79, 127, 144, 155
Social responsibility 78, 127, 145, 146,
    147, 148
Sosa, Adam F. 58, 59, 60, 64
Soteriology 14, 61, 140, 169, 170
Speer, Robert 7, 8, 9, 10, 15, 16, 17, 22
Steuernagel, Valdir 127, 137
Stoll, David 137, 138
Stott, John 57, 112, 146
Strachan, Kenneth 41, 65, 66, 67, 68,
    69, 70

T

Tamez, Elsa 166, 194, 195
Theological dependency 93, 106, 107,
    153, 183
Third World 90, 110, 120, 141, 155,
    156, 166
Thomson, Diego 46, 47

Transformation 52, 69, 74, 75, 77, 78,
        82, 84, 85, 91, 148, 149, 176, 177

V

Vaccaro, Gabriel 117, 119, 194, 195
Varetto, Juan C. 46, 47, 194, 195
Velásquez, Roger 35, 36, 134, 135

W

World Council of Churches 51, 127,
        134, 137, 139, 174, 175

Z

Zandrino, Miguel 56

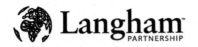

Langham Literature and its imprints are a ministry of Langham Partnership.

Langham Partnership is a global fellowship working in pursuit of the vision God entrusted to its founder John Stott –

> *to facilitate the growth of the church in maturity and Christ-likeness through raising the standards of biblical preaching and teaching.*

Our vision is to see churches in the majority world equipped for mission and growing to maturity in Christ through the ministry of pastors and leaders who believe, teach and live by the Word of God.

Our mission is to strengthen the ministry of the Word of God through:
* nurturing national movements for biblical preaching
* fostering the creation and distribution of evangelical literature
* enhancing evangelical theological education

especially in countries where churches are under-resourced.

Our ministry

Langham Preaching partners with national leaders to nurture indigenous biblical preaching movements for pastors and lay preachers all around the world. With the support of a team of trainers from many countries, a multi-level programme of seminars provides practical training, and is followed by a programme for training local facilitators. Local preachers' groups and national and regional networks ensure continuity and ongoing development, seeking to build vigorous movements committed to Bible exposition.

Langham Literature provides majority world preachers, scholars and seminary libraries with evangelical books and electronic resources through publishing and distribution, grants and discounts. The programme also fosters the creation of indigenous evangelical books in many languages, through writer's grants, strengthening local evangelical publishing houses, and investment in major regional literature projects, such as one volume Bible commentaries like *The Africa Bible Commentary* and *The South Asia Bible Commentary*.

Langham Scholars provides financial support for evangelical doctoral students from the majority world so that, when they return home, they may train pastors and other Christian leaders with sound, biblical and theological teaching. This programme equips those who equip others. Langham Scholars also works in partnership with majority world seminaries in strengthening evangelical theological education. A growing number of Langham Scholars study in high quality doctoral programmes in the majority world itself. As well as teaching the next generation of pastors, graduated Langham Scholars exercise significant influence through their writing and leadership.

To learn more about Langham Partnership and the work we do visit **langham.org**

CPSIA information can be obtained
at www.ICGtesting.com
Printed in the USA
BVOW06s1409120117
473350BV00003B/21/P

9 781783 682065